growgirl

THE BLOSSOMING OF

AN UNLIKELY OUTLAW

Heather Donahue

GOTHAM BOOKS

GOTHAM BOOKS

Published by the Penguin Group

Penguin Group (USA) Inc., 375 Hudson Street, New York, New York 10014, USA · Penguin Group (Canada), 90 Eglinton Avenue East, Suite 700, Toronto, Ontario M4P 2Y3, Canada (a division of Pearson Penguin Canada Inc.) · Penguin Books Ltd, 80 Strand, London WC2R 0RL, England · Penguin Ireland, 25 St Stephen's Green, Dublin 2, Ireland (a division of Penguin Books Ltd) · Penguin Group (Australia), 707 Collins Street, Melbourne, Victoria 3008, Australia (a division of Pearson Australia Group Pty Ltd) · Penguin Books India Pvt Ltd, 11 Community Centre, Panchsheel Park, New Delhi–110 017, India · Penguin Group (NZ), 67 Apollo Drive, Rosedale, Auckland 0632, New Zealand (a division of Pearson New Zealand Ltd) · Penguin Books, Rosebank Office Park, 181 Jan Smuts Avenue, Parktown North 2193, South Africa · Penguin China, B7 Jaiming Center, 27 East Third Ring Road North, Chaoyang District, Beijing 100020, China

Penguin Books Ltd, Registered Offices: 80 Strand, London WC2R 0RL, England

Published by Gotham Books, a member of Penguin Group (USA) Inc.

Previously published as a Gotham Books hardcover

First trade paperback printing, January 2013

10   9   8   7   6   5   4   3   2   1

Gotham Books and the skyscraper logo are trademarks of Penguin Group (USA) Inc.

Growgirl illustration by Heather Donahue

The Library of Congress has catalogued the hardcover edition as follows:

Donahue, Heather, 1973–
Growgirl : the blossoming of an unlikely outlaw / Heather Donahue.
p. cm.
ISBN 978-1-592-40692-0 (hardcover)   978-1-592-40704-0 (pbk)
1. Donahue, Heather, 1973–   2. Actors—United States—Biography.   I. Title.
PN2287.D49A3 2012
792.02'8092—dc23
[B]   2011032920

Printed in the United States of America
Set in Bembo   •   Designed by Elke Sigal

While the author has made every effort to provide accurate telephone numbers and Internet addresses at the time of publication, neither the publisher nor the author assumes any responsibility for errors, or for changes that occur after publication. Further, the publisher does not have any control over and does not assume any responsibility for author or third-party Web sites or their content.

Penguin is committed to publishing works of quality and integrity.
In that spirit, we are proud to offer this book to our readers;
however, the story, the experiences, and the words
are the author's alone.

Praise for
Growgirl

"*Growgirl* is pretty wonderful. Donahue is not only a funny, sharp, endearing narrator, she's downright wise about the experience that is, literally, torching a previous life."
—*The Awl*

"Donahue's hippie-chick sensibilities don't impair her ability to offer droll descriptions of the foibles of the community of growers she lived with for a year."
—*Library Journal*

"Frank and funny."
—*The New Yorker*

"In her quirky, kooky year-in-the-life account, she writes hilariously. . . . Wry, with a nuanced distance from the events, Donahue offers an unorthodox gardener's take on the growing season."
—*Publishers Weekly*

"Everything contained within this 'fish out of water' memoir rings true and reads fiercely and crazily entertainingly. . . . In constructing a book that is both a gentle polemic and a deeply felt, richly developed personal memoir, Heather Donahue shows herself to be an author with talent, skill, and a unique, rich author's voice in which she can wrap them."
—*New York Journal of Books*

"Wickedly funny, insightful."
—*Cannabis Culture*

"The book is a dense and breezy read, full of extraordinarily intimate details. . . ."
—*The Village Voice*

"Her memoir is a hilarious commentary on pot culture and Hollywood vapidity."
—*Los Angeles*

"*Grow Girl* is great if you like your marijuana stories imbued with a general sense of struggle. (And what other kind, really, exists these days?)"
—*San Francisco Bay Guardian*

"An intimate look at a woman's yearlong search for her place in the world."
—*Kirkus Reviews*

"Thank God things didn't work out in Hollywood for Heather Donahue. Otherwise, we'd never have gotten this book. Anyone who's taken a fall will bond fiercely with Donahue's hilarious frankness about hitting bottom. Beautifully written, full of wisdom. A terrific read."

—Katie Crouch, author of *Girls in Trucks*

"Heather Donahue has a gloriously comic voice and beguiling self-knowledge. *Growgirl* will tell you how to grow pot—and how to grow up. It's a hilarious, rollicking, endearing memoir that's also friendly, wise, and thoroughly addictive. I inhaled it!"

—Michelle Huneven, author of *Blame*

MICHELE CLEMENT

Heather Donahue is a writer and actress, best known for her starring role in the 1999 cult classic *The Blair Witch Project*. She has been featured on the cover of *Newsweek*, in *People*, and on *The Tonight Show*, *Today*, *The Daily Show*, and CNN. She lives in San Francisco.

For my parents, Jim and Joan Donahue,

for remaking the past into love

Contents

April's Powers

May I?

June Bloom

Ju Lies

Augustine

September Mourn

Oktoberfest

November Is a Month of
Spring in the Southern Hemisphere

Decembrrr

January Means Camellias in Japan

February's Extra *R* Should Just Let Go

Author's Note

I have sort of composited characters, somewhat altered time lines, mudged the odd fact, basically changed all proper nouns that don't belong to me and Vito, re-imagined dialogue to the point of invention, and otherwise did my best to ensure the reader's enjoyment and the impossibility of this document ever being admissible in court.

But of course nobody portrayed in this book did anything illegal. Everybody portrayed in this book was, as much as one could be in the gray area of legally growing pot, compliant with all state and local laws, including, but not limited to, the Compassionate Care Act and California SB 420, in perpetuity and throughout the universe, amen.

—Heather Donahue
SAN FRANCISCO, JULY 4, 2011

growgirl

"I aimed to be a student not of longing but of light."

—Maggie Nelson, *Bluets*

"Fail again. Fail better."

—Samuel Beckett, *Worstward Ho*

"Where are the men?" the little prince asked, politely.
The flower had once seen a caravan passing.

"Men?" she echoed. "I think there are six or seven of them in existence. I saw them, several years ago. But one never knows where to find them. The wind blows them away. They have no roots and that makes their life very difficult."

—Antoine de Saint-Exupéry, *The Little Prince*

LEAP DAY

THE LEAP

TODAY IS THE LAST DAY OF A SAME THAT WILL NEVER BE THE SAME AGAIN. At least that's what I'm hoping.

Today is leap day. I am moving. Or my stuff is, via some Ukrainians with excellent biceps. If there ever was a day that deserved a fat spank of carpe diem it's this one. February 29—a day that won't repeat for four more years. Thank God. I don't think I could handle such leaps annually. But for now, for this minute, this moment, I'm smack dab in the middle of an empty apartment in the middle of the basin, the Hollywood flats. Not quite obscured by power lines and palms is the iconic Paramount water tower. The ocean lost in smog is technically to my right, though I can't prove it. It's not a clear day. A staunch wall of mountains is allegedly behind me. The air is a color most familiar to dentists.

Today I am a city girl. I was also a city girl yesterday and the 12,478 days before that. Palm trees line the street formerly known as my street. They're so stunning in their towering uniformity that they make you look up. I like anything that helps a person remember to look up. On windy days they sway like drunk sentinels. They bend but don't break. When the wind dies down, they stand tall again. Good for them. That was the thing that sold me on the place, those neat tall guards lined up so straight and long they diminished to specks as the street dead-ended at the 101. I thought they beckoned, saying, *Follow, follow, you're on the path.* I believe in the preternatural wisdom of trees, though I also shave my armpits.

Tomorrow I will be a country girl, with chickens and a dog and a garden full of organic veggies (and medical marijuana). I have never been a country girl before, though I once went on a hayride as a child. Still, I have a very vivid picture of what it will be like: I will wear rubber boots and possibly overalls, and there may or may not be a piece of straw hanging out of my mouth when you least expect it. I will be small and serene among the cannabis and pines that blanket the hills of Nuggettown—they too will sway but sometimes they will break and I will find them more relatable. I will grow my own food (and pot), raise chickens (and pot), and maybe a dog (and pot).

THE CITY OF ANGELS

WHEN MY EX WACŁAW AND I MOVED HERE IN 1998, THIS APARTMENT WAS in an undesirable yet affordable location, gunshots be damned. It was also rent-controlled. It is now in a desirable yet unaffordable location, gunshots be damned. Wacław said, "I don't know. I have a feeling like something bad happened here." Two years later we found out the previous tenant had been robbed then stabbed after inviting a homeless guy up for a beer. I was told he died in the hospital, which was supposed to make it better. "There was blood everywhere," the tenant who eventually told me said. "Everything in there needed to be replaced. Rugs, drywall—why'd you think it was so nice and big for so cheap?" I didn't think. I was a twenty-four-year-old aspiring actress fresh from New York with not so much as a temp job in these parts, and it was close to the freeway. Last year my friend Mr. Kim, who ran the mini-mart on the corner and had a much-beloved Chihuahua named Pinky who sang his ringtone, was shot in the face about a hundred yards from where I was sitting on the red couch, which used to be next to where I'm standing right now before the aforementioned Ukrainians put it in a truck for twice the estimate they gave me on the phone. I cried and got ten percent off the one hundred percent increase. I didn't cry on purpose to get the discount. I cried because it's hard to let go of what you know even when it's threadbare and moth-eaten and formerly bloodstained and generally very last century.

For the last decade I've lived not only in Hollywood the neighborhood, I have also lived in Hollywood the industry/mythic land. I was an actress. I couldn't do anything else. If I had something to fall back on, I would. I stopped thinking about all the other things I might be, because then I might have trouble keeping the faith. If I could just as well be a botanist, psychologist, lawyer, or trucker, then I might not pound the pavement with the requisite verve. And let's face it, none of those options sounds as much fun as being an actress. I made the commitment and prepared the ritual sacrifice, which consisted mostly of headshots, résumés, and the absence of cheese.

When a rough little indie film I did called *The Blair Witch Project* became a turn-of-the-century phenomenon, it briefly led me to believe that I would have a sustainable career, but it was more like a brushfire.

THE GIRL FROM *THE BLAIR WITCH PROJECT*

ONE VIVID NIGHT, I LEFT AN INTERVIEW AND THERE WAS A CROWD OF people waiting with stuff they wanted me to sign, mostly eight-by-tens of me looking happier. I signed for a few minutes, but it was after midnight and I just wanted to go home. The folks who were waiting didn't like this. The publicist ushered me into her car. They followed. She was trying to lose them, but couldn't. We drove past billboards with my face on them. This went on for about thirty minutes. We pulled over and tried to wait them out, see if they'd pass. They waited about a hundred yards behind us. We continued to circle; they continued to follow. After an hour, we found the West Hollywood sheriff's station, and they gave us an escort.

When I arrived at my apartment, Wacław was stoned on the couch, watching TV. He once worked at Successories, peddling pictures of bald eagles illustrating such go-getterisms as "Your attitude determines your altitude" from a kiosk in a New Jersey mall—but that was a long time ago. When we met, he was a square-jawed, Slavically accented director of photography. His primary occupation at this point, four years into our relationship, was stoner. He used pot to open himself up but never managed to bridge his own gap. I hated pot for letting him believe he was present. I loved it for the way it let him be touched.

I turned the deadbolt and bawled. I bawled so hard I couldn't breathe.

That was when a commercial for the movie came on. I bawled harder and Wacław, glassy-eyed, said, "I knew this would ruin us," but held me anyway, not hugging so much as tethering, the way a sandbag tethers a hot-air balloon.

There's this part toward the end of the movie where I'm hyperventilating with snot dripping out of my nose because my character thinks she's going to die. It was part of the commercial. It echoed in the living room, and each stabbing inhale ricocheted around the apartment. The sobs on the TV matched exactly the sobs I choked live. My dream, it could be said, had come true.

I am, to this day, often correctly mistaken for The Girl from *The Blair Witch Project*, who is also Heather Donahue, which is confusing. This began in 1999, with the release of the film. I never saw it in a theater after it played at the Sundance Film Festival. When it premiered at the Angelika in New York, I watched the line stretch around the block from across the street, because I was supposed to be dead. The premise of the movie is that it's the found footage of three student filmmakers who died while they were shooting it. The main thrust of the marketing scheme was to convince people that we were really dead. It worked so well that my parents received sympathy cards.

By the time that line snaked around the block in New York, the movie had already taken on a life of its own that had little to do with me. It wasn't until ticket sales plateaued that the three of us, Michael Williams, Joshua Leonard, and I, were resurrected. At that point, there were a lot of people who didn't believe we were really the actors from the movie. They thought it was the next level of hoax. Despite the fact that the three of us were trained actors who also improvised and shot the film, the marketing angle positioned us as three random kids who were dropped in the woods. It was hard to convince people, both professionally and randomly, otherwise. At no point did any of us think that supernatural forces were really out to get us. I was no more really afraid of the piles of rocks in *Blair Witch* than I was really awestruck at being inside a spaceship in *Taken*. We believed it into being. That's what actors do. They disappear and reemerge through someone else's words. That's another reason why I quit. I wanted my story back.

What really scared me about *Blair Witch* was what happened after. It's a strange thing to be told you're not really an actress when that's what you spent your young adult life training for. It's even stranger to be told that your name isn't really yours anymore, that it's somebody else's intellectual property now. The most basic things that a person roots a self to—name and occupation—were gone. I wasn't an actress. I wasn't Heather Donahue. I was The Girl from *The Blair Witch Project* and I was supposed to be dead.

I'm sure somewhere on the cover of this book will be the words *The Blair Witch Project,* and believe me, I will have tried to prevent that. There's no me without it for any but the people I love. And even with them it takes a while.

Still, it wasn't until I did a movie called *The Morgue* and found myself sprawled on wet asphalt with apple juice dribbling from my mouth and rubber tubing draped suggestively across my face, having just simulated death by mock fellatio, that I had to think, *Maybe this acting thing isn't really working out.* I was a Hollywood has-been. I wanted to begin again.

THE GREAT PURGE

AFTER I REALIZED I WASN'T GOING TO BE AN ACTRESS ANYMORE, I VISITED, as a Californian might, my Ayurvedic doctor. Dr. Iqbal suggested, "When the body is hungry, eat. When the body is tired, sleep." Which seems pretty basic, but who has that kind of time? He also prescribed herbs and some Rumi, a Sufi poet who wrote, among other things, "Die before you die." I took this to mean something like, "Empty your cup so that it may be filled with something more delicious, like an Arnold Palmer, or a root beer float." So I set about emptying my cup. I didn't want to be The Girl from *The Blair Witch Project* anymore, but I couldn't tell where the root of that was so I just pulled hard and deep. I called it The Great Purge.

I gave away what I could. I gave the flannel shirt I wore in the movie to a homeless guy on Gower. He left it behind the fence in the parking lot of the now abandoned mini-mart where Mr. Kim died, so I passed it every day and tracked how it faded in the sun. Only on the first day was I tempted to scale the fence and take it back, maybe sell it on eBay, but I wasn't calling this The Partial Purge.

I drove out to the desert—Joshua Tree. I hadn't eaten anything for twenty-one days. I was there to shed. To shed a skin whole, to shed a story like a snake. My scalp was itchy and my sagging sweatpants sang a stained refrain from the day's munch of miles. Lucy, the ten-year-old four-wheel-drive I bought new from signing autographs, was full of plastic bags stuffed with my last ten years. I had nothing left to lose. Not even ten pounds. I lifted the grill on the fire pit and it sang like a locker door, rusty bones, a maw. I stacked the logs in a perfect Girl Scoutian teepee, filled the empty pit with the first load of résumés, headshots, lingerie, lint, until it was full full full of shit shit shit. Like a constipated belly. Or me.

White buds swelled on the yuccas. We were all so close to blooming.

I sat in a ten-dollar captain's chair from Target with my feet up, smoking the remains of a joint from a previous relationship, drinking the sole beer I brought. It was like one of those Corona commercials, except instead of white sand there was ash. It took a while to get the blaze glowing, but when it did, I was treated to chartreuse, fuschia, aquamarine—bright with the toxic rainbow of my incinerating trash, I was a speck—no—a spark. Photos burn pretty. Ditto lingerie.

My past in embers fluttered up like fireflies, danced around my head. I looked up to the half full moon and everything and no one and said out loud: "Bring it."

LADY GODIVA AND THE TIT WHISKER

ASIDE FROM THE BURNING OF MY SHIT AND THE GENERAL URGE TOWARD change and the lack of career prospects and the utter lack of interest in going to law school like a normal hyperverbal d-bag, there is a man involved, as there often is when a woman relocates. I met Judah three months after The Great Purge.

Like everything, we began in warm water.

I said, "Bring it," so he did.

Like any devout Californian with an urge to transcend, I went to a silent meditation retreat. For most of it, I heard in my head Neil Young's "Rockin' in the Free World," and on entering the lunchroom, the sitcomesque catchphrase "Stop hatin', start tatin'!" by which I meant instead of hating, one should meditate, which was followed, in my head, by everyone in the lunchroom doing the wave, which amused me to no end. That's the kind of thing silence does to me. On the last day, everyone found their tongues again and warm popcorn was served in silver bowls. Fingers brushed and bloomed among the kernels. For some of us, language was wobbly. For others, it came in gusts. I was the former. He was the latter.

He was not the man I noticed in the meditation hall, the one who sat in radiant stillness. He was the fidgety guy to the left. Now he's Judah, a sleepy, blond Barney Rubble/skateboy hybrid with a sprinkle of permafreckles across his nose configured like Orion's Belt. He didn't wait to ask before sitting beside me.

"Where are you from?" I asked.

"Little place called Nuggettown."

Ding.

"Seriously?"

"You know it?"

I did. The first time I went to Nuggettown was with Wacław. After driving through hilly, heady swaths of pine and cedar, we happened upon the bitty burg. As soon as we stepped into the old school Western shoot-'em-up charms of Main Street, I proclaimed with absolute solidity: "I am going to live here." It was on my itinerary for this trip, after the retreat, because I wanted to go back and see if I'd have that same feeling again. "I thought about going there on my way down south."

"On your way down south?" A grin bubbled through his earnestness.

"LA." I stayed stoic. Zen, even.

"Random," Judah said. His eyes were the color and texture of this pair of leather pants I once had and always felt good in.

"Yeah, but it kind of makes sense." Which is the kind of thing you can say after a meditation retreat, when the whole wide world really does seem to make sense for a minute.

"What do you do there?" I asked him.

"I grow pot."

Ding.

"Are you supposed to just tell people like that?"

"I don't usually, but at the moment I feel safe."

This *I feel safe* was a liquid and contagious thing. We passed it around through each other's eyes and that we're-the-only-two-people-in-the-room thing happened and I meant it when I said, "I feel safe too."

"I'm going to a hot spring this afternoon," he said. "You want to come?"

Ding-ding-ding.

When I arrived at the parking lot, after scrubbing toilets, one of the more humbling ways to be of service at the retreat, he was already there, sharing pictures on his phone with a woman who had a scar on her brow. He looked up at me, then quickly down. "She's beautiful," the woman said, and my shoulders climbed a little. "How old is she?"

"Eighteen months," he said. "So are you going to meet me at the springs?" he asked her, and I thought I'd made a terrible mistake. I approached and she said, "Probably not," and got into her Prius.

"Sorry that took so long. You ready?" He slid his phone and its pictures into his pocket.

"Yes." An understatement.

When we arrived at the hot springs, I dipped into a pinkish layer of awkward on discovering that it was clothing-optional. I dipped into a pinker layer of awkward when in the undressing room I discovered a tit whisker under my left nipple. I tried to yank the hair with my fingernails. It curled like the ribbon on a birthday gift, or a pube. I needed tweezers, pronto. I slipped out to my car.

Owner's manual, insurance, registration, seven pens, minty floss, toothbrushing gum (a boldfaced lie), a yo-yo with a bract of heather blossoms entombed in resin, my Triple A card, assorted Band-Aids in filthy wrappers, a corkscrew, but no tweezers. Crouched between the car doors, I examined the hair once again. I once again tugged at it with pinched-together fingernails. It straightened and recurled. After three days of openness, I clenched—an actual physical reaction, the way an eyeball constricts in too-bright light. Over a hair.

When asked what he thought, Buga, my Russian tortoise riding shot-gun in his Tupperware habitat (he's an excellent meditator, if something of a shit machine) gave his usual reply. Something about the answer being in stillness, which despite the meditation I still struggled to understand. I kissed him on the shell.

Emerging from the undressing room clad only in tortilla chips and tit whisker, I ascended the stairs to the meditation pool with as much grace as I could muster. My head hair cascaded around my shoulders in what I hoped was a distracting way. I liked to think my highlights were gleam-ing. Ping. Ting. Emphatic fling.

I caught him immediately among the bobbing heads. Fermata, bird's-eye, corona; I held. He watched me in a way that got absorbed and multi-plied by my whole body before it circulated back out through every pore. I'd never felt so beautiful. I stood straight and strong and descended into the pool, each step equanimously considered. I was not the me I knew as I glided through the warm water toward him; I was more like a preview of someone I might become, or Lady Godiva.

We stood side by side, backs against the wall of the pool, heads resting on the edge, tracing the trajectories of dragonflies. I glanced around at the crowd in the pool. The place was oozing off the edges of the patchouli continuum. A sign explicitly forbade sexual activity, and couples all around us pressed toward the boundaries of each other and that edict. Silence was required, so the fugue of sighs and other intimate murmurs blended with the sound of water flowing in. There were two men floating women in their arms. The women were serene, hearts and breasts offered to the sky, a blend of baby and queen. "May I float you?" Judah asked.

This would put the tit whisker directly in his line of vision.

"Yes." And I said it again: "Yes." He pressed one hand to the small of my back and the other behind my shoulders and my body rose through the water, and I don't remember a time ever in my life when I have felt so completely at ease and at home in myself or so completely in love with a stranger, or so complete in every way at all. I heard Nina Simone's version of "He's Got the Whole World in His Hands," hands so sure and gentle as they led me toward the holes where the water gushed up from so deep under and inside the earth, so warm and steady, and he moved me so that this whooshed up and in between my legs, breath deep and easy as he pulled me close and spun me in a slow circle and I didn't want this to ever, ever end, and it wasn't until I thought this that it did.

He returned me to the wall and let me sink back to vertical. I kissed him on each eye, then his forehead, a tender little triangle of gratitude. He did it back. He opened his arms to me and steered me in so that my left side leaned into his: "Heart to heart," he said. "I think you're my Father's Day present." And we held each other like that for a long time, breathing together. I whispered in his ear, a Sanskrit word repeated as a mantra at the retreat . . . *anicca* . . . *anicca* . . .

It means everything changes.

SPROUT

HE INVITED ME TO HIS HOUSE, BUT I HAD TO DECLINE BECAUSE I WAS ON my way to Lake Tahoe for a three-day free vacation in exchange for being pitched a timeshare. Some telemarketer called and offered and I said yes. There are worse ways to roll. While Buga munched wheatgrass from a juice bar back at the hotel and I was trapped in a real estate office looking at papers I would never sign, Judah sent another invitation via text. He offered "Tortoise accommodations upon request." Buga was not a turtle. He was a tortoise. Chelonian distinctions were lost on most. Once again I said yes.

I arrived in the evening after getting very lost. His eighteen-month-old daughter, Sprout, was there, as she was three days a week. Judah and her mom weren't quite together anymore when Sprout was conceived. I fed her quinoa and veggies, using the airplane technique. Judah leaned on his elbows and shook his head, "If you would have told me that The Girl from *The Blair Witch Project* would be at my house feeding my kid . . ." I didn't drop this piece of trivia. Googled, bamboozled. I jabbed another piece of broccoli.

"What? What would you have done?" I asked, raising the spork high. "This one's coming from Barcelona . . . cleared for landing . . . *Benving-uts!*" Sprout giggled and ate her veggies without fuss.

"You're good at this. Please, stay. As long as you want."

THE GIRLS

"Have you ever been in a growroom?" he asked as we stepped off his porch toward the detached garage. The industrial-strength baby monitor bulged from his back pocket. City girl. Country night. Couldn't see my hand in front of my face.

"I don't really smoke."

"Heather." He took my hands in his. "You made a bong out of an apple last night."

I faltered. "I dated a stoner for ten years. He couldn't pay rent but always had a bag of whatever. Mary Jane was like the other woman."

"Dude, don't say Mary Jane. Unless Cheech just gifted you a Thai stick on your way home to watch *Solid Gold*."

"Sorry, dude, don't know the lingo."

"I'll teach you," he said, and wrapped his arm around my shoulders. "I'll teach you everything you need to know. Then you'll never go back to LA."

He made a faux sinister *bwah-ha-ha* face at me, then threaded his arm through mine.

"You were never here," he said, jangling his keys.

Earlier today, in front of this same detached garage, he put his arm around me and said, "Having you here makes me want to clean my gutters." Now I was never there. We were not skulking about, arm in arm, in deepest night. I heard something—Feds? A bear?—and gripped his arm.

"It's just deer," he said. "You'll learn that sound if you move here." Still, I knew how to take a false idea and run it up and down my spine, playing scales. In my previous occupation it was considered a skill.

He kissed me, rocket-tongued, handed off the flashlight, and fumbled with the key in the lock. He stepped into the tiny vestibule, opened a second door, then swung it back so there was room for me to enter. I did. White sheets of paper in plastic pockets covered the door. "These are my scrips," he explained, "the patients that I grow for." There were purple metal boxes, stacked and humming on some plastic shelves. Thick black cords jutted umbilical, disappearing into a hole stuffed with pink fiberglass. The pink, the purple—my eyes were adjusting.

"Those are the ballasts," he said, and locked the outer door. He was crouching in the vestibule, gripping the tab of a white, crescent-shaped zipper lit from within.

"Why is it curved?"

"So you can open it with one hand."

The zipper was part of another door, this one made of some thin dark skin, kind of like the room was really a giant tent where, instead of lots of pot, inside will be a dancing bear and a sequined girl on a flying trapeze.

"Ready?"

"I think so."

In one giant swoop he split the crescent and it was like death in the movies: I was awash in white light. Except this white light wasn't gentle. It was fierce and completely overwhelming. Nine thousand watts in all. Inside was a sea of luminous, vigorous green, with a million specks of hydroponically juiced resin. It was a nuclear beehive, a homemade spaceship bracing for takeoff. It hummed. The hum was not just from the fans and the ballasts and the power and the light, the hum also emanated from The Girls themselves, their own hungry hum. Each sticky calyx a fingery antenna wanting touch. All flowers are sexual organs, instruments of desire. Thanks, Girls, you made it abundantly clear. My eyes, nose, fingers, toes adjusted and I saw him again, Judah, my Cheshire Cat.

"Sixty thousand every eight weeks," he said, tapping the five-gallon jugs of nutrients, or nutes, into a conical cup, then dumped them into the reservoirs. Practical magic.

"Then how come your phone got shut off?"

He's startled.

"That's if everything goes perfect."

The plants were aligned in neat rows on each of the seven large tables, like some kind of vegetable chorus line. They kicked their limbs into three layered grids of white plastic trellis and kicked me in the nose with their deep piney peat.

"Only Kush smells just like that," he said, of my deep inhale.

"They're like trees!"

"Tahoe trees."

"God, they're so sticky."

"Thank you." He hung his head, like when I complimented his daughter, like he couldn't take all the credit, but said, "Yeah, I'm pretty proud of my Girls."

There was no way I could have guessed that normal-looking detached garage harbored a mechanical Eden. It was a botanical jack-in-the-box— *pop goes the ganja!* Nature and technology had come together to support a mind-boggling amount of plant per square foot, rocking barbarian buds, 'roided out, sweating glitter, and about to blow.

A ball floated and fell inside a glass cylinder attached to a tank as tall as me. "The CO_2 setup," he said, adjusting the tank on its dolly.

Giant foil robot arms connected the lights. "They're air-cooled." He pointed to a fan mounted in a far, high corner of the room, above the row of breaker boxes. It was a smaller version of what propels a jet. There were more familiar-looking oscillating fans mounted on the walls, and desk models gusting at the undercanopy. Every leaf quivered. "Ventilation is key. It makes The Girls strong, and doesn't let pests or mold spores land."

"Thrip traps!" They were the only thing in here that I am familiar with from my parking lot garden in LA. They are simple cardboard rectangles, blue for thrips, yellow for whiteflies, covered in glue. The pests are drawn to the color, and away from the plants. He had a collection of them zip-tied to his trellis poles like prayer flags.

"You don't want to get your hair caught on those," he said.

"Tell me about it," I said, glad to have some common ground.

This is when the pumps kicked in. They were staggered, so as not to flip a breaker. I could hear them. There was nothing to be seen because the plants' trunks disappeared into a thick white sheet of plastic that concealed whatever went on at the root. "Flood and drain," Judah said, and lifted the sheet, which was black on the other side. "The plastic keeps the algae out, and the white reflects the light." Underneath were squishy tan logs with squishy tan cubes set on them. "Rock wool," he explained. "It's like fiberglass." The rock wool cubes were subsumed by roots. After thirty seconds of flooding the tables and saturating the absorbent cubes with nutrient solution, the drain began. "The nutes go back into the reservoir," he explained, and dragged a huge tub from under a table, "where they get aerated again. I dump and refill them every five days. You want to check the pH?" He handed me something like a tagger's Magic Marker. "Just take off the cap and dip the tip, that little glass ball, into the reservoir." 5.6 popped up in the display.

"Is that what it's supposed to be?"

"Yeah," he said, and kissed the top of my head.

NUGGETTOWN

THE RIVER REALLY DID FLOW WITH GOLD. WE PASSED PROSPECTORS—SOME grizzled, some unexpectedly young—working their claims in the sun. We passed clusters of pot families, some of them known to Judah, some not, out at the river in the middle of a Thursday afternoon. You could tell they were pot families partly because they were out at the river in the middle of a Thursday afternoon—jumping from rocks, swinging from trees, floating, swimming, laughing. Dogs swam for sticks; babies were strapped to hiking mothers. Bright towels lined the banks. Smooth granite boulders held napping bodies.

Judah's best friend, Zeus, his son, SaRah, and his girlfriend, Cedara, were waiting for us by the bridge. Zeus was a thirty-year-old country-tyme baller originally from the Pacific Northwest with a face that gave up nothing but stubble. His four-year-old son came into the world via a Costa Rican birthing tub. Despite these serene beginnings, he mostly liked to hit things. Cedara was not SaRah's mother, but she *was* a dead ringer for Snow White, if Snow White had spent some time as an expat in Thailand in lieu of college.

There were lots of people along the banks, but we found a place. Judah, Sprout, and I squatted and bounced in the water. Sprout was surprised by each fish and tried to catch them with her hands. She ran to Cedara for carrots while Judah and I floated. We took in the canopy of oak and madrone, the fluffy clouds chugging off to nowhere quite as good. We dove off the big gray boulders. Cloths were unfolded to reveal snacks. Dirty little carrots were rinsed in the river and bitten with a happy crack. There was seaweed salad and sunflower seeds and roasted beets cut into cubes that we dipped into goat cheese. Our lips and fingers were all stained bright. We dredged up specks of gold and mica with our toes. Fish flashed through the muddy clouds of silt we raised. Dragonflies hummed. Bees bumbled past, investigating lemonade from home. It could be 2007, or it could be 7 BC, but for the brightly colored towels and the Spandex.

Cedara and I spread the cloths out on the sand and put together sandwiches with the bread she baked that morning. A seeded loaf, dense and crusty. We tore out warm hunks and ate them before we filled the crust with avocado, peppers, lettuce, and lemon cucumbers from the garden. Somebody's dog ran up the beach with SaRah's wooden sword between his teeth. He dropped it at SaRah's feet and panted, waiting for him to throw it again. Zeus grabbed it before SaRah could bring it down on the dog's head.

We were hungry again by the time the shadows sent us home. Sprout put her arms around my neck and said, "Feather hold you," which meant she wanted me to carry her. At first it was awkward, but Judah rustled her hair and mine, one hand on each, and we laughed.

We all went to Judah's house, and he and I showed SaRah how to set the table without using utensils to slash and puncture anything but food while Zeus and Cedara prepared a Technicolor goulash.

"So this is what community looks like," I said to no one and everyone.

Cedara smiled. "You in?"

"Oh, she's in," Judah said as he watched me lift Sprout into her high chair.

We bowed our heads and held hands to thank the Mother for the bounty she provided. We thanked the river too, for helping us earn our appetites. We washed it all down with cider from last year's apples.

The kids were tired so their papas tucked them in before heading out to check on the garden in the garage. Cedara and I washed dishes. "Isn't it wonderful?" she said, perched on the counter, drying. "Our men tending the crop, the children sleeping. Our bellies and hearts so full."

"Yes" was all I could muster. *A thousand times yes.*

"It makes me feel bad for most people. This is how we're meant to live. We're not meant to be cooped up in cubicles and cars, looking at screens all day. It's the only reason I can think of why ganja is illegal. The Girls let you know what life is supposed to look like. Smoke them, grow them, they show you how things can be. Can't let the word spread too far or the whole system would fall apart."

"Don't you worry about getting arrested? The real-world laws still exist."

"This *is* my real world. The Mother's laws are the only laws worth obedience. I talk to friends of mine who work nine to five, not even counting their commute—they're in prison already. There's a risk to growing, sure, but look what we have. . . ." She put her hands in prayer position then pressed them to the floor. She rose, quivering. "Thank you, Mother!" she shouted, throwing her hands ecstatically above her head, and I had to hand it to her, she looked a lot happier than most people I knew. At the moment she looked deliriously happy, in fact. She was twirling in the kitchen like a dervish. I thought about rows of cubicles, empty of me, and I thought, was this—all of this—something they were getting away with? Or was she right, and this was how things were meant to be?

Zeus and Judah returned, pungent from the garage, and we smoked some of the Blueberry Cheese that he experimented with last round.

"If we both grow for a few years, we'll be able to retire, move to Bali or something." Judah's words slid down his chest into my ear.

"Maybe for a year," I said.

"And after that?" Zeus asked me. What we all had in common was no plan B.

"I can take care of you," Judah said. My cringe was submerged under the deep Indica stone.

Cedara nuzzled into Zeus at the other end of the couch and stared at me, nodding. The lamplight from the end table conjoined their heads, seeped into a halo.

"Trust," she said.

A THOUSAND TIMES YES

AFTER THEY LEFT, JUDAH AND I LEANED AGAINST THE DECK WITH A BOTTLE of red, looking out over his land. I was studying a pine that skewered a teddy bear, the way the shadows laid, when he cracked the quiet. "What's your definition of love?" he asked me.

I paused. "Respect, compassion, passion, acceptance, laughing together—"

"You do love me then," he said, and I wriggled a little under his double-barrel gaze—looked down at the moons on my nail beds, up at the one in the sky—and everything went still.

"Yeah, I think I do."

He took my hands. "I see you," he said, underlining the *see*. Being seen is different from being recognized by strangers on the street. We don't see ourselves, so we say we see others. I liked that he saw me; it meant he was paying attention. It was the toll for that particular bridge, the back-bended crazy girl fuck. He pulled me into him, enveloping me like fur. His hands went white around my shoulders, then dark again on the slide back down. My hands went white on his shoulders too, slid over lobes to nape and pulled. *Welcome.*

"I see you," he said again and freed one hand to cup my cheek. He wiped a trickle with his thumb; so much was falling from my eyes.

"Do you want to stop?"

Don't stop, I didn't say but he could hear me anyway. The match of heat and wet smeared up everything between us. *Yes. A thousand times yes.*

WE LOVE PAPA

THAT WAS JULY. BY JANUARY HE WAS CALLING ME HIS DREAMGIRL. THE One. Things like that. He said that if things didn't work out with me then maybe he was just meant to be alone. After my relationship with Wacław ended, I vowed never to live with anyone I wasn't married to ever again. Mama always told me they don't buy no cow when they're getting free milk. So I lived with Judah for eight weeks. It started out as only November, but November was pretty shaky, so we added December. We called it The Trial Period, and it included a pot-growing apprenticeship as well as a thing we called Creative Hour, where we drew from bags of prompts we made for each other and then set a timer for one hour. I'd write a story, he'd write a song, and then we would come together to share what we made. He wrote me a song called "Ladybug" about how I was a blessing to his garden. I decorated Sprout's tiny kitchen table with the alphabet and spent the better part of an incredibly satisfying week shellacking it. The Trial Period also included building fires, baking flourless chocolate tortes, bathroom scrubbing, snowshoeing on his land, babysitting, cooking, shopping with his mother, much humid afternoon delight, laundry, singing Beatles songs in his living room, and one unfortunate incident where I gratuitously stabbed a frozen chicken that I was trying to fry during a power outage.

Once, when he was at a men's circle or a workshop about intimacy or a sex party in the city, I watched Sprout and we gathered pine needles and acorns in a basket that may or may not have been woven by her mother. With the needles and nuts and glitter glue and construction paper we made him an enormous sign that read, WE LOVE PAPA! It took up all the space next to the French doors.

Sprout and I hung the sign, and when I put her to bed with a story and a kiss and "Golden Slumbers," she said, "I love you, Feather." I told her I loved her too. Because I did, beyond reason. As a duo, she and her Papa were sweetest kryptonite. It was hard to separate out my attachments. My love for Sprout was so simple and bright it blinded me to a lot of things that shouldn't have been hard to see. I liked being the lady of the house. It felt grown up. It felt full when LA had left me hungry.

After Sprout was asleep, I went downstairs and Windexed each panel of glass—each spiderweb, each moth carcass. The glitter glue, the windows—everything shone. I left the porch light on for him. There was no way he could miss the sign when he came home, even before he got out of the car. He didn't. I was in the bathtub when he arrived and heard how long it took for him to come in after he pulled up. I waited in the tub all the time it took for him to find me after he finally came in the door. I saw how red his eyes were and how much he didn't want me to see exactly that.

He got into the bathtub with me. I had a fire roaring in the woodstove downstairs and his daughter was dreaming in her bed—everything about this was warm. He said, "That's the nicest thing anyone has ever done for me," and I didn't think he was lying. I kissed his face and licked my salty lips. "This house needs you," he said.

DELIVER ME FROM POT WIFERY

The Trial Period came to a close and I had to decide what to do.

"I think you should move here. I think you should let LA go," Judah said. "Aren't you happy here?"

"I am," I said, and leaned into him on the couch. "But what would I do?"

"You could live with me. You could help out with the garden. We could put veggie beds right over there." He pointed through the window at a flat spot next to the little corral I built for Buga.

"I could be like Cedara, you mean? I could be your pot wife?"

The pot wives are not The Girls. *The Girls* refers only to the marijuana plants, who are all female and strictly prohibited from contact with males.

Nor is a pot wife actually a wife. She is a girlfriend, typically a cohabitating one, who does all of the traditional 1950s wifely things—but she does them in the name of the Divine Feminine. She is like a Beverly Hills trophy wife with more body hair. She is like Betty Crocker if Betty were a vegan who garnished everything with seaweed and gogi berries. She grows food, but she usually has very little to do with the money garden. Rutabaga is cheaply replaced; The Girls, not so much. Let the lady have her farm fun on less serious crops.

Frequently, she is a semiretired massage therapist. She often does yoga, belly dance, makes her own granola, and takes care of her man's baby from a previous relationship with a woman who was also not his wife, but could be considered his ex–pot wife, whom he also takes care of, in what begins to develop into a sort of mini-empire, or at least a harem. There is no jealousy; there is not even mild annoyance. All of these women get along great because they are all manifestations of the Goddess.

Where do they come from, you might ask?

Or perhaps you're wondering: How can I get one?

They are selected from Uncle Harvey's Trim Parade, the annual harvest season pageant where young hopefuls come from as far afield as Hawaii and Costa Rica, grape scissors in hand, to trim the ripe outdoor bud crop and vie for a grower lover who will finance their self-exploration in exchange for lending crystals, crafts, and quinoa to an otherwise abject growhouse. It's not easy to have coziness and industrial agriculture in the same house; these ladies make it happen.

When they tire of their situations and want to go out on their own, maybe have their own scene and not just cook meals and watch his kid, they wind up as sharecroppers for their man. Often, these women don't have the credit to rent a house on their own, so their grower boyfriend cosigns. Usually, he hasn't shared much of the how-to of actually running a room (or she just hasn't been particularly interested), so he provides the start-up costs, equipment, expertise, et cetera, and she will pay him a sizable percentage, which, after overhead, leaves her with very little money and no more ability to roam. The Girls keep you on a short leash. The wives become kept twice over.

The pot wives can't really understand why I would rent my own house and have my own scene. They made fervent arguments for "embracing abundance mentality" because I "deserve these gifts he wants to give me," that I was "being granted this opportunity by the benevolence of the universe." I almost gave in to the narcotic tug. But I didn't know any forty-year-old pot wives, and I was already thirty-four. Where middle-aged pot wives ended up was, I imagined, similar to the place missing socks go when they disappear from the dryer.

Sometimes I think we should send pot wives to teach the Hutus and Tutsis or, perhaps more apropos, the Janjaweed militia in Darfur about abundance mentality and the benevolence of the universe. I would watch that documentary, but for the gore.

"Would that be so bad?" Judah snuggled me into the couch in a way that suggested the Vicodin prescribed for his back had kicked in.

"What if I got my own house?"

"To grow in?"

"Yeah. To grow in."

"It's not easy. As you've seen." He stroked my cheek and his hand kept sliding—throat, chest, belly.

His Girls had struggled mightily while I was there. Turns out it was the offgassing of the new veg room Hydrohut, a plastic stand-alone shelter he'd bought to make a veg room under the house. The Girls, it seems, are sensitive to invisible forces. Which is why other thoughts passed first—like I was the opposite of a blessing to his garden.

"I don't need easy. I just need something that's mine."

"You're welcome here. You can have the loft just for you." His hand was still sliding—chest, belly, thighs.

"Thank you. I appreciate that. But maybe we could date in the same town? Instead of this thing where we're either hundreds of miles apart or together twenty-four/seven?"

"If that's what you want." I should mention that Judah was the kind of man that makes a word like *want* echo in your bones. I should also mention that he knew this.

"I want to get married, have a family. I'm tired of renting," I said.

"I'm not ready for that."

"You already have it."

"And it's as much as I can handle. I like my life the way it is. With you in it," he said.

We wrapped our arms around each other in a mutually groany squeeze.

"I'm not gonna let you run. I'm gonna hold you just like this," he said. When he wanted to be, he was the most present man I'd ever known. His eyes were like the air above a car hood in July. I was in the woods again and not sure whose breadcrumb path to follow. Birds long since ate the one I laid.

I said, "Let me throw the coins."

Since The Great Purge, this is almost exclusively how I made decisions—the I Ching. Ancient Chinese divination, sure, but basically a coin toss. Somehow the fact that it's two coins tossed six times made it feel more legit. The ancientness didn't hurt either. I wrote on a piece of paper: "What will happen if I move here and rent my own growhouse?"

"Seriously?" he asked.

"How do you make decisions?"

"I think about them. I meditate. I listen to my heart."

"My heart loves you and would enjoy being your pot wife. But my brain will not let my heart live with someone who is 'not ready for that.' Because my hands have a tendency to do laundry and scrub bathrooms and generally feel like the lady of a merely rented house and then my liver overmakes the bile of resentment." I kissed him.

He laughed and kissed back. "Throw your coins."

I do.

"Oh. Huh."

"What does it say?"

I read from the Wilhelm translation, my handy yellow hardback with fingerdirty edges: "Deliverance. The obstacle has been removed, the difficulties are being resolved . . . These periods of sudden change have great importance. Just as rain relieves atmospheric tension, making all the buds burst open, so a time of deliverance from burdensome pressure has a liberating and stimulating effect on life. One thing is important, however: In such times we must not overdo our triumph. The point is not to push on farther than is necessary . . . If there are any residual matters that ought to be attended to, it should be done as quickly as possible, so that a clean sweep is made and no retardations occur."

No retardations. That would be new.

"Did you hear the part about all the buds bursting open?" The deal done, I laid back on the couch.

"Did you hear the part about not pushing on farther than is necessary?" He rolled on top of me. I loved making mouth fondue on a Tuesday afternoon. I much preferred it to a cubicle.

"All I have to do is find a house."

"Later."

THE HOUSE AT THE END OF THE ROAD

I WOKE WITH IT URGENT IN MY HEAD: *GO TO NUGGETTOWNHOUSES.COM. Go to nuggettownhouses.com.* I clicked on the site and there it was, a three-bedroom, two-bath with an attached garage. "Enchanted Forest! This beautiful home won't last long! The ultimate in end-of-the-road privacy, this elegant house also offers a hot tub and fire pit on the massive cedar-shaded deck, and an above-ground pool! All this and more on three and a half forested acres. Live like you're on vacation all year round! The clock is ticking . . ." I woke Judah. "I think I found it. I think I found my house."

I showed him the page. "Looks good," he said, but he wasn't subject to my easily enflamed enthusiasm. "Let's check it out."

"It's five hundred dollars a month over my budget."

"Don't worry about that. The Girls will have your back."

"But what if I don't want to do that?"

"You'd rather waitress?"

"Can you believe it has a pool *and* a hot tub?" I asked him as we drove.

"You know you can never use either of those things. Or the washer/dryer or the dishwasher."

Right. That's what *Marijuana Horticulture: The Indoor/Outdoor Medical Grower's Bible* (or, as it's called in The Community, simply *The Bible*) said. Rent a house with as many energy-sucking accoutrements as you can find and then don't use any of them. You want them for cushion so that when you start racking up $1,500 electric bills, it won't seem so shocking to the power company or anyone else who might be looking.

We passed it. Twice. The road was marked only with a white post and a vertical arrangement of stickers. Very easy to miss. "That's good," Judah said. We drove down the street, no, a dirt road, no, a lunar surface. We passed two houses right across from each other and continued down the road, waiting for the house to show up, but it was another eighth-mile. We passed a gate at the final bend. "It already has a gate," Judah said. "Wow."

We passed the pool on our right. "Look! Look!" I said, pointing like a five-year-old on her first trip to the zoo. We came around a final curve and there it was, cuddled by trees like it was their kid—which it sort of was. It was like a reconstituted treehouse with its unvarnished horizontal siding, formerly known as trunks.

"This is definitely the end of the road," he said, and I tried not to hear that for the metaphor it was.

"Oh my God! This is it! This is totally it!" We got out of the car.

The house was in a large gully with hills rising up around it. If I had known more about feng shui, such a feature might have been less appealing. There was only one other house even remotely visible, and it was way up the hill, mostly obscured by oaks and manzanita. And look! There was one particularly magnificent cedar whose boughs shaded the deck. The ancient Egyptians used cedar for shipbuilding and coffins. I sniff it—thick, green, grand, strong; incorruptible as the gold its taproot likely tickles. I have a crush on it already, this tree. I will put my rocking chair under it and drink Sierra Nevada and practice becoming an old lady some twilights in August. "Oh, this is it," I said again. I was digging in. Judah lifted the door of the electrical panel, checked the gauge of the main wire. "It's the best grow rental I've seen. Better than my place. Pretty perfect," he said to me and smiled. "And so, you know, Blair Witchy. You. Out here. At the end of the road. In the woods. Perfect." He laughed.

Last year, when I went to community college to try to figure out what to do with my life, I took a philosophy class where I learned about Nietzsche's idea of eternal recurrence. He suggested that life was circular and would keep repeating on you like cucumbers or chili, with nothing new in it, until you came to love your life so well that these repetitions would seem not like a curse, but an eternal confirmation.

Whatever I meant by *bring it* that night in the desert, I thought, was being brought.

POLAR

BUT FOR NOW, I AM STILL SITTING IN THIS YELLOW DRYWALL BOX THAT I have not yet painted back to unbloodied white. I am sitting in the middle of the thousand-square-foot room on the cheapest available taupe carpet, staring without nostalgia at the pimpy push-button faux stone fireplace while trying to find a dog on Petfinder. I have rented that house in Nuggettown and the only problem I see is one of security, as there will be bears and large spiders and men who wear overalls without irony, and I will be a woman living alone at the end of the road (with a medical marijuana garden in her garage). Ergo, the dog. It's preferable to a shotgun. So far. Although the idea of me in a bonnet and calico dress cracking a Winchester on my front porch shouting "Git off m'land!" does have a certain appeal. Luckily, a loyal dog snarling by my side can only add, should I decide to go that route later.

I'm getting a rescue dog. I don't want a puppy under any circumstances. I don't want to housebreak a puppy, or train a puppy in any way. A puppy won't know it should be grateful because I saved it. A puppy will just assume that I've always loved it and life has been good and full of walks and cuddles and organic treats. No. I want a dog who's been through the wringer and will appreciate what I have to offer, in case what I have to offer turns out to suck. I want a dog who knows things could be a lot worse, so if I should happen to screw it all up the dog will think, *Well, things could be a lot worse.*

I found him. I knew as soon as that picture of him—one ear up, the other down, frolicking in the snow—popped up on my screen. His name is Polar. He's half German shepherd and half golden retriever, exactly what I wanted. This choice might be indicative of some commitment issues I may or may not have. I want a guard dog, but one that's also blond and cuddly and fetches and drools. His page opens with: "This is Polar, but mostly we call him Bi-Polar. A temperamental mixed bag of both his breeds, he's very smart, and sometimes cuddly! With the right handler and continued training he might eventually be a stable family pet! He's at the top of his class in obedience school!" That many exclamation points usually suggests to me a sense of desperation, but see him frolic! And he's nine months old! Mature enough to already be housebroken, but young enough to bond with me!

GIVING BIRTH BY YOURSELF

TODAY, SMOG-CHOKED CITY GIRL. TOMORROW, POLLEN UP MY NOSE, SEEDS in my pocket, living off the fat of the land. Sure, this living off the fat of the land business might seem like a tall order for someone who has never lived in a place with a population under a million, but I think it's probably doable. I both established and tended a little four-by-six-foot garden in the parking lot of my apartment building. The jasmine and gardenias I planted there to mask the exhaust functioned a lot like the matches of my childhood that my dad lit after taking a shit—the aromas layered rather than mixed, each scent asserting a defiant, snobby sort of purity. In the country, there will just be well-integrated breezes weaving manure and blossoms and sunshine and soil (and skunk). Also, I have a copy of *The Encyclopedia of Country Living.*

In these allegedly pre-apocalyptic times, it's a must-have. Carla Emery (may she rest in peace) tells you everything you need to know to live off the land. The section called "Giving Birth by Yourself," for example, has an informative part called "Toilet Babies." It's a handy reference for urbanites as well, as in the part called "How to Kill, Pick, and Clean a Pigeon." My favorite passage is sort of random and snuggled between how to preserve herbs and how to make herb butter. It's just kind of snuck in there, like she doesn't think anyone will read close enough to find it. It says, "God, if I deserve it, make me a better person. Guide me, Lord. Sometimes things get so confusing. Sometimes I'm not sure what it is You really want me to do. Help me get everything done that I've got to do. Thank You for the joy to come." I'm not so big on God with a capital G, but otherwise, Mrs. Emery, my sentiments exactly.

Right in the introduction, however, is this: "The easy way to do things is to do one thing and do it well. But if you commit yourself to this kind of life, you're committing yourself to trying to do a hundred incompatible and competitive things, and like as not, in your first year seventy-five of them will fizzle." And Mrs. Emery, as far as I know, never grew pot.

MARCH ON

LIL DICK

I TURN OFF THE FREEWAY TOWARD THE SIERRA NEVADA. NUGGETTOWN IS nestled here, tucked away in the foothills. I wind my way up Judah's road and hear a vaguely angelic chord as the hill crests and his ten acres open to the sunset in front of me. Pine tops wave. *Welcome, welcome . . .*

Judah runs up the hill from the porch to greet me. He is pulling on the door before I get Lucy into park. "So no more trial period—you're officially a country girl! Congratulations!" He lifts me up and spins me around, plunks me back into the driver's seat.

"Where's my overalls? I thought I got a free pair of overalls," I say, but he's already at the passenger door.

"Beer first!" he says, getting in.

"Wait, I at least want a piece of straw to put in my mouth."

"Let's just go get beer."

"I just drove nine hours. Why can't you drive?"

"You want me to drive Lucy?" He's back out and over, lifting me from the seat again.

"What's wrong with Shark Attack?" His Subaru.

"Lucy's bigger." He takes the keys from my hand.

"You're getting a keg?"

"Just get in."

I do.

Lucy's tires shriek as we turn off of Judah's road onto the asphalt. "Your car has like zero pickup." There is an old blue 4Runner in the rearview. Judah glances up like he expected it to be there. Lucy's engine revs hard before turning over. I pat the dashboard to console her.

"Are you high?" I ask. A chronically relevant question in these parts.

"Hold on." The 4Runner is still behind us. There is no way to lose it on this narrow highway. Judah tries anyway and crosses the double yellow to pass the pink water truck in front of us.

"What the fuck?" I yell at him.

"Hold on." The 4Runner is behind us again. The water truck driver lays on her horn. Judah pulls up to Mountain Mama Mart. The 4Runner pulls up beside us. Dust. The water truck passes, giving us all the pink acrylic finger.

Two men get out of the Toyota. One is in his late thirties, big eater, glossy white track suit. The ganja leaf T-shirt underneath is probably not supposed to reveal his midriff. This is Lil Dick: middle-class kingpin. The other is his henchman, in a plain black XL Columbia fleece.

"So, boy think he in business for hisself," says Lil Dick, his blackcent picked up cheap at Justin Timberlake's garage sale. "What you driving your girlfriend's car for, you scared little shit? Where my money? Huh? You forget who da King of Kush in this county?"

I'm sure the alliteration is unintentional, but sort of lovely nonetheless. I think that is a good thing for me to focus on right now, because otherwise I keep alternating between being scared shitless and feeling like I'm in an *SNL* sketch about rural gangstaz. Lil Dick's sidekick doesn't do anything except stand on my side of the car with his hand in his jacket pocket, the one inside.

"What the fuck is that?" Lil Dick gestures to the backseat.

"Looks like a fucking turtle," says Fleece, hand unmoving.

A turtle? What the fuck? I clarify: "It's not a turtle, it's a tortoise. His name is Buga. It means *universe* in the langu—"

"Shut the fuck up."

Other cars pull into the parking lot, and I wonder if I should scream. I try to catch Judah's eye for some clue, but Lil Dick's head is inside the driver's side window, so it's sort of tight quarters. Hard to send a message without it getting intercepted.

"What are you looking at?" Lil Dick asks me.

I am looking at the white dust sticking to the hairs of your right nostril. I say nothing. "Tha's right," Lil Dick says.

"Leave her out of this." Judah lets go of the steering wheel, kills the engine. A woman picks up her little boy and scurries past Lucy, trying not to look.

"Let's go for a walk." Lil Dick, a gentleman, opens the door.

"You stay here," he says to me. Judah affirms this with a somber nod. The three of them stroll away so casually that I almost expect them to hold hands. I want to rewrite their dialogue because it's so clichéd. It's like I've stumbled into a sandbox where some little boys are playing *Godfather* and I have no idea how committed they are to their game or what props may be involved. They disappear behind Mountain Mama Mart. I press my hand to Buga's shell. My fingers tingle. The window fogs.

Fifteen very long minutes have passed. It's getting dark, and I get out of the car. Lil Dick and Fleece are coming toward me. Judah isn't with them. Fleece's hand is no longer in his pocket.

"I thought we told you to stay in the car," Lil Dick says, and laughs. The pot leaves stretched across his belly dance.

"You did. I'm—"

"Tha's right." Lil Dick and Fleece walk on, letting my knees be joints again.

Judah is sitting on a milk crate beside a Dumpster with his head in his hands. I kneel beside him. Broken glass shivers and reflects the moon. There are no street lamps here. This is the country, dammit. He puts his arm around me and seeps a brittle whisper, "I will do whatever it takes to protect my family." *Yeah! We're a family! Fuck that guy! Fuck that Lil Dick!*

I don't say this; I don't say anything. Judah's phone rings and he turns away.

"Hey man, some shit's hit the fan. . . . No shit. . . . Oh. . . . Shit. . . . No way. . . . What the fuck? . . . Fuck that shit. . . . That's bullshit. . . . No way. . . . Don't do it, man. . . . Just breathe. . . . Keep your center, man. . . . Fuck it. . . . That won't solve anything. . . . Hold the space, man, hold the space. . . . Breathe. . . . Okay. . . . Arrightbye."

CIRCLING THE WAGONS

WE DRIVE TO ZEUS AND CEDARA'S HOUSE. SARAH IS RUNNING AROUND the living room brandishing a small saw. He charges at me. I duck.

"Rah, cut it out," I tell him.

"RRRRRRAAAAAHHHH!" he growls, and charges again.

Zeus lilts, "Okay, Rah. That's enough." I am squatting in a corner. The small yet very real serrated blade is suspended like a guillotine in SaRah's little hands.

I look him in the eye and whisper, "Do I look like someone you want to mess with?" He brings down the saw, holds it to his chest, considering.

"Yaaaaaaaaaaa!" he shouts. I tuck and do a front roll out of the corner as the blade whistles down.

"Ah, are you playing with Auntie?" Cedara says. I move behind her.

"No, I'm killllliiiiiinnnngggg herrrrrrrrrr!" he growls.

Cedara turns to me. "He's not bothering you, is he?" SaRah, seeing me distracted, takes this moment to pick up his wooden sword and hit me behind the knees. They buckle, then throb.

She cradles SaRah and pours a mantra in his ear. "You're not a killer, you're a healer, you're not a killer, you're a healer, you're not a killer, you're a healer . . . What are you?"

"A killer!"

"Do you have beer?" I ask.

"It's in the fridge. Let me just put him to bed. Meet you in the hot tub?"

They turn to go upstairs and the kid sticks his tongue out at me. Much of me wants to give him the finger, but he's only five.

Ed arrives, his arm in a sling crafted from old plaid flannel, jammies maybe. His shoulders are stooped and his fists clench harder as he mutters something with *fuck* in it. If he were in a comic, he would perpetually have @#$%! in the thought bubble over his head.

He waves his flannel arm at Zeus. "Tell me you didn't give that fat fuck money." Everyone knows he did. He's the only one who could, the only one consistent enough to have something socked away.

"It was diplomacy," Zeus says.

"It was being a pussy," Ed scoffs.

Judah has stepped into the center of the living room wielding the talking stick, which is adorned with obsidian, feathers, boa bones, quartz. He plants it in the living room floor like a flag. It becomes, incontrovertibly, his turn to speak: "Ed, just chill—we need to stick together. We're here to make a plan, not to act like assholes." His eyes continue to scan the assembled. "We need to do whatever it takes to protect ourselves. I realized today how much I have to lose." Judah looks at me when he says this. My chin rises, puckers. His elbows come away from his sides and his eyes pass like a church donation plate to every person in the room.

"Whatever it takes," he repeats, reaching his fist out for the other guys to bump it, one at a time. *Wonder Twin powers . . . activate! Form of . . . a warrior!*

"Whatever it takes," they all echo. Zeus straddles his djembe and beats it for a minute. Judah whoops. Ed drinks more beer.

Zeus asks me, "Isn't Cedara waiting for you in the hot tub?"

"Fuck him, we could just grow Sour D," Judah says.

Time for the menfolk to do manthings.

"We'd lose a round a year, dude. Two extra weeks to ripen, plus that shit is larfy," Ed says.

Time for the pot wives to go to the hot tub, where they belong.

I reach around the kombucha and grab another cold Sierra.

HOTTUBBIN'

CEDARA AND I ARE SMOKING A SPLIFF IN THE HOT TUB ON ZEUS'S DECK. The jets are on and it's hard to hear and I am glad because this is my first day as a country girl goddammit and I am clad in a million tiny bubbles, sopping up a billion vellicating stars.

"Do you think they'll get guns?" I ask, vague and loud.

"No way. That'll just bring gun energy and that's not our scene," Cedara says.

"That would change things," I say, because it would for me, at least.

"Would you still do Kush?" Cedara asks.

Kush is what the boys grow. It's the most consistently valuable strain, but it's nearly impossible to find solid OG Kush seeds, at least in this community, and it's too risky to buy them online. So to fill your garden you need clones, which come from cuttings and take constant care to root. Lil Dick has provided the clone supply in exchange for taking everyone's manicured medicine at rock-bottom prices. Though the prices Lil Dick pays are still higher than what other strains would fetch, the gents are attempting to liberate themselves from his tyranny. Ergo the multiple injuries. Ergo the djembe-fueled kibbutz in the living room.

"Lil Dick doesn't really know me . . . ," I say.

"Yeah, he probably wouldn't think you're doing your own thing. Plus you're not gonna do hydro, so he wouldn't be interested in what you'd grow anyway," Cedara offers. "Cute new bangs, by the way."

"Thanks. They help with my fivehead." I demonstrate how my forehead accommodates five fingers, with room to spare. "And, you know, new life, new hair. It's nice to actually see something different in the mirror. Like, see that? I'm changing."

"They should infect Dick's room with spider mites."

"Ooh, that's cold," I say. I've seen what spider mites can do. They are smaller than a pinhead and suck the life out of a plant. Then they weave webs like a freeway system, so they can suck some more. They are harder to get rid of than a fear of commitment.

"That is not the way to fix this." Cedara twists her black hair into a bun. "We need to come from a place of love. He's scared, but we can't validate his place of fear. We just have to transform it with our prayers. And yeah, I wasn't havin' it when he was gettin' all up in my face over here, but it's important that we hold space for him and let him know that he's still a member of our Community."

"You think that will work?" I ask.

"I think it will work better than putting spider mites in his room. He's not an idiot. He has Floramite," Cedara says.

"I'm adopting a dog," I say. "I found him online. We're going Thursday to pick him up. He frolics in the snow and everything—you should see the pictures!"

"I want a dog!"

"Me too!"

"I love dogs."

"Yeah."

"Dogs are awesome."

"I don't want a puppy."

"They protect you."

". . . the shit."

"Yeah."

"That's a lot of shit."

"And pee."

"No shit."

"That sucks."

"Totally."

We laugh our asses off because that spliff is done and puppies make a lot of shit and pee, and that really does totally suck.

The menfolk arrive.

"You ladies been keeping it warm for me?" Judah says, taking off his pants. He saves his shirt for last—because he has a personal trainer, because of his back. He pauses like a model at the end of a runway before he gets in.

"We get it man, you like your cock. Just get in the fucking hot tub already," Ed says.

Zeus huddles himself into a demi-squat and doesn't pause before submerging.

Judah stretches out his arms along the rim of the tub, encompassing both me and Cedara. Ed drinks tequila.

"God, this is great!" Judah says. "Get in here, Ed."

"I ain't getting naked with your hippie ass."

Ed drinks more tequila. Cedara sits on the ledge of the tub, her ass against Judah's arm. She undoes her bun, shakes out her hair, wiggling.

"It's hot!" she says, as if to explain.

Judah watches the water gather and drop from her nipples.

She tries to roll another spliff. "I'm too wet!" she says and stands, gets out of the water, and walks over to where her towel is. She bends over with straight legs to dry her hands, holds the fold.

Her pinks and furries are a bull's-eye in Judah's line of vision.

He won't take his eyes off her dripping target.

The other guys look away.

Ed sighs and goes inside. The sliding door reverberates more than it should.

Cedara is still bent. She's still drying her hands. Judah's still watching. She lingers still longer before rising. Lingers again before wrapping the towel, holding it open for a moment to frame her yoga sinew, then pulls it from side to side like the veils she belly dances with, drying her arched back.

Zeus looks to the sky.

"My goodness, I am a raisin!" I say, sounding like a schoolmarm, clenched. "Can you pass me a towel?"

"Oh, don't go, stay, stay, come on, stay," Cedara says. "I was just going to go in to get my tobacco."

"We need to get going too. I had that nine-hour drive today. You coming?" I ask Judah.

"Uh, I'm just gonna hang out here for a couple more minutes."

This is because his cock is rock hard. I pretend not to notice. I want my underwear.

My skirt is already up as we pass through Judah's French front doors.

"I'm so happy you're here for real," he says and shuts his eyes tight as he bends me over the dining room table.

Now we're on the floor, the wood flat and hard on my back, the wood flat and hard inside me. I take a deep breath and stop moving and watch him fuck me for about thirty seconds, head thrown back, knuckles simian beside my ears. He doesn't even notice I'm just lying there, and I know it's a bad idea, but I say it anyway: "Are you fucking Cedara in your head?"

He comes immediately. Okay. I have my own house.

"That wasn't fair," he says as he rolls off.

"True," I say. "Is there a paper towel?"

Welcome, welcome . . .

EVERYTHING ABOUT THIS IS PERFECT

I PASS THE TWO OTHER HOUSES ON MY STREET, PASS THE EMPTY FIVE-ACRE lot for sale that borders my land, making my isolated cul-de-sac more like eight vast acres. I have not, to date, had a real backyard. I pass the gate, following the bend, letting the manzanita branches tickle Lucy's ribs. If I kept driving I would land in my living room.

I turn the key. The house is empty and cold and mine. We are finally alone together, this house and I. We should get to know each other better. I slide my hand along the low wood wall that separates the dining area from the living room. There is allegedly ivory carpet from wall to wall to wall to wall—all of it tattooed by red dirt and cat pee. Even the bathrooms are carpeted. The carpet in the guest bathroom has an unappetizing grey ring tracing the base of the toilet. The word *septic* comes to mind. A spider the color of old pork chops dangles from the ceiling fan.

Out on the deck, I am dwarfed by the forest. I'm outnumbered by trees, birds, lizards, spiders, squirrels. The hot tub is sunk into the far edge of the deck, just outside the master bedroom. I lift the cover and discover several bloated lizards in varying states of decomposition. I turn it on anyway. The lizards come apart from the force of the jets, unaware that I'm trying to sustain an idyllic reverie here.

I take wood from the piles stacked against the house. There's tons of it—seasoned oak, not pine. At least that's what the owners said in the note they left. I have no idea what they mean by seasoned. Have they sprinkled something on it? Or is it just old, seasoned like Robert Redford is seasoned? I gather fallen pine needles. There is no shortage of these; the property is thoroughly blanketed in them. I fold up my skirt and pile them in like a peasant girl with ruddy cheeks from some Bruegel painting just before the virile young shepherd comes and bends her over a hay bale. I gather some sticks, some firmer fuel to ground the flames.

Proof that I live in the country: I am making a fire in my woodstove. I kindle the tinder, add the sticks. I wait for the sticks to flare and calm a little, steady their breath, before I add the log. The log hesitates. I add another and arrange them so they lean on one another, but not too close—there must be space for air. I learned that this past winter while visiting Judah, when I thought I might live with him. I like to think that maybe the lone log second guesses itself, isn't sure burning is such a good idea until another shows up, and then they're in it together, cracklechatting, dancing in their red shoes.

I have no idea how long I've been sitting here in front of this fire, but it's dark, and I've added two more logs. The sound of Judah's tires on the gravel road is a cutting, amplified version of the wind in the trees. I jump, shore up my pudding limbs, run to the front door, fling it open to find him standing in the road, looking up.

"It's perfect," he shouts. "Everything about this is perfect!" I go to him and take his hand. "I could sell my place and we could buy this one," he says. "We can put the veggie beds right down there by the pool. I mean, we could do outdoor there too, but I think we should do veggies. And Sprout's gonna love the deer. I don't know, man, it was hard to see at my place, but I can see it here. Everything we talked about. The whole thing. Sustainable, you know? Freedom for real. Chickens running around and everything." By keeping the homesteader part of the dream alive, we keep our nobility intact. It's not just a six-figure work-from-home job we're after—it's a new stamp on a very old paradigm. Some days, like today, I believe this completely. We hold each other, full of all that pulsing right under our skins. It takes the rumble of the moving truck to budge us.

UKRAINIANS WITH EXCELLENT BICEPS

"You definitely mooft," says Gustav, the Ukrainian with excellent biceps. "We miss you street twice, have to back up thee truck. Which was, like, eempozeebull."

"You were looking for a street. It's a road," I tell him, with newly adopted NorCal pretension.

"You are to be living out here yourself? For reals?"

"Hey, I'm Judah."

Gustav gives a sly "So you make boyfriend here."

"Uh, yeah, actually." The excellent biceps are not lost on Judah.

"How you make money here?" Gustav asks me.

"I don't know yet." I avert my eyes because I'm a terrible liar, and leaving out the short-term pot plan is not insignificant. I am going to have to get comfortable with half-truths. I am going to have to change.

"How *you* make money here?" Gustav asks Judah directly.

"I'm a kitchen consultant."

"What kind of job is thees?"

"A pretty good one." Judah retreats to the deck.

"You look more happy already," Gustav says to me. "Where you want thee couch?"

When the Ukrainians are halfway through, I'm about to offer them a beer, but I check in with Judah first, ask if he wants one too. "I'm just going to stay out here," he says. "It sucks, with my back," he says. "I wish I could help."

"I do too," I say, because it's true and I'm not done moving.

SHELTER

WE'RE TAKING A LITTLE ROAD TRIP TO GET POLAR TODAY. THE ANIMAL shelter is about two hours away, so we're packing lunch and making a day of it. We'll have a beautiful drive through the Sierras, sing songs, and make each other laugh. It's fun when we're all together.

I slept over at Judah's last night. It's hard to want to go back to the boxes and the forest when there are animal videos and trampolines and guitars and loved ones here. I wake up alone, as I always do when Sprout's here. I get up and go to her room. I crack the door and it's like opening a jewelry box. I can almost hear a melody, delicate and tinny, as they are revealed, sleeping in a glimmer of motes. Judah is curled around her, she the germ and he the husk. I no more fit into that picture than I fit inside a regular jewelry box. My eggs scream just looking at them. I want to be allowed to crawl into that bed and have our dog jump in too because he needs to be walked but first he will lick our faces and we'll say *ew, gross* and then maybe we'll go to the park or on a hayride or plant some seeds or roll down a hill or throw a snowball or put glitter on something or everything or make macaroni necklaces and chicken parmesan. I want this (any of it, all of it) so much that I had to get my own house so I can try to want it a little less, so as not to confuse things. I can have the dog, at least.

Sprout opens her eyes and watches me framed in limbo. "Feather go away," she says. I ride a flash of sad, which is dumb because she's two and it shouldn't matter.

"Don't you want to get the doggie?" I ask.

She forgot in her half-sleep, but now she remembers. She pushes her snoring papa back and forth. "Go go go for doggie!"

"For what?" he says.

"Doggie!"

"What?" We look at each other and act like we have no idea what she's talking about.

"Doggie doggie doggie doggie!" she says, jumping on the bed.

He barks at her and does raspberries on her belly and now that everyone is awake I don't feel like a spy. I belong here enough to pass through the door. We make a giddy, growling tickle pile on the bed.

"I want something." Sprout has been in her car seat for over an hour now.

"What do you want, sweetie?" I ask.

"I want something." Sprout is writhing, pulling on the straps. "I WANT SOMETHING!"

"Sprout . . ." Judah is using his paternal warning voice, code orange, usually an effective strategy.

"NOOOOOOWWWWWWWWW!" She is red.

"What do you want, honey?" he asks, but she can't hear him.

"AHHHHHHHHHHHHHHHHHHHHHHHHHHHHHHHHHHHH-HHHHHHHHHHHHHHHHHHHHHHHHHHHHHHHHHHHHHHHH-HHHHHHHHHHHHHHHHHHHHHHHHHHHHHHHHHHHHHHHH-HHHHHHHHHHHHHHHHHHHHHHHHHHHHHHHHHHHHHHHH-HHHHHHHHHHHHHHHHHHHHHH!"

"Would you please give her something?" Judah says to me.

"What? What do you want me to give her?"

"There's stuff in that bag, give her something from the bag."

"AHHHHHHHHHHHHHHHHHHHHHHHHHHHHHHHHHHHHHH-
HHHHHHHHHHHHHHHHHHHHHHHHHHHHHHHHHHHHHHHH-
HHHHHHHHHHHHHHHHHHHHHHHHHHHHHHHHHHHHHHHH-
HHHHHHHHHHHHHHHHHHHHHHHHHHHHHHHHHHHHHHHH-
HHHHHHHHHHHHHHHHHHHHHHHHHHHHHHHHHHHHHHHH-
HHHHHHHHHHHHHHHHHHHHHHHHHHHHHHHHHHHHHHHH-
HHHHHHHHHHHHHHHHHHHHHHHHHHHHHHHHHHHHHHHH-
HHHHHHHHHHHHHHHHHHHHHHHHHHHHHHHHHHHHHHHH-
HHHHHHHHHHHHHHHHHHHHHHHHHHHHHHHHHHHHHHHH-
HHHHHHHHHHHHHHHHHHHHHHHHHHHHHHHHHHHHHHHH-
HHHHHHHHHHHHHHHHHHHHHHHHHHHHHHHHHHHHHHHH-
HHHHHHHHHHHHHHHHHHHHHHHHHHHHHHHHHHHHHHHH-
HHHHHHHHHHHHHHHHHHHHHHHHHHHHHHHHHHHHHHHH-
HHHHHHHHHHHHHHHHHHHHHHHHHHHHHHHHHHHHHHHH-
HHHHHHHHHHHHHHHHHHHHHHHHHHHHHHHHHHHHHHHH-
HHHHHHHHHHHHHHHHHHHHHHHHHHHHHHHHHHHHHHHH-
HHHHHHHHHHHHHHHHHHHHHHHHHHHHHHHHHHHHHHHH-
HHHHHHHHHHHHHHHHHHHHHHHHHHHHHHHHHHHHHHHH-
HHHHHHHHHHHHHHHHHHHHHHHHHHHHHHHHHHHHHHHH-
HHHHHHHHHHHHHHHHHHHHHHHHHHHHHHHHHHHHHHHH-
HHHHHHHHHHHHHHHHHHHHHHHHHHHHHHHHHHHHHHHH-
HHHHHHHHHHHHHHHHHHHHHHHHHHHHHHHHHHHHHHHH-
HHHHHHHHHHHHHHHHHHHHHHHHHHHHHHHHHHHHHHHH-
HHHHHHHHHHHHHHHHHHHHHHHHHHHHHHHHHHHHHHHH-
HHHHHHHHHHHHHHHHHHHHHHHHHHHHHHHHHHHHHHHH-
HHHHHHHHHHHHHHHHHHHHHHHHHHHHHHHHHHHHHHHH-
HHHHHHHHHHHHHHHHHHHHHHHHHHHHHHHHHHHHHHHH-
HHHHHHHHHHHHHHHHHHHHHHHHHHHHHHHHHHHHHHHH-
HHHHHHHHHHHHHHHHHHHHHHHHHHHHHHHHHHHHHHHH-
HHHHHHHHHHHHHHHHHHHHHHHHHHHHHHHHHHHHHHHH-
HHHHHHHHHHHHHHHHHHHHHHHHHHHHHHHHHHHHHHHH-
HHHHHHHHHHHHHHHHHHHHHHHHHHHHHHHHHHHHHHHH-
HHHHHHHHHHHHHHHHHHHHHHHHHHHHHHHHHHHHHHHH-
HHHHHHHHHHHHHHHHHHHHHHHHHHHHHHHHHHHHHHHH-
HHHHHHHHHHHHHHH!"

"Jesus, give her something!"

"AHHHHHHHHHHHH . . ."

"I don't think it's a good idea to give her something just because she's screaming."

"AAAHHHHHHHHHHHH . . ."

"Oh my God, she's blue, is she blue?" Shark Attack swerves; Judah glances in the rearview mirror.

"AHHHHHHHHHHHH . . ."

"It's just because she's screaming—sweetie stop screaming," I say. "Use your words or just breathe okay or just . . . shhh . . . okay? You're okay . . ."

"AHHHHHHH . . ." She stops, breathes. Her face returns to ruddy olive. I think I have sudden onset tinnitus.

"Okay, that's much be—"

"AHHHHHHHHHHHHHHHHHHHHHHHHHHHHHHHHHHHHHH-HHHHHHHHHhhhhhhhhhhhhh . . ."

"There's finger berries in the bag, give her finger berries . . ." Judah has all the desperate urgency of a junkie as played on, say, a particularly subpar episode of *Law & Order*. I take the raspberries from the brown bag and put them on my fingers. "Look! Finger berries!" I wiggle them around in front of her face. I do a berry-infused version of "Where Is Thumbkin?" and realize that the melody is the same as "Frère Jacques" and wonder why I've never realized that before. The kid isn't buying the finger-berry puppet show. She's blue again, purple even. I haven't screamed like that in ages. Really, how often do you get to scream like that after three, maybe four? Never, if you're a city girl. Cops would come, for sure. I'll have to try it at the new house. It looks strangely satisfying. Thinking these thoughts puts some much needed distance between me and the sound.

"IwansumingIwansumingIwansumingahhhhhhhHHHHHHHHHhh-hhhhhh . . ."

We approach the 7-Eleven conveniently situated at the entrance to Squaw Valley.

"Don't get her anything. Seriously. You'll never survive her teen years if you get her something now."

He looks at me like I just clubbed his kid with a baseball bat as he takes her out of the car seat. She's kicking and clawing and crying. They come out of the 7-Eleven with plastic Easter eggs, the kind that you fill with surprises and hide. My own eggs, incidentally, have shut the fuck up.

At the shelter, I say, rosy and bright, "We're here to see Polar." The kennel attendant takes in our little family. "I thought you said you didn't have kids."

"I don't. She's his."

"He doesn't do well with kids."

"Neither did he, apparently," I say, nudging Judah, "but look at him now!"

"We see doggie!" Sprout barks at the kennel attendant.

I have cut up treats into little pieces and put them in a fanny pack, for convenient dispensing, as advised by numerous training manuals. I strap it on. Judah looks away. There are some things a man shouldn't have to see. A grown-ass woman in a fanny pack is one of them. But I have read a lot of books about dog training, and I want to do this right. I want them to let me take Polar home.

The kennel attendant nods to me, "You first, see how he does," then to Sprout and Judah, "Then we'll see if you two can go in." I will rename the kennel attendant; let's call him the Warden. The Warden unlocks Polar's cell and ushers me in. The door clanks shut. I ask Polar to sit. He does. I give him a treat. He is sweet and his tail wags for me, and really, that's what I'm looking for. The Warden asks if I'd like to take him outside. I do. I put him on the leash I brought and he heels automatically. I give him a treat for heeling and he licks my face—*ew, gross, woo-hoo.* I knew he was the one.

"He's perfect!" I shout down the hall to Judah and Sprout. They approach and Polar snarls and lunges, trying to eat Sprout's foot. The Warden alpha rolls him. "No!"

I take Polar outside. He does down, down-stay, shake. The ad was right, he is great at obedience.

"Before you keep going, you should bring them in again," says the Warden.

I gesture through the window to Sprout and Judah, and they come into the yard. Same as before. He is not just Polar. He is bipolar.

Sprout is crying again, but she does still have her foot. "Take it away!" Judah says, clutching Sprout. The Warden is already on it. Polar looks back at me as he's led back to his cell. "You can't get that dog," Judah says.

"He did really well with only me."

Judah just stares. I'm single and childless yet my towels smell like balls and Polar will not be coming home with me.

We eat the remains of our brown bag lunches in the parking lot outside the shelter. "Why Feather crying?" Sprout asks.

"I want something," I say.

She hugs me and hands me a pink plastic egg.

THE PLANNING COMMISSION

THE NEXT DAY WE REPORT TO ED'S FOR THE PLANNING COMMISSION MEETING. The planning of my growroom. In which I will grow medical marijuana. Which is, technically, if you go with the federal version of things, illegal. Which means, in some states, this meeting would be about launching my life of crime. But this is the Republic of California, so let's try again: The Community is coming together to plan and build my room—not unlike an Amish barn raising—where I will, with much TLC, grow medicinal THC—in full compliance with the Compassionate Care Act and all other applicable state and local laws, including, but not limited to SB 420, which shows a sense of humor on behalf of California's senate—for a few of California's medical marijuana patients. I am becoming a caregiver, noble bringer of the good green love.

See? Isn't that better? With a little rephrasing, I like the job I'm taking on. When I see it dressed in fuzzy flannel under a starchy lab coat—wholesome as a kitten, righteous as a nun—when I can excavate it from last century's dusty propaganda, it feels right. America's Declaration of Independence was drafted on cannabis. Mine too. Sure, it was paper made of hemp pulp, but you get the idea.

Ed is not just the resident loose cannon, he's also The Community builder. He's the one you go to when something tangible needs to be done, whether it be punching someone in a bar or building your grow-room.

Zeus is here to assist with the design. He is resplendent in a three-quarter-length faux fur coat and orange Crocs. In the shadow of his fedora, a half-inch bamboo plug impales one earlobe. His newly rescued puppy sleeps in his lap. Everything about him says *I am the postapocalyptic emperor.*

"What are you going to call her?" I ask, gesturing to the puppy.

"We're torn between Ganesha and Kali. You know how all those dispensaries in LA that didn't get popped in that last big raid all had statues of Ganesha?" His head drops. "But Cedara likes Kali." The puppy licks his mouth. She is sleek and tawny with big green eyes. "Weren't you getting a dog?" Zeus hands her to me. She trembles when anyone but Zeus holds her.

"It didn't work out." The puppy settles in my arms, opens her eyes, then lets them drift shut again because everything is okay.

"There's three more from her litter at the shelter. Go there tomorrow as soon as they open, ten o'clock. Tell them I sent you. The lady there loves me."

"Oh, I don't want a puppy."

"Ten o'clock," Zeus repeats.

"I'm gonna need a smart dog," Ed says.

"Dude, what are you talking about? She's smart. This dog is gonna be big and smart." Zeus is pink.

"Dude, that's four kinds of big dumb dog. But she's cute. I'll give you that."

"Why you gonna insult a puppy? Just talk about what you know, dude." Zeus kisses the puppy's head.

"So the setup is going to run, including equipment, construction, nutes, and tanks, around ten thousand dollars." Ed hands me the design plans and equipment list he's prepared. It's five detailed pages. "Your bloom room will be right at the county limit of seventy-five square feet," Ed explains. Nuggettown's county put its own spin on the six mature

HEATHER DONAHUE · *48*

plants per prescription allowed by the state. Here, you can have six plants *or* seventy-five square feet of canopy per prescription. People can very well have six plants that exceed seventy-five square feet or thirty-six plants that are under, and growers have been busted for falling on either side of that, *or* depending on the mood of the officer.

The other limitation that everybody here respects is the ninety-nine plant maximum. Anything more than ninety-nine plants comes with a mandatory federal sentence, so everybody in this Community is a ninety-niner. Not to be confused with a forty-niner. In a community of ninety-niners, there's more for everybody because everybody stays within the bounds of the law. Everybody grows only what's allowed for the number of patients they have prescriptions for. As with any crop, some harvests are more successful than others, and the surplus is sometimes given to a dispensary in exchange for a donation to the grower in keeping with the law that requires medical marijuana to be a nonprofit enterprise. Everybody in The Community takes only the piece of the pie allowed them by Prop 215 and SB 420. This means that pot is the one cash crop whose wealth is still widely distributed at the mom-and-pop level. Medical marijuana is taking care of a lot of people who would otherwise be unemployed or stuck in a job they hated, in addition to helping patients. Ninety-niners don't seek fortune, just freedom.

"Ten thousand," I gulp. "And then fifteen hundred a month for power?"

"In July, more like seventeen with the AC." Ed is puffy with facts.

"It's a business," Judah tells me again. "You have to think of it as a business."

"I thought it was caregiving. I'd like to think of it as caregiving. Are we sure LEDs would be impossible?" LED lights take very little electricity to run, and with less power going in, less escapes as heat. They're more expensive, but the power savings over time would make up for it. "The technology just isn't there yet," Zeus says.

"Don't they use sixes in Europe?" I ask. Sixes are six-hundred-watt lamps. These are generally preferred over thousand-watt bulbs in places like Amsterdam, where going big or going home is not so much a matter of national identity. "Why do I have to juice it American-style?"

"You won't pull a pound per six. You'll be lucky if you pull a pound per thouie your first year anyway," Zeus tells me, using the nickname for thousand-watt lamps.

"It's not too late to do hydro instead of soil," Judah offers. He does hydro, and thinks my urge toward soil is a fool's errand. Soil-grown buds generally don't turn out so glittery with resin as their hydroponically produced counterparts. The Girls produce resin under stress, to seal in scarce water and refract excess light. It's where most of the THC (the compound that gets you high) is, so more resin means more THC, which means a more valuable nugget, but it's like The Girls' form of flopsweat.

In soil you generally can't stress them into producing the amount of resin that a hydroponic grower can. On the upside, soil is a natural buffer, which buys you time to fix mistakes before they go too horribly wrong. When you grow hydro, you can play God—direct and efficient—but one false move, one broken pump when you're away for the weekend, and it can bite you in the ass.

"I want a buffer," I tell them, because under stress I will not produce resin, only anxiety, and this will not make me a more valuable nugget.

"Nobody makes money their first year. Keep that in mind and you won't be disappointed. Your rent will get paid and you'll eat some sushi, but you won't make money." Zeus grows in soil. And he's the one who never gets his phone turned off, so I'm not worried about this particular decision.

"I thought it was supposed to be a gram per watt," I tell Zeus.

"Even with hydro I haven't pulled that yet," says Judah.

"Yeah, you should just put that out of your head. OG Kush isn't going to give you that," Zeus says, stroking the puppy.

"Look, we're talking about what's proven," Ed says. "If you want to come in here and reinvent the wheel, that's up to you, but we're giving you a way that works."

"There are a hundred ways to grow great weed," Judah says. "Just get the technical side taken care of, and then you can find your own way, one round at a time." It sounds almost Zen, like what I am embarking on is more than a temporary fix. "I'm only doing this for a year anyway . . . ," I say. They try not to laugh at me, unsuccessfully.

"Okay," Ed says. "You got your down payment?"

I put cash on the coffee table. They don't give me a receipt.

CUTTINGS

I'M AT JUDAH'S WHEN ZEUS CALLS TO TELL ME HE HAS LAUNDRY FOR ME, IF I want it. Weedworld phone talk is an art I'm eager to master, or rather, make up as I go along, which is what everyone seems to do. "Help me with a six pack?" isn't an invitation to beer, as I first thought. It's an inquiry as to whether you might know someone interested in acquiring six pounds of weed. I turn to Judah. "Zeus has laundry for me if I want it?"

"Tell him to bring it over."

Zeus pulls a large black plastic contractor bag from the back of his Corolla.

"My laundry?" I reach for the bag.

"Inside," Judah says.

Inside are branches in varying shades of yellow and green. "I cleaned up my moms and thought you might be able to use this." By *moms* he means his mother plants, the outstanding Girls he clones from. The ones he kept hidden from Lil Dick. "No charge, but you'll have to plug them tonight," Zeus adds. Judah and I had a date planned.

"You're on their watch now," Zeus says. "You want to put down some roots? Here's your chance to put down a whole bunch of them." The boys used to talk to me of "livin' the dream." There was much mention of eggs Benedict with jalapeño Hollandaise and swimming in rivers that flow with gold. And autonomy. Now they mostly mention how I can't really use my hot tub, or take a vacation, or be away from the house for more than forty-eight hours without hiring a sitter for The Girls.

"They keep you on a short leash," Judah says, head hung.

"Well, they're girls, right?" I offer, just to talk.

I squat and contemplate the bag. My future hidden in black plastic. This bag is not a toy. Judah supplies me with two black plastic trays and two matching inserts that have a grid of squares for the brown Oasis cubes. He hands me a pair of white-handled grape scissors, the industry standard for both cloning and trimming. The branches are in varying stages of wilt. Judah is not impressed. "Maybe we can just go to the Bay and get you something more . . . usable."

"That sounds expensive."

"This looks time-consuming." He is searching through the bag. "And I'm not sure it's gonna work."

We scan each branch for a viable cutting. Obviously the yellow parts won't make it into the tray, but not every green bit has plant potential either. Judah and I have done this together before, as part of my winter apprenticeship. It's my favorite part of the process. In the beginning, when nothing has gone wrong yet. The first date with your future crop—or not—the excitement of not knowing. "What do you think of this one?"

"Too skinny. Won't even stand up in the plug."

I try anyway. He's right.

"I do know a couple of things, you know."

We do a rough cut of each potential candidate, then trim off the lower leaves, leaving a few inches of naked stem. He cuts the leaves toward the tops at an angle. "That's butchery," I say.

"You want to lose all your water through transpiration?"

"Isn't that why we're putting those domes on top? To keep the moisture in?"

"Yeah."

"You don't really know why we have to cut the leaves do you?"

"The clones root faster when you do it. No, I don't know exactly why, and to me, it doesn't really matter."

"I'm being a pain in the ass."

"Kind of."

We cut stems at forty-five-degree angles, just below nodes, little knots of potential along the stem. We scrape the bottom half-inch to reveal the cambium layer, the cells that will transform from stem to root, though they don't know it yet.

"I don't understand why there aren't more women in this business. It seems like such a natural fit," I say, wishing each little cutting well before I stick it into an oasis cube.

"It's not about nurturing; it's about production."

"I think nurturing leads to production."

"You don't need to wish each cutting luck. It's genes. They'll make it or they won't."

"These are clones, so of course they all have the same genes, but not all of them will make it, and those that do won't all do well. What determines that?"

"Luck."

"Define luck."

"Do you want to smoke? It'll make this more fun."

"Okay, so don't define luck."

"Don't overthink this. You'll just make it harder."

"Right." I hold another cutting in the Dip'N Grow cup, 1-2-3-4. "Good luck little cutting, may you flower abundantly."

Dip'N Grow, which sounds innocent enough, playful even, is a rooting hormone. This chemical basically clues the cutting in that it's being destroyed, and so this lone piece of plant—just seconds ago part of a branch on a whole other plant—declares a state of emergency. It can die or it can rally—flip the chemical switch to becoming a new plant and push out roots where there were none before—or nap sludgy in the compost bin. This little fragment has it inside, somehow, to become a whole. Just add adversity.

"Sometimes I really wish you didn't get your own house."

"And then sometimes you are very glad I did."

"Yeah."

"Sometimes relationships are the price we pay for the anticipation of them. I can't remember where I read that . . ."

"That sucks." He flicks the tip of a clone back and forth with his thumb. "You're changing."

"Like a twig in a tray."

"I feel like you're not attached," he says.

"I love you," I say. "I just don't need you."

He looks sort of crushed.

"Is that bad?" I add.

"It's probably not supposed to be. Probably that's more enlightened or healthy or something. But it feels cold."

"You want me to need you?"

"Yeah. I do."

"Okay." I kiss him.

Soft.

"Thank you," he says and hugs me out of the chair, like a chiropractor or a bear.

Hard.

PUPPIES!

I AM WATCHING BUGA MUNCH ON DEWY CLOVER WHEN ED AND HIS SOME-times girlfriend Liz meet at my house to have a look. Their relationship has been on-again, off-again for longer than I've known Judah. Their mutual pragmatism is a challenge to romance. Liz is the most sincere prac-titioner of radical acceptance that I've met up here. Her signature gesture is the warm shrug. As a grower and a single mom, it has to be.

"A hot tub *and* a pool?" Liz says.

"You know you can't use either one," Ed says.

"I've heard."

"You can clone in here," Ed says of my office, on the tour.

"I'm hoping to do that in the veg room," I say, calling the spare bed-room by its new name.

"Too bright. You need fluorescents."

"I was thinking a dim corner of the veg room? I was hoping to grow in my live house, rather than live in my growhouse."

"It never turns out that way," Liz says.

"The Girls are bitches," Ed adds. Liz gives him a spank.

They are coming to the shelter with me today. Puppy fever is sweeping The Community. We are none of us immune to spring. That, and people around here tend to have free time, and a jaunt to the animal shelter is good country fun. Judah and Sprout will meet us there because people who have been together for nine months collaborate on big decisions like choosing a dog. There is the thought that it will migrate into *our* dog.

Some dogs press against their cages, teeth scraping bars. Others are resigned, lying limp in corners with bowls of food and water, puddles of urine by their side. Only the puppies in kennel thirteen are somewhere in between. One naps, two wrestle—none of them respond to my high-pitched "Who wants to be my little puppy? You? Are you my puppy?" They have no interest whatsoever. They're so small. They can't protect me. Judah, Sprout, Liz, Ed, and I make our way along the concrete floor through the bleach- and bark-filled air. *Are you my dog?* I see a nice Australian shepherd in kennel six. She snarls at me. A young black Lab licks my hand. I return to the lady with the dun blonde braid. "Can I walk the Lab in 23?"

"He's not available. He got here yesterday and we're still waiting to see if his owners come." She registers my disappointment, and the lines around her eyes and mouth swerve into a solution.

"We just rescued an entire litter of Aussie/border collie mixes. No one's seen them yet; they just came in last night. We spent the whole night defleaing them and getting the feces out of their fur. All eight were kept in a cat crate. Their gaits are all bad from worms, and they have kennel cough. All eight. You want to look?"

One of them stops everything he's doing and comes to the front of the kennel before we even arrive there. One eye brown, one blue. The blue one in particular says, *I'm your dog.* He licks my hand and jumps up against the metal and sticks his wet nose between the bars. I reach over the gate and pick him up and he folds into my arm, tiny, calm, and soft. *I'm your dog.* He looks up at me and I pick the blue eye to look in, blue like mine. His chest is covered with the whitest, cloudiest fur I've ever touched.

"What do you think we should call him?" I ask, trying not to under-line the *we.* "How about Felix?" I suggest. "It means happy in Latin. Or Sweetpea or Walt. Or not?"

"How about Vito?"

Judah drops this idea with lots of space around it, like he knows I'm going to love it. "Like the Godfather. And, of course, the pizza." He looks at me with the leather-pants eyes again when he says it. Our love was sealed over slices of Vito's. I can smell it even here, in the kennel, where turds reign. When Judah came to visit me in LA, he introduced me to this most authentic dislocated New York slice.

When I visited last summer, I brought a pie on the plane. He told all his friends, astonished by what an amazing girlfriend he had. "She brought me a *pizza*. On the *plane*." That alone made it worth the effort. As a bonus, it turns out people are incredibly friendly when you're carrying a pizza. It puts a smile on the face of the grumpiest TSAers. An asshole wouldn't carry on a pizza as their personal item. Only an inherently approachable person would, so everybody asks you for a slice. "But it's not even hot anymore!" I'd laugh, tossing my hair as only a gal in her mid-thirties on her way to see her boyfriend dressed in a fifties skirt with garters underneath carrying a pizza through an airport can.

A curbside checker asked me for a slice and I told him it was for my boyfriend who was cooming any minute to pick me up. "Ooooohhhh . . . ," he said, "you gonna toss a salad with that?"

"Yeah! Definitely!" I said with oblivious enthusiasm, not realizing that he was talking about analingus until Judah explained it later, gently.

"Vito?" I say.

"Vito," he says and puts his arms around my shoulders. I fall for him again every time he looks at me like this, like we're being shot in one of those 360-degree orbiting pans popularized by Scorsese. I can almost hear the definite yet delicate cracking of the outermost crust as it is bent in two. The way the tender dough inside is preserved, protected even. The seamless integration of tomato, dough, and cheese, each preserving their unique identity even as they surrender to the unified state of pizza. The rest of the world is blurred to oblivion and we might actually just fall down and fuck each other's dazzled brains out right here.

"Yes! Vito! Two syllables like the dog books suggest. And it means something like *life* in Latin."

"Plus you could shout, 'Hey, Vito,' and people might think you had a hitman in your guest room. 'Cause, um, that's not really a guard dog."

"Yet."

"This is my dog," I tell the braided lady, and she paints a claw on his left paw with blue nail polish to match his left eye. She hands me a clipboard and several forms. I fill them out with one hand, while the puppy sleeps in the other.

"We can't adopt him out till he's been neutered, but you can foster him if you like."

My heart jumps and I guess the pup can feel it because his eyes open. He doesn't flinch at all; instead he puts his paws over my shoulder, nuzzles his head into the crook of my neck, and melts Velveety across my chest. "Sweet things, all of them," the braided lady says. "Born on Christmas Eve." Just two days after Pop-Pop died. Great. "Walt?" I say, because that was Pop-Pop's name, and the puppy turns to look at me with his disconcerting brown/blue gaze. I'm handed Vito's antibiotics and told to bring him back when he's well enough to be "fixed," like he's not perfect already.

Judah and Sprout head off to Mommy and Me and I duck into the restroom. When I return, a stranger is holding my dog. "That one's mine," I say.

"The lady up front said they were all still available."

"Not that one. See the blue claw? That one's mine."

"Do you mind if I take him out in the yard?"

"Why don't you bond with one of the available puppies?"

He's taunting me now. Hanging on to my puppy in one hand while he strokes others. My eyes slit at him. I in no way wish to imply that I'm proud of this.

I believed that the puppy right there, with the one blue claw, chose me. Now he's busy licking someone else's face. I've already committed to being with him for the next fifteen years, and he's already licking someone else's face. I could leave here and never come back. Maybe I should. I don't want to anymore. I want something. I want my dog. *Unhand my dog*, I want to say, but I don't want to be a d-bag, or, rather, I don't want to seem like a d-bag.

After thirty seconds of foot tapping and withering gaze, I don't care anymore, so I say, "Vito!" and the pup strains against the stranger's grasp. "See? My dog."

Vito sits when I say "sit" and hold a treat above his nose. I didn't know it could be that easy. I run and he runs beside me. I stop and he stops too. He wants to please me; I want to please him. He even stays. I give him more treats. I give Ed and Liz some treats for their new dogs too. Everybody's found something and it's perfect and round and smooth and full and fragile. We're just a carton of eggs out here in the play yard.

"So you coming for those other puppies?" Liz asks. She means the little ganja plants that I am supposed to buy from her, because I am getting started. My bloom room is scheduled to be built in two weeks. It will need to be filled with plants that are ready to flower. To be ready, they will need to be vegged until they're between eighteen and twenty inches tall. The ones Liz has are about six. Not a problem; in the veg room's thousand watts of simulated spring they can grow about an inch a day. It's not just about height, though, because that would be up to the grower, and blooming is up to The Girls. They'll let you know plant puberty has kicked in by sprouting white fuzzy pistils at the nodes where the stems branch from the trunk. Trying to get them to bloom before this won't make them flower any faster. For all the technology in play, it's still a collaboration.

"Yeah. I think so." This step makes it official. These are not little cuttings. They have roots. Biologically, legally, incontrovertibly; they are plants. Once I take them home, I am in. No *Oh, this indoor garden is so I can have tomatoes in February, Officer.*

"I have other people asking about them," Liz tells me.

"I'm kind of trying to put that off until I, you know, at least finish unpacking."

"You're gonna need to get them going if you want to flip them when your room is done."

So now I am at Liz's and we're boxing up six young Sour Diesel plants. Not enough to fill my room, unless I wanted to veg them for the next three months, but enough to get me started. Enough to make it official. We put the plants in my car and the new puppies are playing and I am on my second beer.

"You should probably go," Liz says. "You don't want a DUI too." She gives me a big hug, but doesn't say anything like *congratulations*.

Instead she says, "Just remember that worry won't change anything, okay?"

LARRY AND THE BEAR

A SHERIFF'S CRUISER TURNS IN FRONT OF ME ONTO KINGSNAKE IN THE direction of my house. I turn the other way, pulling into a parking lot. It's a church. If it were Catholic I might consider confessing. Wait. I'm not a criminal. I'm a caregiver. Adopter of shelter pups. Sacred nurturer of green gratitude. Heroine of the abundant journey crystal leaf dream-catcher goddess paradigm medicinal bluebird intention seeker path. Something like that. Remember that time when I was being car-chased and the sheriff gave me an escort? That was so nice. This is not that.

From here on out there are some possibilities I will train myself not to consider. Example: Because there is a box of ganja plants in my car, that deputy was sent here to follow me to my house. My pulse and breath be-lieve this even though I doubt the logic. Logic has no chance against the reptilian reflexes of the cavebrain. The fight-flight tug-of-war begins without me. I grab my foot and press it to the floor of the car because it needs to stop shaking before I can drive again.

I startle a family of deer loitering in front of my house, eating the lawn and the shrubs outside the windows. Actually, we startle each other. I stop the car in the middle of the road—I mean it's not like anyone's coming this way anyway—and we all move back toward the house. I'm glad they're vegetarians, because they're really very large.

"Hello," I whisper to them. "I live here now."

That's when I notice the box on the doorstep. It has "I WUV U!!!!!" scrawled on it with thick, black marker. Pictured is a Hydrofarm Xtrasun Mondo Reflector. Behind it are two other boxes, one with a metallic pur-ple Lumitek ballast inside, another illustrating the chubby radiance of an Eye Hortilux metal halide bulb. There's a note inside the ballast box, writ-ten in all caps on the back of the receipt from Nuggettown Hydroporium.

CONGRATULATIONS! it says. I THOUGHT THIS WOULD BE BETTER THAN PAYING FOR HALF OF YOUR MOVE. I prop open the screen door and scoot the boxes inside. I stare at them, in awe of Judah's deep abiding wuv.

I take the plants from the car, Velcro puppy at my heels. That's when I hear the footsteps. I am where the deer were when I pulled up, and I am trying to seem more casual about this intrusion than they were. No chance of me scurrying up the hill with this box in my arms. "Hi there!" the man says, approaching. He waves and I remember why we humans evolved this gesture, to say, *I come in peace, no weapons, see?* I glance at the open screen door and the reflector box, clearly visible. Sure, hydroponic equipment is used to farm things other than pot, but that's usually in large-scale greenhouses. One lady living alone at the end of the road with a new mondo reflector either has a serious wheatgrass habit (in which case she would probably use a more compact reflector) or she's setting up her veg room. And so I'm sorry that deer aren't carnivores now, stampeding in to send this stranger back whence he came for at least the next ten minutes.

I put down the box and go toward him. "Uh, can I help you?" It's not aggressive exactly, but it has definite shades of "git off m'land."

"I'm your neighbor down the road on the left!" He's cheery. I realign. Let's not be the crazy cooter at the end of the road, huh? *The Bible* suggests that with neighbors, you should be calm and kind, but unencouraging. That establishing firm yet friendly boundaries early on will encourage respect and diminish curiosity.

He extends his hand. It's large and rough and doesn't match his gentle blue eyes. "I'm Larry. I rent the house down the road from Fred up the hill." After we shake, he keeps moving toward the house. "Nice pup. Shepherd?"

"Yup." I don't move toward the house with him. I remain by the car, in front of the plants, which are still tucked discreetly in their box. Vito presses on my leg.

"Still gotta lotta boxes to unpack, huh?"

"Always more than you think."

"Yeah." He takes a few steps closer to the house, his eyes pass over the box by the door. I am rooted, but in a calm, kind, unencouraging way. I alternate between putting my hands on my hips and crossing my arms in front of me. My hands usually flail more, in illustration, but I'm trying to seem more like I could feasibly have a gun rack in the garage. Like I have some way of defending myself should Larry choose to maraud.

"Welcome to the neighborhood," he offers.

"Thanks. Glad to be here."

We exchange more niceties and basic biographies and I am wondering if he's ever going to leave.

"What I came down here to tell you was . . . I mean, I didn't know whether I should or not, now I hear you come up from LA, and living back here on your own and all . . ." I'm hoping he'll say, *I grow ganja in my garage, so if you smell something skunky I'd be much obliged if you didn't call the sheriff.*

Instead he says, "There's been a black bear hanging around down here the past week or so—called the federal game warden and he said if the bear sticks around much longer he'll come on out and tag him, but for now, we should just go ahead and keep the trash locked down."

Two words at the bottom of my want-to-hear list are *bear* and *federal*.

"A bear. Well, Larry, I guess that's good to know. Good to meet you, neighbor," I say, extending my hand.

"You too, neighbor." He looks at me like he wishes I would be more neighborly, invite him in for a beer, like he's got soft things to say. Or maybe that's just how his eyes always look. And I would, Larry, invite you in, if I lived where someone would hear me screaming.

BABY'S FIRST MELTDOWN

JUDAH CALLS AND, INFORMED OF WHAT I'M NOW CALLING THE BEAR SITUation, invites me over. I decline, then realize I should sound more grateful about the reflector set and its accompanying wuv. Instead, I drink a beer alone. I open the box with the plants inside and examine them. These little lives are contained for the moment in keg cups, red and plastic—the kind you'd use at a frat party. Too contained. Fuck the bear. I'm going back outside.

It was never this dark in LA. I walk as far as the gate then remember the bear. But the forest is so quiet, and bears are so big. I would surely hear it coming from a mile away. I sit in the middle of my road, cross my legs, close my eyes. Try to sit still.

Vito curls against the small of my back. Nothing bad is happening. See? This is going to be a wonderful learning experience. I will learn how to relax. Yes. That's why people move to the country. To slow down. To simplify. Wait. Maybe I wouldn't hear the bear what with the wind picking up in the trees like it is. The branches flex and hiss.

So, yeah, here I am isolated deep in the woods, fearing unknown threats from beyond, hearing strange noises in the dark, unsure how to defend myself from mysterious attackers, near'bout ready to shit m'pants, pretty much crying and just generally prepared to acknowledge that I have probably told you this story once before. I am Heather Donahue. I am The Girl from *The Blair Witch Project*. Things will repeat on you until you love them, or forgive them—preferably both.

I start to run back to the house, then stop midway, remembering that if you run, a bear will chase you. I slow down. Vito does too. I go online and find the headline BLACK BEAR BREAKS INTO HOUSE, EATS CUPCAKES. I hide the plants in the bathtub and leave the light on for them. I pin a towel around the bathroom window so no one will see them.

I drink another beer. But wait. Why would someone hang a towel on a bathroom window unless they had something to hide? I take down the towel, turn out the light. I sleep the sleep of brandy-addled babes, round my wheezing pup—he the germ and me the husk—for about an hour, when I'm jolted awake by the wind outside, by the pine cones punching the roof. And by the absence of Buga.

He burrows, Buga does, and the last time I saw him was before I left for the animal shelter. He's been on his own for twelve hours. A Russian tortoise can dig himself a burrow in that time, easily. I can't hear the subtle rustling that usually gives him away if I'm quiet enough. It's freezing. If it weren't I would just go back to bed, look again tomorrow when he would be out of his burrow, grazing. He can survive on nearly nothing, but freezing can do him in. There's only so much even the most durable creatures can take.

Now I'm outside, burrowing too. Pushing my hands through the litter of pine needles into the hard red clay. My headlamp slides down my face. I stomp my feet three times. Buga's whole underbelly is his ear. He can feel the slightest vibration. Maybe he'll feel me missing him. He is supposed to outlive me. That was the deal. I was supposed to be able to take good care of him for the rest of my life. It was only half of the rest of my life, really, when you consider the whole hibernation arrangement. He's only really an "active" pet from April to October. I was supposed to learn how not to just give up on things and move to the next. I mean, the care of a tortoise really couldn't be simpler, as pets go. Now I'm supposed to give this puppy his forever home and I don't know what either of those things means.

Buga and I met right after The Great Purge. At first I just went to see him regularly, visiting him at the Petco on LaBrea. No cohabitation until I was sure. One day, it was right. I took him home, but didn't feel like that was rushing things. We would still take it slow. That was his nature. I figured his hibernation would give us each a little "me time." We could have space to appreciate the relationship, to miss each other, time to forget the daily shits and remember the fine summer days spent eating dandelions and rubbing vitamin E oil into the rougher parts of shells. Wherever I was going next, I was going to get there slow and steady like him. Maybe become vegetarian, like him. Do less, like him. In ancient stories a tortoise carried the whole world on his back. He could do this because he was stable and slow and did no harm.

Maybe this time I should call Judah. Maybe I should say, *I need help*, like Sprout does. I say instead, *No problem, I can do it myself.* It's three thirty now and Judah is sleeping and I think I probably should have just moved in with him. But I didn't. I don't need him. I'm not needy. Look at me, comfortable in my skin. So fucking Zen, crawling with radiant humility. Keep looking.

Stop, just stop.

Where's Vito?

Gone. I run toward the main road first, because that's what I'm most afraid of—that he's gone there, that he's gone. I don't see him. Down the dark road or back to the house? I run back to the house. I yell his name even though he probably doesn't know it's his. I go inside. Maybe he didn't follow me out. I don't see him. I do stupid things like look in the shower. The plants are fine. I yell and nothing happens except the sound gets bounced around the gully, sucked up by the trees. Predator ticker tape creeps behind my eyes. Could a raccoon get him? Probably. Owl? Maybe.

Coyote? Definitely. Bear? Shut up. I dash back around the deck and there he is. Quietly sitting in front of the sliding glass door. He doesn't move from his spot as I approach, his tail just sweeps a wilder crescent. Only as I bend to pick him up does a whimper escape, and then a lick. I hold him and tell him he's a good boy until our pulses slow. I put him back down, slide open the door. He trots on in like he already knows where home is.

APRIL'S POWERS

THIS IS HOW THE FUTURE'S DONE

MY SEEDLINGS ARE MUSH. EVERYTHING BUT THE RED RUSSIAN KALE. Russians. Hardy. That row alone stands proud and purply, jeering at the forty-nine other rows of sludge, perhaps taking some vegetable equivalent of vodka in the name of their fallen comrades. Along with the chickens I have already ordered, they were my assurance that I'm a country girl rather than just a pot grower. Yesterday, in the warm morning, I put the trays of fledgling vegetables outside under protective plastic domes for what *The Encyclopedia* calls hardening off. It's when your tender little sprouts are supposed to toughen up, adapt to the environment where they will eventually be planted. Mine are not hard and vigorous; they are soft and brown. The plastic domes were not enough to keep each little cell of each little seedling from freezing and expanding to the point where it exploded each cellulose-tough cell wall. Apparently I'm having some kind of cross-species April Fool's Day.

"Oh, yeah, you don't put anything out to harden off until late April. Don't put anything in the ground until Mother's Day weekend." That's what Larry says when I pass him on the road.

"Everybody probably knows that, huh?"

"Around here, yeah."

You don't have to know anything in LA. Except how to drive. You just turn the tap without worrying about your well pump or how much residual mercury might be in the groundwater from the gold mining days, or how much of the herbicide your neighbor uses to keep the poison oak at bay might be poisoning you. The city invents its own hazards. The hazards of the wilderness are replaced with, say, the hazards of wearing bad pants. There needs to be some kind of threat, otherwise I might just sit on the lawn and do nothing. Maybe that's what money's for, keeping threat alive.

I fear neither frost nor bear this morning because it's April and, despite my sketchy start, I will bring the spring. I'm going to resow Cherokee Chocolate tomatoes, Sun and Moon melons, Rainbow chard. I bought lots of seeds. Right after I find Buga, I will replant. He's been gone for twenty-four hours now, so I put out my own personal APB.

Between ten and eleven thirty a.m. is his busy time, if by busy I mean awake. Usually he's out and about in the late morning, dining al fresco on fescue and clover. I sit, with the sun on my face, waiting for him, but he doesn't come. I'm not so good at letting go lightly. I usually need to accompany it with some grand ceremonial gesture, like a fire. I light a match, tell Buga I miss him, blow it out, leave it where I saw him last. It feels kind of lame, but maybe it's an improvement, not all blazes and ash. Just a marked thought, whiff of sulfur, plume of smoke. Vito sniffs at it, lays his head on my knee. This is how the future's done.

BUILDING

MY HANDS HAVE BLISTERED THROUGH THE GOATSKIN GLOVES. VITO IS NAPping in the shade of an oak. I've been tilling for four hours now—preparing the veggie beds—and it's not quite ten. Maybe it's because what I've known as soil has always come out of bags, and what I'm trying to loosen here is not so much soil, or even dirt, as it is a large sheet of terra-cotta (no, that would at least crack, this is something altogether harder and more unified, the opposite of loam), but every stroke of my ladies' hoe (yes, that's how it was labeled at the hardware store, this little steel triangle on a stick) just kicks up another poof of dust. I pull out the hose and soak my rented land. Now I kick up clods. Clod. He's a clod. This expression has new vividness; a clod is a heavy, raw, unpleasant thing. Nothing can grow in a bed of clods. Love can't grow in bed with a clod. There are lots of expressions I never realized were agricultural until I made this move. "A tough row to hoe," for example, which I always thought was "a tough road to hoe," but you don't hoe a road, you hoe a row. Or "Let's call a spade a spade" and not, say, a clod, a hoe, or a rhododendron, for example. Would a spade be better suited to this job? No. It's only ten thirty. It's already eighty-five degrees and my hands are bleeding and each stroke of the hoe leaves visible trails.

The phone rings. "The soil truck is coming at noon," Judah tells me.

"Noon? Today? The beds are nowhere near ready."

"So have the truck dump the soil next to them."

"I see. You think you might have consulted me on this."

"You told me you needed soil for the veggie beds, so soil is coming. I'm trying to help."

I don't say thank you.

Ed and Scooter, a tall, pale, hot new arrival from Costa Rica who once slept with Sprout's mom after she and Judah broke up, resulting in an unacknowledged high level of competition between them, are disassembling the shelves in the garage, the ones that will have to be put back as they were before I move out. "Wait, I haven't photographed them yet. How will I know how to put them back?"

"They're shelves," Ed says. "We'll figure it out. Where do you want me to stash the garage door opener?"

"Um . . ." I'm struck deery, then recover. It's not a difficult question. "How about under the deck?"

"You should really just go get yourself a roll of black plastic mulch," Ed suggests. "Save yourself some sweat." I don't know what that is. Shit. I don't know shit. This has all been a terrible mistake and as the words *black*, *plastic*, and *mulch* float in my head, I see this clearly for the first time.

"What is that?"

"It's mesh that keeps the weeds from coming through."

"Oh."

I should get in the car and go buy myself some black plastic mulch. This is what I should do. No. I will continue hoeing. I know how to do this. I know how this works and, hamster to wheel, I'll stick with it. I'm pretty sure all of this will work out somehow, but right now the only thing that can really, feasibly work out, as far as I can see, is the hoeing of these beds. I'm making visible progress. Good. Plus, the repeated swinging of the hoe and the resulting shiver up my arm, through my shoulders, and down my spine, is vaguely satisfying. So I stay put, sweating, bleeding. Everything about me is salty. I'm hardening off.

The dump truck arrives at twelve fifteen. "Where you want your dirt?"

"In front of the beds, I guess." I'm almost done clearing the first bed, but not quite. I will have to shovel double.

"When can I plant in it?" I ask the truck guy. I know that new soil needs to sit sometimes, or it can burn roots from an excess of nitrogen. Thanks, *Encyclopedia of Country Living*.

"Veggies or marijuana?" he asks. It's so matter-of-fact. It makes me consider changing my mind. I could call off construction right now and put those plants I got from Liz in these beds, try and sell back all that equipment I just bought, grow outdoor instead of indoor and call it a day.

"Are there different requirements?" I ask.

"Veggies could go in right away. You'd want to let it sit a week before you plant your marijuana." He adds, "Great spot for it." I dislike the way he is scanning the gully.

"Oh, it'll just be kale and tomatoes," I say, swiveling my hoe. "Fingerling potatoes, Rainbow chard, New Zealand spinach . . ." I keep naming things that aren't marijuana and keep swiveling my hoe because if I do change my mind I don't want this guy to show up come harvest time and rob me while I'm out. Pot thieves have been known to dress up as DEA agents and cut everything down while you watch. This guy, helpful deliveryman today, could be a thieving bandit come harvest time, so I continue my litany of vegetables. ". . . Easter Egg radishes, Slenderette beans . . ."

"I got it," he says. "You're doing veggies." He climbs back into the dump truck and wishes me luck.

I need a shady spot where my humming arms can rest. I choose the berry patch, where my bare-root plantings have been eighty-five percent successful. It's ninety-five degrees and the sight of my hoe makes me gag, or maybe I'm just thirsty. Yes, definitely thirsty. I look at the pool, just beside the beds, the only area of full sun on this land, and wish that I was just living here like a regular person so I could take the cover off and let that water glint and Judah could shout "Marco!" and Sprout could shout "Polo!" and I would try to find them. Instead I hear Ed's saw ripping through two-by-fours to frame out my growroom. No pool. The power that would normally go here will be diverted to the garage. I am The Girls' bitch.

The walls are almost completely framed. I'm paralicited. Can't choose between paranoid, paralyzed, and excited. Can't think. Must do. I water the plants in the veg room. This is the room formerly known as the spare bedroom. This is where the plants I bought from Liz reside. This is where phase two will happen. Phase one is the nursery in the office closet—that's where the trays of plugged laundry cuttings rest atop heated mats to sprout roots. Phase two is the vegetative stage, where those new, fragile individuals find homes in one-gallon pots until they hit puberty, at which time they'll be moved to the garage for the big show, phase three: blooming.

Mounted to the ceiling in the veg room is the Mondo Reflector Judah gave me, down are the ceiling fan and original light fixture that came with the house. Inserted in the window is a piece of plywood with a hole cut in it to vent out the freestanding air conditioner. The wood is just wide enough to support the vent tubing and positioned so that it can be somewhat adequately hidden by the Star jasmine in front of the window, unless someone were to come up and look closely. In that case, I'm doomed. The preexisting jasmine is a plus. For the four weeks it blooms it will be more than enough to costume any Girlstink. Ed tells me if anyone asks I should just say I'm running a clothes dryer. In a bedroom.

I've cut a hole in the blind for the vent tube to fit through. The blind is just one of the things I will need to replace when I move out. Panda paper is stapled all around the window to prevent light leaks and the edges are sealed with black gaffer's tape. I stare at the ceiling fan covered in plastic on the upper shelf of the closet, then to the ceiling, trying to find patterns in the black constellations left behind from Judah's attempts to hang the reflector before Ed showed up with his stud detector. Yes. There will be a lot to do when I move out. This thought is squatting on my breath. I'm already chest-high to a duck here, which is different from drowning, so that's what I'll call it. Let's water the plants. This much I know how to do.

I am supposed to fill the thirty-two-gallon trash can that is the new veg room reservoir to feed the six small plants that are vegging under a thousand very expensive watts. This is overkill, all of it, but I am making a concerted effort to follow directions, to not insist on doing things my way, to be a good Community member. I'm to remove whatever seeps into the tub with the twelve-gallon shop vac I was instructed to buy for this purpose. In a fit of autonomy, I halve everything, but even at half capacity, the tub that the pots are sitting in is full of runoff. The two-gallon watering can would have done the trick. But wait Grasshoppa, go in humility and get your shop vac. I suck up about a gallon before the lights go out.

Ed calls from the garage, "What the fuck?" He and Scooter are balancing a giant piece of Sheetrock on their heads.

"It's just I was watering and—"

"Check the breakers."

I stare. Ed continues: "The metal box on the side of the house with the switches inside. See if one of them is facing a different way from the others and if it is, make it match."

I am glad the Sheetrock is on his head, so he can't shake it at my stupid.

"I've lived in apartments . . ."

"Just check the box. You'll be doing it a lot so it's good for you to get used to it with someone here."

"Thank you for helping me," I say, and sure, I'm paying him, but I'm getting The Community price, and he is actually giving me clear instructions that make sense. For a change, I am relieved to be told what to do. Ed attaches the Sheetrock to a frame while he explains it all:

"This whole job is problem management" *nail*

nail "Things never go as planned" *nail*

"For more than about forty-eight hours" *nail*

"Max" *nail*

nail "There's no problem" *nail*

"That you don't have twenty-four hours" *nail*

nail nail "To solve" *nail*

"Unless it's a heat problem" *nail*

"But you're not going to have to worry about that"

nail "Except maybe in the veg room" *nail*

"Sooner you learn to take it in stride" *nail*

"The better this will all work out for you." *nail nail nail*

Thinking mostly of crucifixion, I successfully flip my first breaker. Which is when the post office calls to tell me that my chicks have arrived.

CHICKS!

"You're the one with the peeps?"

"Yes, I am!" The handful of people who were waiting for stamps now surround the counter where the noisy box has landed.

"They've been going like that all morning," the lady says. "Sure can't wait to take a peek . . ." Now the other employees have gathered too. The scrape of the corrugated cardboard flaps reverberates through the tiny huddle, and a collective *awww* mingles with the chirping.

I'm not supposed to name them, so I only name one: Lilybird. She has what looks like black eyeliner around her eyes, and she is clearly the bossiest. She takes to the gel that came with the birds before any of the others. I have lined the box that the Mondo Reflector came in with shop towels—absorbent but disposable. I bob the back of their heads over the water and food bowls until the first few start eating and drinking. The others learn by example. In under an hour they're all pecking and bobbing and shitting on their own. "They'll be hopping out of that box by the end of the week," Scooter tells me. "My family kept chickens. You wouldn't believe the dust."

I decide to worry about that at the end of the week. All of it. For now, I'm making a concerted effort to enjoy something, so I bring Vito and the chicken box inside the office and shut the door. *The Encyclopedia of Country Living* says the first thing a chick sees is what they imprint as mother. Probably this is someone at the hatchery but I hover over the box anyway and try to make eye contact with each one. I hold them, one at a time, and look them in the eye. There are twenty-seven. I only wanted seven, but the Murray McMurray Hatchery required a minimum order of twenty-five, so that they keep each other warm during shipping. I've received two bonus chicks for no apparent reason. I'm glad the bonus chicks aren't making up for dead ones.

With the bonus, I justify naming two more. Rosie has a big V on her head, and Daisy's head is all yellow. Okay, three. I'll let myself name three. After a few minutes it's hard to keep track of which ones I've held and which ones I haven't. I don't know how long I'm supposed to look at them until they imprint. *The Encyclopedia* offers no details on that. I hold Vito while he checks them out. When he peeks over the edge of the box they all instinctively run to the opposite side. He regards them more as a curiosity than, say, lunch, but they don't seem to be imprinting on him as mother. I put Vito in a down-stay while I bond with Lilybird. I trust that he'll hold it like we've worked on, and he does. The room is humming—and not just from the heat or the fans in the veg room next door. The seeds of the dream are thriving.

Judah knocks on the door with an Italian rice ball in his hand. It's my favorite: rice hiding meat, breaded, deep fried, smooth marinara on the side. Judah and I are joined in food. We share all kinds of hungry. "I didn't hear you pull up."

"The nail gun is pretty loud," he says. "It echoes through the gully."

"Do you think the neighbors can hear it?"

"It might be better not to know. Cute chickens."

"This is Lilybird. She's my favorite."

"I thought you weren't going to name any. Hey, Mr. Vito!" He gives Vito the boroughs accent and hand gestures. Vito remains unperturbed. Judah places the food at my feet and I hand him Lilybird.

"Two hands, you need two hands!" He holds her as I stroke her downy head with my finger. She's skittish. So's he. He hands her back.

"You want to hold Daisy?"

"I'm good." He slides open the closet door to check on the clone nursery.

"I think what you really want is a baby," he says, lifting lids on clone trays. The way he drops it while doing something else makes it hard to tell if it's an accusation or a conversation starter.

"I want roots."

"I think you got that covered." We laugh, looking around the office. In this one little room are five trays of replanted vegetable seeds, two trays of spindly ganja clones, twenty-seven day-old chicks, a sixteen-week-old puppy, and a glitter-crusted macaroni necklace I made with my god-daughter, proudly displayed on the shelf.

"Maybe you're right probably." This is what you should never say. It's best to seem blind in your long-term eye, be more fun. Adore the moment and him, nothing more.

"Do you have a turkey baster?" is what he asks.

"Yes. Kitchen. Drawer beside the sink."

"You've got way too much water in those clone trays," he says, lifting the Oasis cubes.

Two of them have shaggy white beards, others mere stubble, most have nothing white at all, no sign of rooting. "These two need to be transplanted now. Do you have soil?" he asks, as he leaves the room with the earnest efficiency of a brand-new ER intern.

"Yes." Lilybird's heartbeat is very fast against the palm of my hand.

"What kind?" He's back with the baster and a purple plastic bowl.

"The Ocean Forest I was using for the strawberry boxes."

"Zeus is on his way over. I'll ask if you can use that." When he finishes clearing the trays of their excess, he hands me the bowl so I can dump it. He won't put it down on the floor. It floats there sloshing, blocking his face, pulsing at the end of his strong straight arm. I have to put Lilybird back in the box, waking her, to take the bowl. He goes next door to the veg room. I hear, "What the fuck?" He returns, irked. "Where's your shop vac? You can't let the plants sit in that much water."

"I started to vac them and the breaker flipped and then the post—"

"You can get molds, fungus, all kinds of shit can breed in that standing water. No standing water, remember? How long have they been sitting like that?" He hovers above me. He's told me. I've read it in *The Bible*. No standing water. But the breakers—the chickens—the hoeing since dawn.

For eighteen hours a day the veg room hums next door. Sometimes this hum breaks down into its component parts—the high ping of the bulb, the midrange of the AC, and the warbling chant of the fans—but that only happens when each of those sounds has found joints in my skull to jimmy, like now. The veg room reverberations are tweaked by the panic of chicks.

I don't eat the last bite of rice ball. I bite my bottom lip instead, to steady it, because my quaking chin is dented like a peach pit or the moon.

"Thank you for the rice ball," I tell him.

"You're welcome." He stares at me, sitting on the floor still holding the bowl. "I really hope you build character up here."

BOXING CEDARA

ZEUS AND CEDARA DRIVE THEIR COROLLA TOO FAST DOWN THE GRAVEL road. I watch through the window as they alight from the Toyota, emerge from the dusty cloud of their own velocity, and approach the house. I watch through the window as Cedara takes it all in, puts her hands together, and bows to the boys in the garage. Judah goes out to greet them and I close the office door behind him. Vito sniffs at the purple bowl of undumped waste, then lays his head on his paws and sighs. Cedara taps on the closed door but doesn't wait for a response before opening it. "Such abundance! What did I tell you? The universe is conspiring to shower you with blessings!"

I stand. "Yes! So much abundance all at once that it's easy to mistake for anxiety!"

It is unlikely that she will not touch the chickens. But I can delay it, let my face sink in for them a few seconds more before she brings her presence to the box.

"Oh let me see let me see let me see!" She pulls her ankles up onto her thighs in full lotus and with gentle reverence reaches into the reflector box, wuving endearments still shouting from its sides. She has selected an anonymous chick, livestock. But still, after about a three count of her gaze bearing down on it, stroking its downy head, I take it from her and recommend she hold a different one. I don't really understand the imprinting thing and don't want to take any chances. I'm the Divine Feminine in this house. She can go bless her own fucking temple.

"Can I pick my five now?" Zeus and Cedara have agreed to take five of the chicks.

"I don't know how we'd mark them."

"This one is so pretty."

"That's Lilybird," I say, not even giving her a three count. "This one I'm definitely keeping."

"You seem a little closed today," she says, "a little tight around the heart."

"This whole thing is stressful."

"This whole thing is beautiful, perfect, just as it is."

She takes a long, deep breath and, as she exhales, turns her palms up on her knees.

"Do it with me," she says. "Take a cleansing breath."

I sit like her, facing her. She rests her hand on my sternum, the heel of her palm between my boobs, and presses against my inhale. "Yes, open the blockage, release the tension. Keep your heart open. Choose gratitude." Cedara closes her eyes and briefly hums a blissy "ommmmmmmm-mmmm . . ." then, "Let's get in the hot tub." I regret removing the lizard corpses. I regret my decision to use all available appliances until the bloom room lights come on, so there won't be a sudden jump in the power bill.

I don't exactly feel like getting naked with a construction crew in my house, even if they are mostly members of The Community who have already seen me naked on numerous other aquatic occasions. It's nothing against nudity; I just feel quite vulnerable enough already, thank you. See? I'm choosing gratitude.

"I have to finish shopvacking the veg trays," I explain.

"Judah said he'd do it for you, while you play with the chickens."

"I think I might feel better if I did things, rather than getting in the hot tub right now."

"Then we'll just stay here and breathe together," Cedara says, and I can see Zeus "holding space" for Judah through the window. Judah has his forehead against a pine and Zeus's mouth moves as he circles him. He hands Judah several pine cones and Judah hurls them into the gully as hard as he can.

"He's getting sick of me."

"Yes, yes, he is." She is still looking at me in that way that doesn't change no matter what I say, no matter what she says. She's playing hippie chicken with me and I'm not in the mood.

Hippie chicken is when a hippie looks you right in the eye in a way that is, I assume, meant to generate a deep, if momentary, bond and to somehow connect you and said hippie like some kind of psychic fascia. It's sort of like a staring contest, but those are funny, so no—it's more like having someone stick a bayonet in your eyes, or drill a core sample through the back of your skull, or pin your pupils to a specimen box. It's different from mere gazing, and like pornography, I know it when I see it.

"I really want to center with you," Cedara says, putting her hand on my shoulders, because she hasn't won this round yet. "You're really emanating imbalance." *No shit*, I think, and look away—she's won!—at my bare feet, then my hands, dirtier than they've ever been in my life. Dry. Cracked. Always dirty no matter how many times I wash them or soak them in olive oil and lemon juice. The lines are brown and fine, like the skeleton of a leaf. Three cuts, five blisters at the current count, and nothing in the ground yet. Her hands move from my shoulders and wrap around me. Goddessdammit. The ante is upped. We're now firmly in BOA territory: belligerently oppressive affection. Which, I believe, is self-explanatory. I of course return the hug, not wishing to be that sad, closed-off girl from LA. "I love you," Cedara says, and I should have seen it coming, but like Tyson and the ear, I thought she would know where to stop—but no—I'm on the ropes—she has completed the fatal hippie trifecta: chicken, BOA, and the gratuitous use of *I love you*.

"Thanks, I really appreciate your support," I reply. Fancy footwork. She pulls out of the hug and we're in round two of chicken—the eyeball uppercut. She's relentless. I want to be open and compassionate and universally loving, but I can't afford to cheapen these words because they're all I've really got to root with in a lot of important situations. If I just start saying *I love you* all over the place to every casual acquaintance then how will I still be able to tremble when I say it in a trembleworthy context? She ceases blinking. The challenge coagulates in the whites of her eyes; her nostrils flap slightly with each deep inhale and exhale. Even her breathing is hegemonic. Vito's in my corner, presses on my leg, *You can do it, kid*. Cedara tilts her head slightly; is that curiosity? At first I can't tell, because the dark matter of her pupils is sucking me into the hippie event horizon. No, it's not curiosity—not gentle like that—it's pity, and fuck that. But wait—where is my compassion? She is sorry for me, sorry I'm such a love miser. Summon your compassion. I've got nothing else left. "I love you too," I say.

The corners of her mouth rise like charmed serpents. She touches her forehead to mine. "Blessings, sister. Now let's have our ablutions."

UNI UNAGI TEMPURA TORO KOI

"YOU LADIES UP FOR SOME SUSHI?" ZEUS ASKS, PERCHED ABOVE THE hot tub.

"Girl soup!" Judah says, as he slips through the gap in the sliding glass door and lines up beside Zeus. It's a little like that bar in Florida from the fifties where ladies dressed as mermaids would swim in tanks behind the bar, except I don't have the benefit of a tail and the way the hot tub is sunk into the deck means that Zeus and Judah loom over us, rather than a more equitable eye-to-eye leering. We look up to them.

"You guys coming in?" Cedara asks. The hippie hottubbing is easier when everyone is drunk and/or high. It's not like going to a hot spring where everyone is wholesomely naked.

"I took care of the veg tub," Judah says. *Choose gratitude choose gratitude choose gratitude.*

"Thank you," I tell him. He is staring from me to Cedara as if we were playing tennis, which we're not.

"Mmmm . . . mackerel," Cedara says. It seems she is up for some sushi.

"Ahhh . . . albacore," Judah replies.

"Oooohhh . . . uni," she adds, needlessly.

"We would need to go like now," Zeus says.

Ed and Scooter slip out next, pouches of organic American Spirit in their hands. "Nothing wrong with naked chicks in a hot tub at the end of the day," Ed says. He has a real talent for unscrewing the NorCal lens and stomping it with his steel-toe boot.

"Leave it to you to make a mockery of everything," Cedara tells Ed.

"Leave it to me to not be full of shit," he says, taking a drag on his rollie. Ed and Scooter approach, tenuously, not sure if it's boyfriends only in the front row or general admission. "You guys done for the day?" I ask, begging the obvious.

"Yeah," Ed answers, not even bothering to look at my eyes. I give him the *Hey, here are my eyes* gesture. "Dude, I'm not going to pretend it's not hot like these pussies. You two should make out." Scooter shifts his weight, moves to the outdoor table several feet away, and sits. Ed taunts him, "Hey, Woody, you got a light?"

"You're an asshole," Scooter says, but throws him the lighter anyway.

I look at them all, just standing there. Ed seems to sense my self-consciousness and says, "Do you want to just wait and pay us out tomorrow?"

"No, no, I'll go get your money." I take the quietest of breaths, suck in my stomach, and scuttle from the hot tub like a mutant crab.

"Uni unagi tempura toro koi . . ." Cedara chants this, contemplative before the menu. Zeus asks how I'm holding up and rubs behind my shoulder blades to coax a reply. Judah is pouring everyone more unfiltered sake. "It's challenging," I say. Zeus and Judah are unified in their insistence that one of the great benefits of this job is learning to be cucumber cool in the face of adversity. It seems to me more like you become accustomed to chronic low-grade anxiety, but then I think that maybe these are the same.

"It seems like you're really taking on a lot, what with the veggies and the dog and The Girls, and now all those chickens," Zeus says. I try to explain that I like a challenge, but the way I am draining those irritatingly small cups of sake would suggest that what I'd like right now is obliteration. Zeus adds, "We all agree that you could use some help."

"Who is we?"

Judah and Zeus indicate each other, using edamame.

"You guys have been really helpful already, with the tubs and all. I wasn't expecting the chick—"

"You are going to encounter a lot of things you aren't expecting,"

Zeus says, rubbing the Chinese coin that fills the hole in his earlobe. Cedara moves away from him and takes the seat beside me.

"Pretty much daily," Judah says, and pours me more sake. Cedara nods gentle assent and puts her hand on my knee. Judah puts down the sake and puts his hand on my other knee. Zeus, sitting across from us, continues to rub the coin as he clears his throat and looks pointedly at Judah.

Judah moves his hand to mine, interlacing fingers. "I really think it's best if Zeus becomes your consultant. He'll give you plants, because I'm not sure how many of those laundry clones are going to work out. He'll bring his expertise, be on call for whatever problems you may have."

"I thought you were going to help me," I whisper to Judah. I'm whispering because I'm of the opinion that this was something that perhaps should have been a topic of discussion for him and me, not him and Zeus.

Cedara chimes in, "It's so much better if your consultant is someone other than your lover." They all laugh, because Cedara had a growshow in Berkeley with a friend of hers, and Zeus was their investor as well as their consultant. They never did very well. Early on, Cedara calculated the nutrient measurements and wrote them down in what I can only imagine was careful, looping cursive on an index card that was pinned above the reservoir where the nutrients were mixed. These Girls were never able to reach a reasonable yield, and they were leaking money in power bills and rent. No one could figure it out. They repeated mantras as they watered. They told The Girls how much they loved them. It was only when Cedara and Zeus dropped out of the operation that her friend, drawing up a new nutrient chart, discovered that all feedings under the previous regime had been given at a quarter dose. Three people had been trying to problem solve for a year—except no one had checked the math.

"I'm not really sure I need a consultant," I say.

"Everybody has one for their first round," Judah says. The other two solemnly nod.

"I didn't think people who pony up their own cash and have already done an apprenticeship at their boyfriend's house had to have a consultant."

"I do hydro. You're doing soil. I can't help you with that. He's the soil man," Judah says, pointing a chopstick at Zeus, who has his chin in his hands and a grin on his face of the shit-eating variety.

"That I am," he says.

"So you would just help out a sister of The Community like that? That's really nice," I say, and look to Cedara, who is looking at Zeus, who is looking at Judah. I leave them stuck in their hippie chicken daisy chain and drain another cup of milky sake. There is going to be a price. I am not going to like it, but I am going to have to pay it. Just because I worked in Judah's room all winter, trimmed and bent and stripped in the glittering Live Girls! emporium in his garage—that is still way below the normal sacrifice. Apprenticeship is not a sufficient entry fee. Have I never seen *The Godfather*?

"Am I obligated to have a consultant?"

"You want one; you just don't know it yet," Zeus says.

It's entirely possible that he just wants to help me. But since I am, after all, both Heather Donahue and The Girl from *The Blair Witch Project*, and what we share aside from an affinity for the woods is an unpleasant mix of know-it-all attitude and emotional instability, it's entirely possible that the job of being my consultant will be a pain in the ass, worthy of compensation.

"How much?"

"Twenty-five."

"Twenty-five hundred?" I ask.

He leans across the table. Judah is still holding my hand.

"Twenty-five percent of your gross."

For twenty-five percent I had a manager and agent and a lawyer in LA. Unlike the folks who shepherded my acting career, Zeus will actually see that percentage, and soon.

"I think we should begin that cleanse tomorrow," Judah tells me. "We really need to release some toxins."

I really need to make new friends.

LAUNDRY ORPHANS

There's a time as the clones begin to root when it looks like they're dying. At first it weakens them, this transformation. They begin to yellow. The lower leaves drop off. They don't yet know how to be what they're becoming. This has been especially true of the yellow orphans in the nursery, the ones that came from Zeus's "laundry" bag. The ones Zeus would have thrown out, the ones I wouldn't have bothered to root if I'd had other options. Only now that they've rooted do they really look strong. And so I'll move them along again. That's how it goes in the growhouse: As soon as you thrive you get pushed again. Tonight I'm putting them into one-gallon pots and moving them into the veg room.

Soon I'll be taking clones from them. Before I put this round in the bloom room, I'll cut the bottom branches off and those branches will become the new clones, and so on . . . There was a perpetual garden in that bag. A livelihood. Just add care.

Only the clones with thickest stems rooted, but I can't bring myself to throw the unrooted ones away and it costs little to run the nursery, so I keep them, though they're unlikely to root at this point, and if they do, they're unlikely to catch up to their sisters. Not really sisters; that would imply some genetic difference. These are clones in various stages of life. Same material at different places in time. The Girls are not so much sisters as alternative selves, living parallel lives all over the place. Some of their other alternative selves are in Zeus's garage, and Ed's and Judah's, and some are ash in a bong. They don't need legs; they get around on desire.

The Girls persist despite any one grower's error because they're a colony, or a sort of borderless nation. They're defined more by their far-reaching presence than by any one individual. And yet they're all differentiated individuals, with immune responses that mark the end of themselves and the beginning of another. I wonder if any one of them prides herself on her independence. She probably shouldn't.

In between pottings, I scratch Vito on the neck where his fur is thickest. He's still coughing at night, but he's getting better. I can't tell yet if the chicks have imprinted on me as mother, but they seem pretty happy to see me anyway. For a girl who didn't want to cohabitate, I sure have a shitload of roommates. These are relationships too, among my most mutually intimate.

I notice these things now, out here where it's quiet. I didn't in the city, not to this extent. This job requires constant attention. Attention is what money buys you out of. You pay money instead of attention. Food, pot, wine, clothes—in the city I just bought them, subsidizing someone else's attention. But to do what with that time? This is no less humbling a way to be of service than scrubbing toilets at the meditation center. Paying attention is the joy of this job, that much I'm already learning.

They're already turning toward the light. It's what plants do. They can't help but choose awesome. It's why they're not considered intelligent. They have no ability to make bad choices. I've come to squat too long in shadows; it comes from getting burned.

I still don't have enough plants to fill the room according to the original schedule, but I can give them more time in the veg room. But really, six plants would be enough to fill the room if you veg them out long enough. They will stay in vegetative mode until they get the light signal to begin flowering. Until they get twelve hours of light and twelve hours of dark they will just keep getting bigger. Letting these plants veg until they can fill out the room would put me behind and make it harder to recoup what I've already spent, but I'm not racing. The one-year plan isn't etched in stone; it's sketched in sand. Besides, the upside of Zeus being my consultant is that he'll provide plants to fill in the gaps. It's not all up to me.

The schedule that has been laid out for my growshow is based on a modified sea of green setup, which is what the guys do. A true sea of green would be done with more, shorter plants, which the county's canopy law makes possible and the ninety-nine-plant rule makes manageable. In a true sea of green, veg time is only a week or two, or when they hit about eight inches in height. This means they'll have just one main cola, or main budding stem, which makes for less yield per plant but a faster turnaround. The way a large number of small plants looks in tight quarters means you see nothing but a sea of green. This technique means not necessarily waiting for The Girls to show preflowers, tiny filaments that mark plant puberty, so they're pushed to flower before they're naturally ready. This stresses them beyond the already heavy stress they're already bound for as indoor plants. This, to me, is too much. Of course I want yields, and I know they're only plants—but they're also my Girls and I want them to be good medicine, not only for the patients who ultimately take them, but for me too. The modified sea of green that I'm doing allows the plants to veg out until they preflower and hit between eighteen and twenty inches, allowing four main colas and more yield per plant and fewer plants in total, to keep me well within the limits of the law. Their schedule will make my schedule. This extra veg time, the guys tell me, leads to a better crop. For me, it just feels better. I need to nurture something and they're it. My cup wasn't empty for long. It filled with surprises—not what I would have imagined, not on the finest hallucinogens, but here we are. The Girls, chickens, veggies, Vito, and me. We are here.

STINKERBELLE

JUDAH AND I ARE ON OUR WAY TO SAN FRANCISCO TO GET MY PRESCRIPTION.

Judah is handling Ed's calls about the construction at my place. They don't bother to call me when a decision needs to be made. I have absolutely no authority, which is somewhat pleasant. It's nice to take a load off. What concerns me is that I am not there to understand how the room is put together, but I will be running it alone. This, I guess, is why Zeus is involved now. But what about round two? I don't want to think about this, so I've unzipped Judah's pants. Before long a minivan shares the gridlocked space beside us. "Oh, shit, there's kids in there." I stay secret, stay down. He takes the first exit in Berkeley and we end up in the parking lot of an Indian restaurant when he comes. I suggest lunch, as they are advertising a $6.99 all-you-can-eat buffet, and maybe that would be a nice thing to do after the drive that consisted mostly of silence and sucking and sucking silence. He hands me the water bottle filled with a watery mix of lemon, maple syrup, and cayenne pepper. We are on day one of our cleanse.

"Besides," he says, "Stinkerbelle's expecting us."

This much is clear when she opens the door, wearing a stamp-sized square of Hmong embroidery lashed to her back with some hemp twine. On the bottom is a gauzy sarong, slung below creeping pubes. Radiating from her armpits are her signature curls and their accompanying pungent wafts. This is a version of hippie chicken I hadn't considered, one in which you can dominate a person's space using scent, whether it be patchouli, sandalwood, or just unsoap. She wraps her arms around Judah and they rock slightly. She looks at me, then Vito, then back to me and asks Judah, "When did you get a dog?"

Vito has unfurled and shredded toilet paper all over the living room. He has created chaos with a single roll and he looks really happy about it. I am relieved that I have to clean it up; it gives me something to do rather than watch Stinkerbelle give Judah the hippie hippie snake.

The hippie hippie snake is another weapon in the hippie arsenal. It is mostly used by women but can sometimes be seen in lankier men. A hippie would probably tell you this slow meandering in place is the result of tremendous kundalini energy that they have spent careful hours of meditation and several previous lifetimes cultivating, that this energy is their life force magnified. An unusually high allotment of the universe's energy courses through their yoga-honed vessels. Their spinal fluid is where earth's gravity and the cosmos's weightlessness meet in, like, tidal flow.

The feet typically remain planted, joints loose, knees slightly bent. Much as a charmed snake rises from a basket, so too the hippie seems to rise from the ground, head rocking like a pendulum. When combined with hippie chicken, it is a claustrophobic strategy. It is often accompanied by suggestions, another borrowing from the hypnotic repertoire. The hippie body will nudge your orbit and pull out again, leaving you feeling like you have just spent the afternoon on a boat, having embarked, perhaps, on a particularly rough and disappointing whale watch.

"Did your dog eat my cat's food?"

"He might have," I say. She's lost the hippie snake. Her movements have grown as angular as the shoulder blades jutting out from under the zigzagging hemp as she peels the foil off a fresh container of Sheba and my stomach rumbles. Vito goes for it immediately and I put him on my lap. "Didn't you bring food for him?" She's spitting little darts.

"It's in the car." My shoulders round over Vito, making myself a cave for him. "Isn't it almost time for my doctor's appointment?"

THE GOOD DOCTOR

THE WAITING ROOM HAS A DENTAL QUALITY—INNOCUOUS BEIGE, A TABLE fountain—but the magazines on the waiting room table are *High Times* and the NORML newsletter and a list of local dispensaries, none of which the office can officially recommend. Two girls rise from chairs to give Judah big hugs. They are from Nuggettown. "Looks like scrip season is here again," he says.

"You know it," says the short one.

'Tis the season when folks line up to get their prescriptions renewed, so they can be a patient in someone's outdoor co-op. Growers need enough scrips to legalize their indoor grows too, but there are a lot more plants around now, as outdoor season arrives, and open-air patches are much more vulnerable to checking by patrolling helicopters. By giving a grower your prescription, you become part of their co-op. The California grower can then legally grow more plants, and you get your prescription filled with a pound of marijuana at harvest time. Any surplus from the plants grown for your scrip is your donation to the grower to cover their expenses, risk, and careful tending. A pound of medicine from a dispensary would cost a whole lot more than the hundred and fifty dollars it can cost to get your papers.

The Good Doctor is a dashing metrosexual who never takes his eyes off of the prize. "I just got back from LA," he says, hiking up the Seven jeans under his lab coat. "They're creating a reality show around me." I think the glasses he's wearing do not have prescription lenses, and I am fairly sure he doesn't need to wear that lab coat here, or the stethoscope, or use the clipboard, not really. I'm also fairly sure he doesn't need to use that little mallet on my knees. My reflexes are fine and have nothing to do with anxiety, insomnia, PMS, or any of my other potential qualifying conditions. Though he's a real physician, he reminds me more in every way of someone you might find beside you in the waiting room at a commercial audition for Advil. But there they are, his degrees, dangling off the studs of the tiny office.

"What was it like going to med school in Honduras?"

"Humid." He hits my knee again, too hard. I gasp and kick his chair. "I guess you know what that whirlwind is like, the biz . . . ," he says. "Always on the edge of your seat."

"Kind of like the lottery." The blood pressure collar hippiehugs my arm.

"I am in it to win it this time. We're supposed to go to Gabon to shoot the pilot on Iboga." The Good Doctor's show revolves around him and a sidekick going around the world and exploring alternative medicines. The Good Doctor is better suited to television than this tiny office, though it's hard to know which might be more lucrative in the long run.

I put my medical records on his desk. They consist of one-off illnesses that don't necessarily qualify me for a medical marijuana card, but they were all that was readily available. The person who booked the appointment for this particular prescription-granting franchise told me I must bring medical records as proof of my qualifying condition and I am trying to play by the rules, sketchy as they are, as best I can.

"You don't have to worry about this," the Good Doctor says, patting the manila folder. "It says here on the form you filled out today that you have PMS, insomnia, and anxiety." Of course I didn't have the second two until I embarked upon my new career.

He gives me the state-mandated spiel about how I can never take my medicine on an airplane, even if the flight is within California, and that I can't carry my medicine over state lines, even into another medical state. Because he has determined that my condition requires a dosage of an ounce a week, my scrip will allow me to have a pound in my possession at any given time and I can grow six mature or twelve immature plants, unless my local laws allow for more, which they don't. Not exactly.

One hundred and fifty dollars and fifteen minutes later, I am a card-carrying medical marijuana patient, licensed to grow.

CLIFFHANGERS

CEDARA AND ZEUS ARE AT STINKERBELLE'S WHEN WE GET BACK. THIS IS Cedara's old place, so this is where they crash in the Bay. We enter the kitchen. The air is thick with Nag Champa incense, pot, sweat, pale ale. I would very much like a beer. Very much indeed. But you see, this cleanse. Cedara offers me a beer. I pull the small bottle of cleansing solution from my purse. "Are you sure this is the best thing for you right now?" she asks. "You've kind of got a lot on your plate, and you might want to keep your strength up."

"Yeah, that would make sense."

"Come outside with me," she says, and I do because it's feeling pretty claustrophobic in here with the glitchy beats blaring on the stereo and ten people I haven't met yet and a boyfriend who's not really speaking to me. Cedara rolls a cigarette to go with her beer. I take a sip of resentment from my spicy maple lemonade. Yum. Cedara burps and the smell of food and beer is appealing even in this windy, recycled form. "You don't look happy," she says.

"Yeah. Thank you," I say, because I'm practicing gratitude.

"Just because he is all about a spring cleaning for his body right now doesn't mean you have to do it too. I think the last thing you need right now is another challenge, especially one that you didn't really choose."

"You have a point. This might not be the best time for me to be starving."

"Cleansing is very valuable, but so is your sanity right now."

"I'm not very nice when I'm hungry."

"You can address the strengthening of your character as time goes on. You have done enough for now, it seems. You should take your rewards as you see fit." Cedara looks like a fairy goddessmother to me right now. What she's saying is I should drink a beer, I should eat some of those raw almonds, those carrots, that hummus. I am definitely very hungry if the possibility of eating raw almonds and baby carrots strikes me as a great indulgence.

"You're right. You are so so right. I'll be right back."

Cedara takes a deep drag on her cigarette. "You go, girl!"

"What are you doing?" Judah asks, when he sees me pull the beer from the fridge.

"I am having a beer and some hummus and carrots because I think this is not a good time for me to be doing a cleanse."

"But—we made a pact." The triangle of consternation again contorts his brow.

"I don't think I really thought it through completely," I say, and avert my eyes, using them to locate the bottle opener. I pop the lid. "I really have a lot on my plate right now." He looks at me like he just caught me making out with his dad. "Please don't be mad," I say, and grab a baby carrot on my way back out the door.

"Don't be mad? You promised me we would do this together."

"You chose to fast now. I don't want to anymore."

He pulls me around a wall into an empty bedroom. "Like you changed your mind about living with me? Like you changed your mind fifty different times about whether you were going to grow or not?" The carrot is crunchy, cool, and sweet. I put my beer down and stand there for a minute, palms out in supplication. He doesn't come toward me, so I step into him, wrap my arms around him, and there is a melting. There is not a merging, but there is a melting. We don't mean any harm, neither of us. We both just like to complicate things; it helps us believe our lives are interesting.

Later, I hang off one side of the bed, with my hand on Vito. Judah clings to the opposite edge. We are cliffhangers. The sleeping position of doom.

We are still hugging the edges when he wakes at dawn. He gets up and brushes his teeth for a long time. Spits and rinses and pauses some more. He stands in front of the bed like he is about to give the State of the Union, which he is.

"I think we should just be friends."

"What?"

"I think we should just be friends."

"Okay, I heard you."

/

~

. . .

.

Cedara cuts through the fog he just made and announces they are going to brunch. "Okay," I say, "I have to brush my teeth." Vito follows me into the bathroom and lays on my feet.

"What do you mean you think you just broke up?" Cedara asks, and Judah mumbles something that I can't understand. My gums are bleeding. I moved here six weeks ago. I made a crucial error: I needed him. I needed him in a vague and inarticulate way that involved a lot of crying. I thought he would wait it out until I was more myself again, but this is myself too; this baby-hungry, puppy-substituting, beer-swilling, thirty-four-year-old unemployed tangle of chaos is me too. I have been capable and effective, but if you'd met me in only the last six weeks, you would be hard-pressed to believe that. I was trying to take the message of meditation to heart, the part about surrender, anyway. I kind of forgot the part about detachment, the part about disentangling from negative emotions, the Vulcan part. I thought when he said he loved me that it was okay to need him in this weepy way, to be insecure—to allow the rug to come out from under my feet because to resist it would just be fear. I wanted to be brave. I want to be brave now. Maybe he doesn't really mean it.

I THINK *FUCK YOU* BUT SAY "I LOVE YOU" AND MEAN IT

I reach my hand across the center console and squeeze a little on his knee. "I'm sorry," I say, aware of the hole it punches. Maybe the silence was a better option, but I continue. "Moving up here has been a challenge."

He doesn't know what to say. He's not certain this is the right decision. I know him well enough to know he's thinking this. I'm thinking it too. I'm calculating the odds that we'll be friends if he dumps me six weeks after I move here. The sum is negative, according to my calculations. He holds my hand. Calls come in as we drive and he doesn't take them. He doesn't even look at the phone. We're both interested in stretching this taffy silence. Taffy is not resilient. It does not snap back like rubber. Taffy is so sweet it will hurt the least sensitive teeth, get wedged in gums, and make a dull clang.

The road to my house seems especially long. These are what you might call the boonies, if you were a city girl. Vito licks my face and then makes his body back into an O on my lap. He and I are in it for the long haul. He just wants to be friends too. The difference is, we will be. For fifteen years, at least, if things don't go the way of the tortoise.

Judah, too, caresses Vito. "Hey, buddy" and "How you holding up, buddy?" Things he won't ask me are directed at my proxy. "I know you want to be a mom. I see how you are with Sprout," he says, finally.

"I want someone to belong to, I guess. Even just a place maybe. Independence is kind of overrated."

"But it's who you are."

"By necessity. Like now. Again."

Getting out of the car is a step toward finality. So we don't, at first. We take each severing step slowly. I don't expect him to open his door, but he does. We stall again, this time just before my door. The number of spiders here is even greater than the population inside the house. All kinds, but mostly wolfs and black widows. It's not an omen; it's just nature. I want to hold him. He can tell, and we melt chests, wrap arms. We've made a mistake, but I don't know where its borders are. "I'm sorry I've been horrible," I say, because it's true. Somebody needs to tell us that we all are one and it's our egos only, playing at rejection. Where's a hippie when you need one? "You haven't—I'm just—"

"Are you? Just?" There's a rock by the door I'd like to bash his skull with, but I can't, because we're still hugging. *Fuck you*, I think but say, "I love you," and mean it. He doesn't want another child or a person to belong to. He does sometimes, but he doesn't now. His mother told me several times *He's like the weather in Texas.* I didn't really get it then.

"We'll find our way."

"Sure."

"Just not together . . ." I'm checking if he's changed his mind.

"Sad." He hasn't.

"I miss you already."

"I'm not worried about you."

"That makes one of us."

He laughs. "You're like my best friend."

"I hope not."

"I hope we can be friends. I mean, I hope we can continue to be friends. I'm just not ready."

"Ready for what? For what you already have? Plus me? Your Peter Pan Underoos are kind of tugging at the seams, you know."

"Just have to get a jab in, don't you."

"Sorry," I say, because I am.

"You would have come up here eventually anyway. You didn't need me. Not really."

"You didn't want to be needed. Not really. I should probably go check on the chickens."

"Can I come in?"

"Of course."

I don't know why I said "of course," like it was obvious. Vito sits nicely, waiting for me to cross the threshold first.

He checks on the plants. I check on the chickens. The pale blue shop towels are loaded with shit. Ed was supposed to have changed them. I don't change them either. Instead I mutter to the baby chicks, "Get used to it," and shut the door against the stink.

"Maybe if you could wait three years." He strokes his chin. "What if we started trying in three years?"

"What if you said this all over again then?"

"Maybe five?"

"There is one thing I am sure of." Everything I do with my hands feels strange, so I leave them by my sides, let them dangle. "No one will love you and Sprout more than I do. And if you're lucky you'll find someone who loves you just as much." I mean it, I think. I don't know. There will always be times when I can't tell the difference between a new life and a new role.

He leans against the breakfast bar and after a great whooshing exhale he straightens and says, "Thank you. Thank you for making me a better father, for your sense of humor, thank you for being smart and solving problems with me. Thank you for sharing your life with me for ten great months." We stare at each other in a way that does not resemble hippie chicken. We are mutually humbled, mutually lost, mutually exhausted by ourselves and each other.

"You'll make the right woman very happy one day." I don't know what else to say, so I borrow from the playbook of clichéd closers to delay his departure a little.

"Yeah. Sprout."

The part of me that wants to punch him in the face is failing, and I'm sort of glad. The softening scares me and I'm hard again. "You're not gonna turn me in are you?" The occupational hazard, already etched.

"For fuck's sake, no!" He's startled. "Wait—I don't have to worry about that, do I?"

"No!" And just like that, we're two pot growers who used to be in a relationship.

"Good. No. I didn't really consider that."

This, I realize, and viscerally, is what will keep me safe, what will keep me in the fold. "Guess I can trust you, since you're the one with more to lose," I say.

"But you make a better story. 'Girl from *Blair Witch* Busted for Pot.'"

"So I guess we're both safe."

"Sucks, that it comes to that."

"Does."

He takes water to my clones. He pulls the excess with my turkey baster. If he changes the chicken towels I will try to kiss him. He doesn't. He just looks at me. I just look at him. We just sit there on the threshold, at the end of the road, looking at each other. "You should probably go now," I say, though there's nothing I want less. What I mean is *Please hold me and let's just forget this stupid day ever happened.* We plow through to a hug again. It is long and warm and I am fairly sure that, unadulterated, he has never held me quite like this. His hair is dense and warm between my fingers. His arms are very strong.

He doesn't bother with a three-point turn, and his Subaru nearly falls into the gully. The dust he raises is not enough. His exit is completely clear.

MAY I?

MOTHERLODE

Nuggettown sits on one of the richest gold deposits in the California Mother Lode. The shafts stretch for miles, and not all of the gold was removed from the hard rock—it's just that the price dropped and it wasn't worth the trouble to keep mining. Gold has been valuable to all humans throughout history; it's a way of touching the sun, wrapping it around your fingers. A whole world of buried light is under my feet. This is what I'm trying to think about, sitting on the lawn with Vito curled against the small of my back, when my mom calls.

My mom doesn't say "I told you so" like she could after the family intervention at the bagel place last December, the day after Judah left to go back to Nuggettown. My dad and brother did not mince words, saying things like, "Are you insane?" and "I don't get it." My dad, red-faced and tugging on the brim of his baseball cap, said, "Jesus, he's not even handsome!"

My mother was gentler about it, but no less final: "You're getting older and you really don't have this kind of time."

My sister kept her eyes on her extra-sweet coffee, grateful she wasn't in my seat.

So Mom would be within her rights to throw down an all-caps *I TOLD YOU SO,* or even a muttered *thank God.* She doesn't say much, but when she does, her Philly accent is a comfort, almost as much as Vito is. "He dumped me," I tell her, "and now here I am with a puppy, twenty-seven chickens, and a shitload of veggie seedlings."

Yes, there is something missing from this list. I never quite got around to explaining the pot part. My parents' response to finding out it was what Judah did didn't really leave me anticipating a very open reception to this news.

My mom is rarely so silent. She's not sure that response is really what I need so she transitions into the neutral maternal. "Oh, hon . . . you're not gonna stay there are you? In the woods? By yourself?" She doesn't know the growroom was financed with everything I had left.

"Should I take twenty-seven chickens, veggie seedlings, and a puppy back to LA?"

"I'm not worried about those chickens. I'm worried about you."

"Taking care of everything is helping me. I have daily funlets. It's what I call the things I do instead of chores. Because it's fun. And if I call the chores funlets then it feels more like something to look forward to."

She makes a sound that is her own compressed version of *uh-oh*.

"What the fuck am I doing here?" I break and sink into a full-throttle sob. "What's happened to me? I have no idea how to raise a fucking chicken. I don't even say chard right; I thought it was soft like *chardonnay* but it's hard like *cherry*. I mean what the fuck, right? I get why he doesn't want me. Who would? Who could function under the weight of this blobby mess?"

My mom is not having it. "Self-pity? Oh no. Shit in one hand, shovel pity with the other, and see which one fills up first. You got yourself a handful of shit there, sweetyhearts, and you're going to throw it in that fucking garden, okay?"

"Okay."

"You can do that."

"I can do that."

I don't know if I can do that and I'm sorry that she's hearing me not able to breathe. I'm grateful. But I'm also grateful that I have her. She didn't have her own mother at my age. And I remember that now but don't say it because then she'll cry too and understand for only the briefest moment the magnitude of that loss when I was four and my brother was two and my mom was twenty-six and Christmas was a week away. Nanny died suddenly of a ruptured aorta shortly after my mom and her sister found their dad at a hotel with another woman. I feel all of our losses because it's connection, this grief, and I try to breathe them out. The trees take it up and make it fresh. They make it clean again. And again and again and again. They even make it smell good. I think they're breathing with me, supporting me, and it's not such magical thinking, it's just biology made mine. "I love you and I'm so sorry for being such a fucking freak," I tell her. "I wish I was a regular person that wouldn't make you worry all the time. I don't know why I'm like this with all this wanting things to be different all the time," I say, when I can.

"I always knew that you were only on loan to me," she says, and I decide not to wonder if it's because she'd rather not be held responsible. "More than your brother and sister. Your nanny always said you were here before." We're both thinking about Nanny. She has a tendency to show up at times like this. Her memory protects us, but also reminds us that some things don't make you stronger; some things actually just go ahead and kill you.

"Is that some kind of euphemism for crazy?"

I am the loser in the where-are-they-now articles. I am that girl who had "Fails to work to potential" on her report cards. Here I am again, a girl lost in the woods, scared of her own shadow. This is me. Traipsing off another cliff with blind confidence. A fool.

"No. We're coming," Mom says, definitive, "in twenty-one days."

TRANSPLANTING

I walk Vito up and down Red Dirt Road twice in a row, but my skin is still crawling. I'm developing Restless Leg Syndrome. Which is real. And treatable with medical marijuana. And masturbation. The Rabbit Habit vibrator's cock part has a little gingerbread man face under the mushroom cap head. You really have to hand it to the Japanese, they bring the cute where you least expect it, where it really lends itself to a very specific brand of perversion. The rabbit is circumcised—and who makes that decision? Is it the same for bunnies headed to the European market? Hush. Focus. I drench the split ears with adequate saliva and brace myself for solitary bliss.

Nothing.

Not even a slight hum that would suggest a tap against the bookshelf might help, a loose wire that just needs a little nudge. I take out the batteries and put them back in again. Three times, actually. Nothing. Except Vito and Kali wrestling on the deck outside the door, then Zeus behind them. "Rise and shine," he says, holding out a box of lanky Kush Girls. "These Girls are gonna kick the ass of that skinny shit you got in the veg room."

I tie a fluffy knot around my waist. "Uh, I wasn't expecting you."

"I told you I was coming today to show you how to transplant."

"I don't remember discussing a time."

"Is this a bad time?"

"Not anymore."

He goes outside to pee off my deck.

"It's okay, you can use the bathroom."

"Waste of water," he says. "You know how much nitrogen is in urine?"

"No. No, I don't."

"Glad to see you're holding up all right."

"I'm not really sure I want more plants. I'm not going to have time to veg them."

"Just flip them. They'll do great. Look at this," he says and slides a dense shaggy root ball from one of the keg cups.

"Holy shit," I say, because none of the laundry orphans have roots like that.

"What'd I tell you? You gotta learn to trust, girl. Stop needing your eyes to know shit."

Zeus sits on my bed and fiddles with the half-inch agate disc embedded in his earlobe. He lies back on his elbows and adjusts one of the many hats he always wears because there are so few balding ballers.

"Why don't you go out and get things ready, while I change." I go so far as opening the sliding glass door for him and stand beside it until he goes. I get as far as underwear when he comes back to ask about a tarp.

Instead of setting up on the well-concealed side of the house, where you can keep an eye on the gate without being seen, Zeus has laid out a tarp on my deck and dumped three large bags of Happy Frog—a potting soil that proudly states that it's from the Humboldt Nation on each bag—and one larger bag of perlite—a soil amendment used by all manner of gardeners to keep soil moist and airy—onto the tarp or, rather, around it, as the tarp's area is not equal to the exuberant square footage formerly contained by the bags. There is now about a hundred dollars' worth of soil and amendments littering my deck, in clear view of the neighbor's house up the hill, which is, admittedly, about an eighth-mile away and mostly obscured by trees. "They can't see anything from there," Zeus says.

It is only now that I see Zeus has decapitated every last one of my Girls and stuck their heads in a Ball jar. "What have you done?"

"I topped them. You have to. Those tops will root in no time for your next round. You gotta always be thinking ahead. Best to give them a load of stress at once, so they can get over it." I pick up the jar and refrain from telling it I'm sorry.

"What if they—what if they just—don't?"

Zeus takes my hands and turns his eyes a particularly astringent shade of hazel. "Breathe with me."

"No. No, I am not breathing with you. Enough with the hippie shit. We need to move this stuff over to the side of the house right now. This is not where I'm going to transplant, okay?"

"By the time you get the wheelbarrow on the deck and shovel all of this soil into it, I won't have any time left to show you what you have to do."

"I've had gardens before."

"Not like this."

"No, with much harder things to grow."

"You know, Heather, it's not like jasmine or kale or whatever. I'm trying to help you in a way that will be mutually beneficial."

"Community," I say, because this was not my idea of it.

"Yes, exactly. You're still part of The Community." He strokes the tassel of his alpaca hat, the one with earflaps and Incan geometry.

"Isn't it time for your spring hats yet?"

"When it warms up more, in the afternoon maybe." His arms disappear into the pile of soil and rise back up with only moderate resistance.

"You'll know the mix is right when the resistance feels just like this. Here. Try." It's almost as nice as sticking your hand into a big bag of beans. If I had roots, this soil mix would be just the right balance between solidity and air. The Girls and I, we're not so different.

"This feels nice."

"Yeah, soft, right?" He fills the bottom of a three-gallon plastic grow-bag with some soil. "Where's the Piranha?" he asks. Piranha is an expensive brand of mycorrhizae, a beneficial fungus that supports healthy root growth.

"The guy at the Hydroporium said this would be fine," I say and hand him a tub of Chappy's mycorrhizae, which will support root growth for less, but lacks the badassish name and graffiti-inspired graphics that so many of the ganja-specific nutrients with the seemingly inflated prices have. Chappy's can be purchased at Harmonious Hayseeds. Piranha, only at the Hydroporium.

"I said no substitutions."

"They were out."

"So you try another store."

"Can't we just accept what is?"

I've got him there. Hippie rhetoric lends itself to sophist slashes.

"Now pay attention: Caress . . . ," Zeus massages a keg cup in his hands, "slide . . . ," he slides out the young plant, cups the roots, "tuck . . . ," nestles it into its new home, "and pat." He fills the gaps with the mix he's blended and drops the pot lightly a few times on the deck to let the soil settle. "All of it gentle," he adds, and actually it's exactly like transplanting jasmine or kale or whatever, except the plants are more expensive.

A car pulls up. My hearing has grown sharp enough to recognize the sound as Ed's Tacoma.

"What the hell are you doing it here for?" Ed asks, taking in the dirt and perlite sprawling on the deck while Jezebel pees on Zeus's mark.

"More room to spread out," Zeus tells him.

"It's a little exposed," Ed says, glancing up the hill.

"So I guess you guys have it from here," Zeus says and puts his hoodie back on. He doesn't even ask to see the nutrients I bought. At least he's not a micromanager.

Zeus goes to bump fists with Ed. Ed just shakes his head, leaves him hanging. "Thought you were the new partner here."

"What do you think I'm doing here, man?"

"Leaving, far as I can tell."

"Always gotta give everybody shit," Zeus says, topping Jezzie's counter-mark.

LOTTE UP THE HILL

ED AND I HAVE ABOUT TEN LARGE PLASTIC TUBS SPREAD OUT ON THE DECK right now, five of them filled with plants. Nice tall ones. The plants Zeus gave me as part of our deal have twice as many roots as the clones I raised and vegged myself. It is because we stop to admire these lush beardy roots that we don't hear the ball rolling down the hill. It's not until the golden retriever comes to fetch it that we turn and see a lady stumbling after it. Fuckety fuck. "Don't panic," Ed says. "You got all your scrips in order, right?"

"This is really a shitty time to ask that."

"Jesus Christ, you're not legal?"

"I've got mine plus two. The rest are in the mail."

"Just stay calm," he says to both of us.

If the ball had rolled at an angle forty-five degrees to the left, if it had bounced off a slightly different rock, we wouldn't be nearing the neighborly proximity at which one can no longer reasonably be ignored. She waves. The golden retriever is pressed against the fence, snout trespassing.

"What do you want me to do?" Ed says.

"Something," I say, but I'm not sure he hears it because I am already chucking the tennis ball as far as I can back up the hill. The ball rolls right back down on precisely the same path as last time. What are the odds?

Now Vito and Jezebel want in, drawn by the scent of strange dog and slobbery ball. The woman waves to me, losing her balance, but regains her footing, laughing. I look back to Ed, who has turned the five empty black tubs up on their sides, creating a giant wobbly barricade between the fence line and the plants. I take the tennis ball and throw it at him, and one of the black tubs falls down. He shrugs—combination of *at least it's something* and *this isn't really my problem*—and throws it back.

"Hey-lo there, you must be Heather. I'm Lotte, Fred's wife, from up the hill." Lotte extends a warm and tiny hand over the fence. She's plump in a nice-lady way and wearing a T-shirt with a ladybug on it. "I hear you're a movie star!"

Ed shakes his head. All my scrips should be posted.

"Not at all," I say. She has an unceasing smile and friendly salt-and-soil curls, which makes me wish she was my aunt as much as I wish she'd go away, which makes me awkward.

"Getting ready to plant?" she asks.

I pull up my dropped stomach by its throat. "Yes, I have a thing for tomatoes. All kinds of varieties. Little ones. Big ones. Orange ones. Pink ones. You know, lots of tomatoes. Like to have plenty for canning and sauce and stuff. Nothing like opening a nice jar of garden tomatoes in January!" I have never done this.

"Oh, I'm a gardener too! You'll have to come up and see. I even have a Meyer lemon tree in a cold frame." She waves to Ed. "Hi, there!" Ed gives her a flick of his head and tries to sit on one of the upturned tubs while using his hand to balance the one beside it like it's the most natural thing in the world. It slides out from under him. "Goodness, are you all right?" Lotte shouts.

"He's fine," I whisper. "He just has a few, um, disabilities." She nods. Ed attempts to reconstruct the wall, this time squatting on the other side, where he is hidden behind it. "Yes, it's sad, but having his hands in the dirt does wonders for him. He just gets a little funny about protecting plants, they're like his pets, sort of. He is very protective of them until they're in the ground. Then he loves to show them off."

She leans in. "Are you sure you're okay here with him? I would be happy to come over and lend a hand. Dirt on my hands does me a world of good too!"

"Oh no. No, I mean, thank you so much, that's a very sweet offer, but he's not dangerous. They have him very well medicated now. He just has a few quirks, is all." It is not helping the way Ed is occasionally peering over the tops of the tubs. It is not helping at all.

"If you're sure . . . ," she says, because clearly she isn't.

"I'd love to have you and Fred over for dinner sometime, once I'm fully settled in." Lies. Regrettable lies.

"That would be lovely. It would be so nice if our dogs could play together. Is that one yours too?"

"No, no that's Ed's. That's his therapy dog. He's not supposed to play too much with other dogs, because it takes away from his training."

"Really? Do you think I could get that ball back?" I forgot I had it. "It's pretty brave of you to be living out here all on your own."

"Oh, that's why I make sure the gate is always locked." I pass her the slobbery ball and she turns to go then stops herself, interrupting what should have been my magnificent exhale. "So now what would I have seen you in?"

"A couple of guest spots here and there. A few indies. Probably nothing you would have seen. Boring stuff. Long time ago." Often when I put it this way, all cagey like, my inquisitor assumes porn and the questions stop. When it comes to retired porn ladies, most people would rather not know. "Well, gotta get those seedlings potted before dark!" I chirp.

"Can't wait to see that garden come July!" she says, making her way up the hill.

"Me neither!" I say, because it's true.

Ed is still hiding behind the tubs. "Is she gone yet?"

"That was the best you could come up with?"

"If you had all your scrips this wouldn't be a problem."

"It would still be a problem. Don't bullshit a bullshitter."

"What did you tell her?"

"That you have special needs."

Lascivious grin.

"True."

IGNITION

WE LINE THE PLANTS UP IN TIDY ROWS ON THE BRAND-NEW TABLES. THE plants in their new three-gallon bags squat steady on the corrugated white fiberglass. The tables have a little slope, so runoff can flow down the white channels into the plastic gutter along the back wall. The AC runoff goes in here too. All of it flows out under the wall, and the tube ends flush under the center of the garage door. I might not have to empty an AC bucket, but I will be constantly scrubbing the stain that forms on the concrete pad outside the garage door. Every room has its own challenges. This one, however, is mine.

"You got the timer set up?" Ed asks.

"Yeah, seven to seven."

"I'll wait with you, make sure it comes on." He has the courtesy to not acknowledge directly my new loneliness and isolating paranoia. He does it with friendship rather than pity, which I appreciate.

"Thanks," I say. "There's beer in the fridge."

"I know, that's why I offered." He laughs and fake punches my arm and adds, "You ever get too bored out here, know I'd tap that anytime." It takes me a few seconds to get it. I open two bottles, hand him one. We clink. Tacit friendship.

"Thanks, but I'm gonna stick with the self-tap for a while. But really, I've never had so many invitations to the dance."

"Yeah, you should know Scooter isn't drinking anymore since that morning."

That morning was last week when Scooter showed up after an all-night binge wanting to know if I'd like to "get nibbled" because he "wanted to know what movie star pussy tasted like."

Luckily, he didn't realize that he could have just walked around my fence. He stayed in his car with his legs hanging out of it, describing to me how they shone in the sun as if I couldn't see it from the living room. It was partly funny, partly a jarring reminder of just how vulnerable I am out here. Somebody who wasn't worried about how his actions would be received in The Community could have done something decidedly less amusing.

It's for similar reasons that I can't take Ed up on his offer. It's not that he isn't attractive or that I don't like him, but my survival at the moment depends on my place in The Community, continuation of which will have much to do with keeping my nose clean and growing top-notch pot. And besides, Ed is a tendertapper, a man who is eager to please as long as there's no lasting responsibility. But what I want is a cuddlefucker, the holy grail of males: he who maps a long-term trajectory of gentle sweet nothings often shaken and stirred with red-hot monkeyfuckery.

"I give great massages," he says and takes a long slug off his beer. And I think, *Well, if you vampired me right now, just bent my head back and sunk into my neck then we could just take it from there. . . .* For a minute I can't think of anything I'd like more, and then I consider The Community obligations of "dropping in" and "holding space" that would ensue, erasing any pleasure.

"Yeah, Liz mentioned that. The massages. In detail."

I'm the only one in this house with her sex on ice. The Girls are about to unfurl, stack, glisten, and display their unabashed urges with all the shameless exuberance of a pubescent bonobo. The lights in the flower room are on a timer so that they blaze from seven p.m. to seven a.m. This twelve-hour light cycle inspires The Girls to bloom by mimicking the onset of fall, when day and night are naturally even. It lets them know life as they know it is over, and if they want to make it to the next step of perpetuity they need to awaken their inner slut. Like any flower, the ganja bud is a reproductive organ, evolved to tempt in the most irresistible way possible. The Girls have done a pretty bang-up job. Orchids lure specific moths; apple trees plot the seduction of bees. The Girls, however, have gone for the global jugular: entwining their fates with humans for the last nine thousand years. We like them. They like us. Together we have become a real planetary power couple.

"Are you ready?" Ed asks. "It's six fifty-five."

We each stand behind plastic flaps, zippered crescent slices in the panda paper that lines the walls, white on the inside, black facing out, awaiting this momentous moment. The moment of ignition. We wait quietly in the dark, Vito sitting on my feet. We count together, backward from ten. Three . . . two . . . two and a half . . . two and a quarter . . . A click from the timer box and then nothing. Ed grabs my headlamp, scoots one of The Girls over and lifts the gray door on the timer when the first clicks are heard inside the hoods, then the flicker of the bulbs igniting, then gradually dawning to full blaze, then the vibrating hum of the fans. We are standing in what can only be an early twenty-first-century soil-fed, hand-watered NorCal medical marijuana growroom. Mine.

OFFICER LAVERNE

I WAKE TO THE DOORBELL. NOBODY I KNOW RINGS THE DOORBELL. IT'S eight thirty in the morning, and I'm definitely not expecting anyone. The fans in the growroom should be off but I have no idea if the timer works yet. Whoever is at the door does, though. I tie on my fuzzy pink robe. She presses her sheriff's department ID against the glass—the silver badge pings me, then my focus opens to include the gun holstered snug against wide beige bureaucratic hips: OFFICER LAVERNE MALOMANO.

"Okay boy, lessgoforawalkyouwannagoforawalk?" I ask, or rather shout so Officer Laverne can hear just how chipper I am how cheerful I am how much more like Katie Couric than a drug dealer I am. "Okay, Vito—lessgoforawalk!" I crack the door and Vito rushes out.

"Sorry, he's a puppy . . . ," I say, by way of explaining how we are now about a hundred yards from my front door. "Is this your dog?" she asks. A leaden pivot, she scans the house.

"Yesthisismylittlefuzzybuddyyesheisaren'tyoubuddy!" I'm trying too hard, notice it, wait for it to pass. During this speck of time I develop the presence of mind to read the side of the van—the part under the giant golden capitals incarcerated in black: S-H-E-R-I-F and, to reiterate, one final F at you—under which it says, ANIMAL CONTROL. The fans are off and the only thing I can smell is pine.

"Come, Vito, sit," I say, my clammy sheen evaporating into the May morning.

"Actually, ma'am, that's the county's dog."

"I've been fostering him. He's been sick." Vito leans against my leg. I pick him up.

"We tried to reach you all weekend. The dog comes with me. County doesn't adopt a dog out until he's been altered."

"Altered?"

"Fixed. You know. Chop chop." She smiles.

"You're here for my dog's balls."

"That's correct, ma'am."

"I see."

All the maternal energy that I am foisting, sloppily, upon this poor unsuspecting creature shoots up my spine and sizzles every follicle—I beam it out my eyes, let it glance off her gun and say, "He's still sick. He can't have an operation until he finishes his antibiotics."

"Can I have a look at that medicine, ma'am?" And for a throb I think she means The Girls. But no. She means Vito's antibiotics.

She can't come near the house. Okay. I know that. "Sure, um. I'll be right back." I hand Vito to her, thinking that will lock her down. I don't give her time to reply, because I have gripped my robe shut and sprint such a sprint I could not repeat—nor FloJo nor a cheetah—into the kitchen—amber plastic into fist. Vito cannot resist such momentum, escapes Officer Laverne's grip, runs toward me, jumps up, muddying the pink. I present the bottle to Officer Laverne like it's the Ark of the fucking Covenant.

She looks to me, down to Vito, back to me. We are granite. We are steel. We are not breaking up. "Let me call this in, see what I can do," she says.

If I had a hat, I would toss it to the sky like Mary Tyler Moore at the end of the opening credits of her eponymous show because for this one brief moment it would be appropriate to belt out: "You're gonna make it after ah-all!!"

We schedule his testicular lop for three weeks from now. As Officer Laverne gets in the van I say, "Wave, Vito!" and he lifts his paw in what I think is an irresistible gesture of friendship toward Officer Laverne.

"Bang, bang," she replies, pointing two stub-nailed fingers at him. Vito rolls onto his back. I didn't think he had that one down yet. She pulls away through the gate I didn't lock last night. I lock it now. Dog at heel, I click it shut.

"Go on now," I mutter to the settling dust. "Git off m'land."

THE BALLAD OF LIZ AND WILLA

THE NEW VEGGIE SEEDS I PLANTED ARE NOT QUITE MATURE ENOUGH TO transplant, but neither am I and it's time to put them in the ground anyway. Liz volunteered to help me. She bounds out of her car and wields her hoe like a magic wand. "I don't think I've ever seen you look so happy," I tell her.

"I met somebody," she says. There is a little chunk of coal in me that doesn't want to hear this. "He is completely amazing," she adds, and I decide to be glad for her.

"Where'd you meet him?"

"At my son's school—his little girl Petunia and Levi are friends."

"Petunia, daughter of that guy Jake, Petunia? The one that was seeing that waitress from the Eggloo?"

"Yeah, Willa. They broke up a few weeks ago." Liz slides into a story about strawberries and chocolate and feeling like a queen. "I'm so happy for you, Liz," I say, but there are still more details to recount. ". . . and so slow, in this suite in Reno and. Just. All. Night. He doesn't need to rest like evferrrr . . ." as we plant the Dinosaur kale and Green Zebra tomatoes and most of the White Wonder watermelon seeds.

The Eggloo is one of the two main breakfast places in town. It's Sunday and it's crowded, so I take one of the high tables by the bar. Willa is not my waitress. I order my Eggloo usual, the Blackstone Benedict, because I like seeing breakfast's greatest hits all on one plate. Willa is waiting at the bar for a cappuccino, which is when I go up to her and say, "Hey, I heard what happened with you and Jake. Pretty much the same thing happened to me recently, and, well, I'm new here and I thought maybe we could go be single gals on the town together sometime!" I'm eager to put a positive spin on what I assume to be our mutual heartbreak. I'm eager to not seem crazy. I'm basically just eager. My enthusiasm would not appear to be infectious.

"What happened with me and Jake?" She looks confused.

"You broke up," I tell her. She's gunning me down with Uzi eyes.

"No we didn't. Who are you?" Willa backhands her flaxy bangs harder than necessary; they flop back down into her eyes.

I think of Liz, her strawberries in Reno. Shooting the messenger is no doubt a common error in a situation like this. "I think you have me confused with someone else," she says and spills a little cappuccino on her tray.

I keep on with the keeping on when I should probably relent. "You're Willa, right?"

"Right . . . ?"

"Jake has a daughter named Petunia?"

"Please leave," she says and turns on her heel with the tray.

The waitress who runs my plate drops it hard, poached eggs aquiver, puts her hands on her hips. "What did you say to Willa?"

It sucks that the road to hell is paved with good intentions. Asphalt should be considered, maybe yellow bricks. "I think I had her confused with someone else."

"Well, that's great, because now she's crying in the bathroom and we're totally slammed."

I abandon my Blackstone and knock on the bathroom door. "I'm sorry. Willa? I think you're right, I must have you confused with someone else, I'm new here and I really was just trying to make friends, which I guess is sort of awk—"

"Please go away."

I slip my phone number under the door. "If you want to talk about it later, here's my number." I know that I do not have her confused with someone else. There is only one single dad named Jake with a five-year-old named Petunia who goes to the Waldorf school. I try to finish my breakfast, the restaurant staff shooting me hateful glances. I can't finish. I might hurl. I finish the bacon. I might not make it after all.

Willa calls and I am rightly afraid that all of my sentences are going to go up at the end, in the manner of Canadian children. There's nothing I'll say for the next few minutes that can avoid being infused with apology.

"How did you get this information?" I can tell from the formal, stilted way she asks the question that she is reading from a list.

"This girl I know said she was seeing someone named Jake with a daughter named Petunia?"

"Who?"

"A person I know?"

"What is this person's name?"

"I think her son goes to school with his daughter?"

"You think?" She's straying impatiently from the list.

"Okay, I know?"

"Give me her name and her number," she insists, and it could be considered an unreasonable demand, so she adds, "please."

PANTSHITTING

WHAT IS THAT TERRIBLE ITCH? THAT WOULD BE MY THIGHS. IT'S THE ITCHing that woke me, now that I have the good sense to consider. Not so much on the skin as bubbling up from under. The shower will not get hot enough to burn it into submission. I consider using a fork, but instead I walk Vito, who is giving me the herding eye because that should have happened half an hour ago.

I down a fruit punch–flavored energy drink from the fridge, pull on my rubber boots with the peacock feather print, and load my wheelbarrow with circular saw, staple gun, scrap lumber, hardware cloth, and wire snips. With my trusty hound by my side, I will finish the chicken coop. It's time to move those chickens out of any enclosed or semi-enclosed space where air is shared with humans.

The hideousness of chicken adolescence comes so fast on the heel of downy Easter basket sweetness that you can almost still go *aww* just from the memory of cuteness. And then you can't. And you just want to look at them as little as possible until they look less like dinosaurs and more like birds. This activity will also distract me from the itch of the rash that is now down to the backs of my knees and showing the first signs of colonizing my wrists and inner arms.

Who builds a chicken coop? A fucking country girl, that's who. It's a scrappy affair, this door, this missing piece that turns the preexisting tin shed into a henhouse. I've used my circular saw well enough, although it took me a solid fifteen minutes to figure out how to release the safety. It was actually nice to have a problem that I knew could, eventually, be solved with logic. There is nothing mysterious about a circular saw, unlike say, a ganja plant, a puppy, betrayal, or a small chicken.

My construction skills usually revolve around that ever-handy tool, the staple gun, so the coop door has a Frankensteinian quality that might not be aesthetically pleasing but doesn't take anything away from the deep, simple joy of *I made that*, even if I am only telling Vito.

I wipe the sweat from my brow and down another energy drink. It's a new thing, these energy drinks, and I'm hoping they'll make me less jittery than coffee. I've never tried them before, but I got a case on sale. It's my new thing of the day. Every day I try something new, though most days I don't mean to. I'm jubilant as I drain the can. There's nothing like imagining something and then watching it become more real each day to help you avoid a post-breakup spiral. I've even avoided drunkdials and midnight drive-bys. I feel so clear! So fresh! What's that you say? Another? Citrus? Don't mind if I do! My third can of the morning!

En route to the organic farm store, gut music begins. An intestinal duet for tuba and bassoon. It is loud enough to cause Vito to move to the backseat. I park the car in the Harmonious Hayseeds parking lot and polish off another can. I grab the empty jugs I bring here every Tuesday for the last month of Tuesdays to be filled with magic compost tea elixir.

I shake off a cramp, stretch in the opposite direction, breathe into it. I go to the seed section while I wait for the containers to be filled. A tuba solo blares, churns. I decide yes, definitely I will plant some Little Finger carrots. They're short enough that they will be able to grow in the raised beds without needing to struggle into the clay. That's a great idea, Farmer H! And the seed envelope is still in my hands when the shitstream spurts forth in a great gushing maelstrom. Burning past the rash on my thighs, back of my knees, the stream is flooding my socks. I replace the packet of Little Finger carrots, not in the right place, but in front of the Freckles lettuce. Sorry. I keep my eyes glued to the ladybug decals on the floor, follow them out, knees together, calves my only motor. Not unlike Quasimodo. I am not breathing, as even a momentary unclenching could mean a third septic onslaught. I'm not sure what kind of olfactory artifacts are floating in my wake. Luckily, this store specializes in organic fertilizers. There are definitely worse places this could have happened. Really? Continued optimism? I tell myself to take my rose-colored glasses and shove them up my ass. Later.

I'm home. The upside of hosing myself off with freezing water is that it momentarily quells the itch. I will hose myself off then get back on the proverbial horse to get my compost tea, which is essentially shit and corpses mixed with kelp. I can do this because what I have learned so far is that to grow is to eat shit. I return to Harmonious Hayseeds and claim my compost tea. I throw down the pack of Little Finger carrot seeds, because why the fuck not? The girl behind the counter asks where I went. "Oh, I had to take a phone call," I say, trying for casual.

"I looked for you outside . . ."

"Oh, the coverage wasn't very good here, I had to drive down the road a little." I am both repulsed and impressed with the relative smoothness of these lies. I am glad that I didn't change the shorts; it makes my story more convincing. There is no sense of elevated blood pressure. I've jumped through the hoop of shame. Hosed off, begun again. I would give myself a pat on the back, but my hands are preoccupied with tearing open the skin on my thighs.

THE TRIPLE KARMIC VORTEX

"Where were you?" Willa asks. She likes me less and less.

"Got a little held up with errands." Lie? I can't tell. We sit down by the creek that runs along the back of her apartment building and I attempt to roll a cigarette from the burgundy pouch of American Spirit organic tobacco in my lap. Hey, I'm just trying to fit in, adapt to the local customs—like that time I asked for a baseball mitt when I was in third grade. This is equally successful. The conflagration nearly claims my brows.

"Why are you doing that?"

"Smoking? I know, it's a terrible, disgusting habit, but—"

"No, I can sort of understand why you would smoke, but I really don't understand why you would try to roll your own when you're so—when you don't really seem to have it down yet."

"I try to do something new every day," I tell her, which is very nearly true, but not quite, so I add, "Actually I try each day for my life to seem vaguely familiar and fail. Today, for example, I tried to substitute coffee with energy drinks."

She just stares, a tray of sandwiches extended toward me, lingering in midair, requiring me to extinguish the smoke. We seem to have struck a deal. I won't notice that she blames me for ruining her life, and she won't notice that I'm crawling out of my skin. Compulsively rolling these loose airy cigarettes that nearly singe my lashes each time the paper suddenly ignites because the bone-dry tobacco has mostly fallen out before I can put the thing to my lips is what I am doing with my hands instead of scratching my thighs.

She's blonde, and not in an icy Hitchcockian way, but in a cautiously shucksy way that can only be Nordic via Minnesota.

"I suppose I should kind of thank you," she says.

"I thought that's what the sandwiches were for." I mean, I'm really pretty psyched that she's invited me for tea and finger sandwiches, especially since the tea is red and served in bulbous glasses.

She and Liz appear to have bonded. She says she'll tell me the story when we open the second bottle of wine. Fine with me. Better than fine. I explain to her that I am a sister in suffering rather than the messenger deserving of kill. "Do you by any chance have a scrip?" I ask her. She judges me with only the top half of her face. "A prescription," I say, because perhaps she didn't understand the question.

"For what?" she asks, and it's like she's testing me.

"For medical marijuana."

"Why are you asking me that?" The squint of her little ocular hurricanes reminds me that she does not particularly care for my company and has made these spongy white triangles as a sort of penance. An oversized triangular communion wafer.

"Because I'm growing and my friends in LA haven't come through for me yet and I'm beginning to doubt they will."

"No, I don't have one, and you know they're expensive, right? Nobody's going to just give you their scrip, certainly not somebody whose life you just ruined less than forty-eight hours ago."

"I'm sure my friends in LA are going to come through for me. It's just very warm down there, and people lose their sense of time. Do you grow?"

"No!"

"Why not?"

"I couldn't handle it," she says, and I look smug for a second, *ah, yes, not a job for the faint of heart*—when she adds, "Doesn't really look like you can either. It's dumb to not have all your scrips in hand. No offense."

"None taken," I say, and roll another clumsy cigarette that flares up in my face.

"You could really go to jail."

"As opposed to kinda going to jail?"

She holds out the tray of finger sandwiches and refills my wine. I launch: "You want to know why I was really late? I shit my pants at the feed store. I had to go home and hose myself off and wonder how the fuck I have gotten exactly here. I just say this to say you are not the only one who finds yourself in a shitty situation. I came here to make a friend, so let's just not talk about jail or diarrhea or why I feel the need to act like I actually *want* to do something new every day, or that I'm smoking these stupid labor-intensive cigarettes for any other reason but that they're cheaper and I feel like of all the things going on in my life right now, this is something I actually have a fair chance of actually becoming successful at. Sorry. The wine. It's the wine. I'm not normally a weeper. No, in the interest of honesty, recently I am very much a weeper. Okay? So now you tell me something about you—like what happened when you and Liz went to that c-bag's house to confront him. Or about a time in your life when you too shit your pants. Everybody's got a shit-your-pants story. Your choice."

"C-bag?"

"Colostomy bag—like a douchebag but grosser and more serious."

I am determined to listen to her entire story with my hands folded in my lap. I am going to listen so hard that the itching disappears. She tells me about going to Jake's. The gardeners he had there of course called him as soon as they saw Liz and Willa climb through the window. He had, Willa says, "this pile of laundry detergent on a mirror." Her voice is a little more pinched because she really thought it was laundry detergent, and Liz had to correct her by rubbing a little on their gums. Jake had a lot of laundry detergent, and a lot of things started to make sense to Willa that just didn't before—the bitter kisses, the postnasal drip, the tireless fucking, that weeklong excursion to Florida and how he sent her for a massage and she found he'd packed her bag when she returned. She thought little of it, when, upon returning to Nuggettown, he massaged her into a stupor and then also unpacked the bag for her. "I've got it baby, you just relax." She thanked him.

"I was so pissed. So we dug through his closet and his drawers and found it. A lot of it. We took it and we drove away, but when we got like two blocks from his house, we realized, or Liz did really. She said, 'Stop. Pull over. We have cocaine in the car.' So then we just tried to figure out: What is our idea here? What are we planning to do with it? Liz was making some estimates, money-wise but then—no, she has a son. So we drove back to his house, climbed through the window again. One of the workers shouted to us that Jake was coming. Fine, we didn't need much time anyway. I wasn't sure how much the toilet could handle, he's on septic and all, so I took it kind of easy at first, like a quarter of the first bag. Then we called him. He didn't know quite what to say when he found out we were both at his house together. He was pretty sure he didn't hear me correctly. But he did. When I told him I was flushing his laundry detergent down the toilet he said, 'Don't do that. Just don't do that.' It might have been a little harder for me if he'd said, like, *please*. So I said, 'It's already done.' And he hung up. We got out of there fast. Neither one of us has heard from him since." Willa takes a sandwich from the tray. Her teeth fall softly through it. She chews, swallows, adds, "He never told me he loved me."

"What are you going to do now?" I ask, scratching again.

"I think there's really only one thing to do in this situation."

"Which is?"

"Start a band."

I stop. "Huh."

"You want to be in it?"

"I don't play anything."

"So write songs."

"Okay."

"There are these monks that come here every year and make this giant mandala out of sand. They say that this place is a triple karmic vortex.
That you can clear your karma three times faster here than in a regular
place. Can you harmonize?"

"You want me to write a song called 'Triple Karmic Vortex'?"

"No—I mean not unless you want to. What I mean I guess is thank
you. What happened sucks, but it's not your fault and you can be in the
band with Liz and me."

"You sure you don't have a scrip?"

"Don't push it."

"Yeah, I can harmonize."

"You know you have poison oak, right?"

DRUNKY MCSAUCEPANTS AND
THE SPROUTS OF LOVE

JUST AS I'VE MADE A GLOPPY PINK CALAMINE MAP OF MYSELF, CEDARA
comes to the house to help me put up trellis poles to support the growing
Girls. She brings along a bottle of tequila, a small brown bag of limes, and
her little pot of sprouted chia seeds. We each planted a pot of them on the
new moon. We planted what we wished for, what we hoped to do better
at in this new cycle. The seeds, with a little care, are almost guaranteed to
transform and manifest a sprout, so the idea is that we should also be able
to transform and manifest whatever it is we planted with them. Cedara
planted hers for grace. I chose love. Tonight is full moon and we're going
to eat them.

After we fasten the poles to the beds in the garage, Cedara pours out
some tequila on the lawn for Pachamama, then hands me a shot and a sliver
of lime. Putting her hands in prayer position, she offers a bow and a whis-

pered "Namaste." Sanskrit, tequila—it's great to be alive in the twenty-first century.

She hands me my sprouts of love from the kitchen window. "It's time to eat these now, to heal." I wring the sprouts from their roots and eat them in one bite. The dirt still sticking to the roots makes a horrible scrape against my back molars. It's not a lot, this love I've planted, but it grew.

"Take your time," Cedara says. "Chew mindfully, allow all the nutrients to enter you." We chase the sprouts with another round of shots.

"Now," she says, and pauses again. "Now . . . I have some bad news." She puts a leaf from my room on the counter. "You've got spider mites."

"Okay."

"It's not okay, but I'm going to call Zeus now, and he's going to take care of it for you, okay?"

"Okay." I pour a third shot and don't bother with the lime. I have no plan B. I have no money. I have spider mites.

"Hey, babe, I'm over here at Heather's and Flora might come over. . . . I said Flora might come over. . . . You know, Flora—remember when she came to that party at our place last week? Well, she was saying she might like to get her dance on over here. . . . Yup. That Flora. . . . Yup, I know. Who has it? . . . Oh. I see. Maybe you should get it from him."

Cedara is telling Zeus that I have spider mites and she is instructing him to bring the only known truly effective cure: Floramite. He has told her that The Community supply is at Judah's. I've seen it there in a retired kombucha bottle with a skull and crossbones drawn indelibly across the label.

I rest my head on the blue tiles. I don't want to go look at the spider mites. Cedara has brought a leaf from the room to show me. I don't want to look at that either. She slides it into the dark crevasse between my forehead and the counter. "Where did they come from?" She doesn't know. No one ever knows. They are the last remaining argument for spontaneous generation.

"Don't worry, Zeus won't let this destroy the crop—but once they're in your room you're always going to have to worry about them."

I'm ready for bed. I consider what lullabies Cedara might know. I would accept one of her hegemonic hugs if it came with "Rock-a-bye

Baby." Maybe, just this once, we could have a little ritual I could really use. Something as soothing as my head on these tiles.

"You didn't notice the white spots on the leaves?" I am noticing white spots behind my eyes. Pretty. Like comets. Does that count? Heads up. Dizzy. Cedara pours another round. She's out of limes. It's okay because I'm feeling plenty acidic. Zeus calls again and Cedara is silent while he talks. She hangs up, lifts my head with her hands, and says, "Judah is on his way over. Zeus feels this can't wait. You have to get rid of the spider mites before you're through week three."

"I'm not contributing to a race of supermites. All that poison just makes them stronger."

"If you don't take care of this you'll get nothing."

"Why can't Zeus bring it?"

"It's at Judah's house."

"Why can't fucking Zeus just fucking pick it up? He's my fucking consultant."

"This is a wonderful opportunity for you to plant the first seeds of your new relationship. You could have planted anything in that little pot. You planted love. You've eaten it. Now you can show how it's nourished you." I return my head to the tiles. When Judah arrives, Cedara lets him in. I catch my reflection in the sliding glass door—the dirty hair, the swollen eyes, the pink flakes. He's wearing his panda sweater. It's a favorite of mine and he knows it. It has the front of the panda on the front of the sweater like you might expect, but then it also has the back of the panda settled into the bottom corner, wrapped around Judah's hips, eating bamboo.

"The panda sweater," I say, drunk and defeated.

"Yeah," he says, and takes the pump sprayer full of Floramite into the garage.

"You don't have to do this," I say.

"No, it's chemicals; I don't want you handling it." I go ahead and take the shot that's sitting on the counter. There is a thouie bulging in the front pocket of his jeans. In addition to being a nickname for thousand-watt bulbs, this is what he calls the thousand-dollar wad he carries "in case I need to pick something up while I'm out." Like seven hundred bagels or an ounce of gold.

"Chickens'r getting big," he says, and I wish I had already moved them, but they're still so small, and I'm not sure that my amateur henhouse is enough to protect them. Cedara rubs my back as we watch him take off the panda sweater and leave it on the dining room table, then his pants, until he's standing in my dining room in boxer shorts. "Can't afford to risk infestation at my place," he explains and asks if I have a scarf he can wrap around his nose and mouth.

"He still cares for you," Cedara says.

"Uh-huh," I say, alternately whiteknuckling the blue tile and scratching off my crusty pink cures.

"You know that's poison oak, right? You should put some manzanita oil on it," she tells me.

About twenty minutes later Judah is finished. "Keep checking it. It should probably be sprayed again in five days, just in case," he says, zipping his pants.

"So much for organic," I say.

"That was never gonna happen."

"You would know, right? Nothing here is up to me, you made sure of that."

I am drunk. I should shut up.

"You're welcome," he says.

"Oh my God, thank you. Thank you so much. I am so very grateful that you could come over here and spread more poison." I am giving him the Philly Phinger. The Philly Phinger is commonly employed by African-American women, and my mother. It involves encroaching upon someone's personal space while waving your extended index finger as if it were moving through Jell-O. It is important that there be a sense of resistance around the Phinger's motion, to imply restraint. The Philly Phinger is a warning. A sort of pre-whoopass code orange, if you will.

"Heather." Cedara puts her hand on my shoulder.

There is nothing I can do. I can't even put one foot in front of the other. I collapse into the couch, saying, "Tell Sprout I said hi!"

"This is why," he says before he goes. "This is exactly why."

"C-bag."

We listen to the gravel tremble and still.

I say to Cedara, "You know he wants to fuck you, right?"

"You think?" she says. She knows.

"The way he looks at you," I say.

"What?"

"You notice," I say, and it is definitely an accusation.

"I did wonder . . . someone wrote this note in a book that was out during the New Year's Eve party and I always kind of wondered if it was him." New Year's Eve was when he was still asking me to live with him. The New Year's with a pile of molly in some tinfoil on the counter that everyone dipped in and balmed the bitter with the Frangelico whipped cream I made for my torte. Zeus and I watched Cedara massage Judah meticulously in front of the fire. Soon more joined in and everyone was massaging everyone in front of the fire. "Cuddle puddle!" A mobius strip of nerves and skin, like pleasure and freedom were synonymous, and the thought *just lighten up* did cross my mind, but it all felt fake. My teeth started to chatter like they were motorized and I thought they might crack and I didn't recognize the behavior of my MDMA-bathed brain, or my own giant pupils in the mirror. I didn't recognize this face whose bones were so close to the surface. I licked my dry teeth and was acutely aware of them being the only visible portion of my skull, for now. And how that would change. How it was already changing. How I better love now because I wasn't getting any younger. I was as thirsty then as I am right now, and as near to throwing up in my mouth.

"What did it say?" I ask her.

"What was it . . ." She is staring at the insides of her head. "It was something like, 'Cedara is a goddess among goddesses, my love for her will last forever, as endless as her beauty.'" For someone whose face seemed to be searching, she rattles it off like she's got it fairly well memorized.

"Was it his handwriting?"

"It's sort of hard to tell."

"Can I see it?"

"I don't think that would be a good idea."

"I beg to differ. I think it's an excellent idea."

"Shhhh . . . remember the sprouts of love."

BUT THERE ARE A LOT OF THINGS
I CAN'T TAKE BACK

THE NEXT DAY, I DRIVE TO HER HOUSE, AND SHE GIVES ME THE NOTE, WRITten as recited. It certainly looks like his handwriting, though that's the vague block print of people you shouldn't trust. I pocket it.

Then comes Judah's house. He's not home. I check to see if he's left the door open as usual. He has. I post Cedara's note on his fridge with magnets, then take a moment to remember the sprouts of love. I throw in a dash of forgiveness and a pinch of grace. Not too much. Not yet. Then, with a fat black marker I find on his desk, I make him a sign: MAY A WORLD OF PAIN RAIN DOWN ON YOU UNTIL YOU LEARN WHAT YOU HAVE TO LEARN. I like its incantatory quality, like it's a spell or a hex a witch suggested. This is how I'm certain he'll take it, given his mystical leanings, and I do hope it will give him a little skid in the pants. I tape it to the fridge, below the note.

I look around at what I brought to this house. The towels, the sheets, the storage for his daughter's toys, the bowls of forced tulips. I dump the toys into a mountain beside the TV, where they were before I showed up. I load the baskets into my car, ditto the towels and the sheets, which I strip from his memory foam mattress. I take it all back, leaving his dog-eared copy of David Deida's *The Way of the Superior Man* precisely centered on his bare bed. I spend a lot of time getting it precisely centered. It is without relish that I take down the WE LOVE PAPA sign that he hung on a wall in the guest bedroom. I tear it, crumple it, step on it, scream at it, call it a liar, and then stuff it in the trash can. I sit at the little chair by Sprout's table, the one that I decorated with the alphabet and shellacked with seven coats for her birthday last year. I trace the outline of the letter O and the ostrich sticker next to it. I consider taking down the notes on the fridge but don't. I take a last look at the place and go. I have to pick up my parents from the airport in three hours.

I've just finished unloading the car when he calls. "How dare you? How dare you steal from me?" I'm expecting it and am glad he's experiencing some kind of loss, even though it took the material kind to provoke him. It's my turn to be calm and levelheaded. "Those were things I bought for my home. Now they are in my home. The only questionable thing really is the WE LOVE PAPA sign, since Sprout and I made that together."

"You—" He hadn't noticed that yet. "Where is it?"

"In the trash can." The lid lifts. He gasps and I hear the rustle of paper. He's silent. I shouldn't have done that.

A little guttural puff of air escapes him. "That note—that is just sick."

"Okay."

"Okay? That's all you have to say? I didn't write that note to Cedara either."

"She thinks you did. Besides, it doesn't matter, really. It was good for me to come and get my stuff back. I feel much better now. And I'm sure that soon you will be grateful for this opportunity to grow in patience and forgiveness. That's how it works, right?"

"That's breaking and entering, you know."

"So call the cops."

THERE IS NO PEPSI

MY SWEATY PALMS SLIDE ON THE STEERING WHEEL ALL THE WAY TO THE airport. I am down to taking things an hour at a time, and now the hour of my parents is nigh.

My mother's jaw drops. "You're skin and bones!" I feel tiny in her arms. They look a little older every time I see them. Too much time passes. I press more into the hug. They are mine. They are not forever.

"Fit as a fiddle with all the farmwork!" I say. And it's true I've grown ropy and my jeans sag.

"Jesus, what happened to you?" My father is pointing at my scabby limbs.

"It's poison oak! Badge of a genuine country girl! I can't wait for you to see the town, and my house—it's like a little country retreat! So relaxing!" We are all aware of me trying too hard. "And The Community! Such wonderful, generous people! I really feel like I've met people I can count on."

"Like that douchebag you were seeing?" my dad asks.

"Hon—" my mom says, and he's quiet again.

"This is Vito!" I say, and he starts licking my parents before we can even get the suitcases into the car. My canine sidekick is also going a little overboard, like he too understands the necessity of showing how everything looks when we feel good about it. Vito is reluctant to give up the front seat and no one protests. Considering that I'm about to tell them about my new job, I think it's good that they're together in the back, getting used to the idea, before we get to the house.

Once I've negotiated the airport exit, I take a nice deep breath and say, "I just thought it might be good to get this out there right away since there's really no getting around it. I thought we could just have this ride to all kind of, you know, adjust and whatnot. So: I grow pot."

My father's constipated sigh fills the car with toxic disappointment. I roll down a window, let in air, noise. Two more hours until we get to my house.

"With the tenth anniversary of the movie coming up? I mean, what if some journalist wants to do some kind of where-are-they-now thing? And then what if they find you out here and find out what you're doing? Have you thought about how embarrassing that will be? Have you thought about that at all?"

"Hon—" my mom says to him. "We just got here."

I'm actually enjoying entertaining my dad's speculative stress, because it's not real. I like playing this game of what-if. And no, I had not thought about that at all.

"I would probably tell them to git off m'land. That's the great thing about land, you guys—people from cities think they might really get shot dead for trespassing. There is a certain protection in that even if you've never even thought about owning a gun."

He sighs again. It's not just about that. It's about things that were supposed to be possible.

My parents raised my brother, my sister, and me on steady doses of pizza and classic American arithmetic: Big dreams + hard work = success. They've been together since he was eighteen and she was fifteen. He drove a GTO and played guitar in a band. She had an offer to model in New York that her father forbade her from taking. They had me when she was twenty-one and he was twenty-three. She never went to New York, and he stopped playing in the band. My dad did, however, mount a campaign called Richie Ashburn: Why the Hall Not? that ultimately allowed Ashburn, a baseball player who had shown an unforgotten bit of kindness to my dad after a game he went to as a kid, to officially be a Hall of Famer. My dad worked in the same union, at the same company, for more than thirty years until the day, just a few years from retirement, that his job didn't exist anymore—without explanation, apology, or health insurance. The union may or may not still have the money he paid into his pension.

I love and respect my parents more than any other people in the world. They have worked their asses off their whole lives, and it doesn't look like they'll be able to retire with any level of security. (Unless, of course, many thousands of you buy this book. Tell a friend.) There is nothing like growing up in a working-class family to make working for anyone but yourself seem like a form of slavery. If it hadn't been for *Blair Witch*, I'd likely be tethered to a cubicle, tugging on the business end of a student loan debt noose. But still—this was the best I could come up with? Pot growing? They sent me to college for this? I couldn't have just stuck with acting? What is this country coming to? No, really, that's not a rhetorical question.

My dad doesn't say any of this. His sigh says it for him. Instead he asks, "Jesus, this road is all you?" To my city-raised parents, Red Dirt Road is the highway to hell, a path into the heart of darkness. I'm not saying they're wrong, I'm just saying I wish they would be a little less final in their judgment. "Down that little hill to the left is the veggie garden and *the pool*." A pool means you're doing well. A pool means parents can have something good to go home and tell their friends. Sure, it's covered with a sagging black tarp that leaves a handy mosquito breeding pond thick with algae and possibly West Nile virus, but it's dark now and they can't see that.

"Wait till you see the hot tub!" A hot tub *and* a pool? That's celebrity shit. See? It's all good.

"What about wild animals?" my dad asks, eyes shooting around the gully as he takes their suitcase from the car.

"How does the light get through these trees?" my mother wants to know. I ignore these questions because I am bracing for the Great Presentation—like I'm an eager blonde at a car show, and my growroom is a new Tesla. This is how I present the room: a modern miracle, like an excellent appliance. A dishwasher that loads itself using a robotic arm—something like that. As soon as their bags are out I say, "Come see! Come see!" and lead them into the garage. "Chickens!" I say, and yes, my parents agree, stifling a gag, those are indeed chickens, and given the relentless metabolic flowing of the day, not *just* chickens. The AC is going and still, the stink is deafening. Vito won't come in. He lays on the top step with his paw over his snout. He watches this trainwreck every day.

"Are you ready?" The saccharine beams I emit are making my parents nervous.

My father has his T-shirt drawn up over his nose and mouth to keep out the chicken dust. My mother pulls it down. She's holding her revulsion in reserve; she's my mother.

"I said: *Are. You. Redeeee?!*"

"Yeah!" my mom says halfheartedly, but my dad is still staring at chickens he didn't know could be that ugly.

"A month ago they were really cute. Now come on, are you ready?"

"I don't think I should see this," my dad says. "There are some things a father shouldn't have to see."

"Ta-DA!" I say, and open the zipper in one fell swoop. The scalding beams of light call but more attention to the dusty air. My father simply turns and goes into the kitchen where there is no Pepsi.

"Well, that's just amazing, honey. How'd you do that?" My brother often says that if any of us were serial killers, my mom would brag to everyone about how few fingerprints we left behind.

"I had lots of help from The Community. Wait till you meet the people; I think you'll feel a lot better about everything and . . ."

"Where's your TV?" Dad calls from the living room.

"There isn't one," I say.

"What are we supposed to do out here?"

"Really, the farm chores take up quite a bit of time, and I train Vito, and hike, and, um, I do something new every day."

"So there's no cable."

"Ah! There you're wrong! There's cable Internet! You want me to show you how I change the chicken litter?"

"I think I need to lay down. Come on, Vito." He picks up the dog and they lie down on the couch. My dad covers his head with the fleece throw. My mom sits by his feet and pets the dog.

"I love that window seat," she says.

"Would you like to foliar feed with me?" I ask her, and add, "It's really fun!"

"Sure, sweetheart, we'd love to understand what it is you like about being here."

My father grunts from under the blanket like he has eaten something very, very bad. I load up bottles with diluted Floralicious for my mom and me. We spray down The Girls carefully. "It's like taking care of roses," she offers.

"See? It's strangely wholesome, don't you think?"

She won't commit to a solid yes, but she doesn't say no either. I consider this progress and explain the carefully considered airflow. By the time her bottle is almost empty, she is already talking to The Girls like they are sweet violets.

"You're breaking the law in thirty-six states right now," I tell her, and it appeals to the same part of her that got a tattoo that matches mine and sponsored her love of Van Halen in the eighties and makes her dream of motorcycles.

"Huh," she says, muffling a giggle and spraying with a lot more verve. She helps me fill the reservoir and mix the nutrients. She changes the CO_2 tank all by herself. I plug in the pump submerged in the trash can reservoir, and switch open the valve on the watering wand.

"Instead of counting, I say *you are bee-ooo-tee-full*. Each Girl hears this three times, and then you move the wand to the next one." She does the hand watering while I change the chicken bedding and for a brief moment it feels like the family farm I envisioned before I moved up here. Multiple generations coming to the collective realization that privacy is highly overrated and cooperation equally underrated. Mom's *you are bee-ooo-tee-full* takes on the tune of "Baby Love," which I pick up and start singing to the chickens. And for a moment I have to give props to hippie goddesses. As the males in residence currently doze on the couch, females of two kingdoms, three species, one love, are buzzing heady with our own abundance out here in the garage.

"How about a preview?" I ask my mom, shaking the little jar of smalls from Judah's crop that I keep in the freezer. "I'm sure you'd qualify for a prescription. I'm pretty sure jet lag is a qualifying condition in California."

My mom says, "*Life* should be a qualifying condition." I get a fire going out on the deck, brew a pot of tea, roll a joint that will probably not stay lit. We smoked together just once before, when I was working in the other great bastion of pot production, British Columbia. I was shooting a miniseries and the production had most luxuriously and unneccessarily given me a two-bedroom, two-bathroom apartment. My mom and I took bubble baths, high as kites, while my dad watched TV. Two hours later she still didn't want to get out when I knocked on the door. "I'm on vacation," she said, giggling. It's in these moments that I get glimpses of the teenager who danced on tables and hung out at the Dunkin' Donuts. The girl who told her father to go fuck himself when he hit her.

We are happy to be smoking this joint beside this fire, under this cedar, having tended the garden for the last two hours. "It's weird, how awake I feel," she says.

"It's the lights," I tell her.

"Not just that," she says, and then, "I think I understand," and releases a deep drag and we laugh. She understands. She won't say exactly this, because she'd never live it down—but she is proud of me. And I am grateful for this, for her having the courage to raise me to be independent, even though it means I probably won't ever again live in Pennsylvania. "I wish I had your balls," she says.

"I got them from you. Ladyballs. Our ovaries are full of them. All kinds of potential."

We hover over my father so he'll wake up and let me have the couch to sleep on. We hover and watch him snore, each detail amplified, courtesy of The Girls. The suckling of the phantom nipple, the nonsense syllables, the grinding of the teeth. A whole history in five slumbering minutes, or fifty, it's really kind of hard to say.

We are so quiet, taking it in, each in our own way, hovering, both, with great love. So when he wakes with a shout, because there are two creatures hovering over him while he sleeps, we are disrupted and jolted back into the current time line all together and laugh. We are safe. We are loved. We are together.

TWENTY-DOLLAR PANCAKES

Zeus, Cedara, and Kali saunter toward the Eggloo just as we do. Zeus flicks his head to acknowledge our presence, Cedara throws open her arms messianically, but it is Kali that makes first contact, snout to Vito's rectum. My father squeezes out another constipated sigh as it becomes clear that Cedara is about to hug him. There's no escape. Zeus follows the hug with an attempted fist bump that only perplexes my dad. They make a point of hugging my parents before they even introduce themselves. Dad is exuding a *please tell me they won't be sitting with us* that my mother and I can actually smell. My father is a very gregarious man when in familiar circumstances. Around people he hasn't known for at least a year, however, he clams up, becomes red, adjusts his perpetual baseball cap, and breathes tight.

They do, of course, sit with us on the patio, under the mock cherry no longer in bloom. The dogs take their places under the table. My dad sits at the far corner of the six top. Cedara slides in while my mother is still setting down her purse. When my mother finally sits, Cedara is between us. She puts her arms around both of our necks. "Oh! Feel all that divine mother-daughter energy. You goddesses are *powerful!*"

My mother just rolls her eyes at her purse, but my father actually kicks me under the table. Zeus sits on my other side. I am hippieshackled, their hands on my knees. There is no sense in thrashing under their invisible lead, no sense in alarming my parents.

"I was just telling my parents how incredible The Community is up here," I say, while Cedara distracts my parents with her opinion of various menu items. Zeus smiles and nods, then whispers in my ear, "That was your one opportunity to let your freak flag fly." He grips my knee a little harder. "We want to give you support, but if you do crazy shit like that we just can't." The way that Zeus and I are staring at each other suggests a tumbleweed might blow through the Eggloo. My mom holds her menu taut and her eyebrows high and she's not reading. My parents are no longer listening to Cedara's assessment of the menu. He is not a big man, this Zeus, and I keep it in mind as I say, "Taking my stuff back is crazy?"

"That note you left on the fridge . . ." Clearly it had the intended effect.

"I took my stuff back, and I gave Judah my sincerest wishes." His name sticks in my throat some.

"I'm just saying, that was your one shot. We can't have any more of that."

"Or what?"

"Or we're not going to be able to help you out. We need to be able to count on each other. Understood?"

"Understood."

It is a difficult breakfast to digest.

Vito has chewed through his leash, but hasn't wandered from under the table. With his brown eye he says, *Trust.*

Mom's assessment: "They piss me off like they think they're inventing something, like they've got some new idea. They ain't inventing shit. Please. We already did all this in the sixties. Just a bunch a . . ." She makes a blabby mouth out of her hand. "I mean, I support you in what you're doing, but now I'm pissed."

"Don't let them bug you."

"Oh, it's not those two idiots, it's those pancakes. I do not grow pot, so I do not pay twenty dollars for pancakes." My mom is giving those pancakes the Philly Phinger.

"But they're local and organic," I explain.

"They are bullshit," she concludes, like a sassy black bestie from a midnineties WB sitcom. I love when my mom gets her Southwest Philly up like this. It feels like nothing bad could possibly happen.

My parents, Vito, and I go to Kmart because it's raining and my parents tell me that they're not going back to my place without a TV. Rain does kind of preclude the activities I planned, most of which my parents probably wouldn't be all that into anyway. While we wait for the sales guy to bring out the new flat screen that I can't afford, my father wanders over to the gun section. His eyeballs trace the glass case containing an abundance of rifles. My mother says, "I wouldn't trust that Cedara as far as I could throw her."

"You could probably throw her pretty far."

"True. But don't mistake her for a friend."

My parents are taking to paranoia like ducks to water. My father takes in the rifles again, running his eyes up and down them like a murderous chorus line. I am relieved when the TV comes out, and my father turns his attention to picking out the necessary cables so that we can begin watching movies as soon as we get back to my house. It rains for the next three days. We watch *Borat* for the umpteenth time, because it always makes my father happy. So what if I have to hear him crack up as he repeatedly suggests "sexy time" to my mother over the next twelve hours? So it goes with long love.

When the rain stops, my parents help me clean up the land, rake needles, weed the garden. My mother helps me pot up the newly rooted clones and then we plant some pansies around the sugar maple in the yard.

When I wake up the next morning, the last morning of their visit, I see three index cards held to the refrigerator door. My mom's Catholic school penmanship is soothing, almost as much as the words she's written:

Please be wise, smart, and beautiful as you have always been.
Reminder:
One day at a time.
Tread lightly.
Trust in you.
Helpful hints from a mother to a daughter who lives in the woods:

Cell phone with you at all times—no excuses—keep
charged.
Keep something to keep you safe at your bedside.
No dog off leash after dark.
Lock up, always keep your keys in the same place, like
under your pillow. I am sure there will be more helpful
hints to come. I will probably call every night to make
sure you are tucked in safe and sound. [She will.]

Love always,
Your LOYAL and PROUD Parents
oxoxoxoxoxoxoxoxoxoxoxoxoxoxoxoxoxoxo

"You're not to take these off the fridge until you move out of here,"
she tells me.

"I won't," I say, and I mean it. It's relaxing, having my mother tell me
what to do. I almost wish she would stay and keep doing it.

I hug my parents good-bye at the airport and they hang on longer than
usual. Either they've assimilated the customs of the land, or they're scared
shitless for me. We line their suitcases up on the curb, and my father,
whose PEACE TO ALL WHO ENTER HERE picture, complete with acoustic
guitar and daisy, hung by the door throughout my childhood, takes my
hands in his. "Sweetheart," he says, "we think you should get a gun."

Mom adds, "Just a little one."

JUNE BLOOM

DIGGING

I'M DIGGING. DIGGING ENCOURAGES SONGS. AND NOT JUST "SWING LOW, Sweet Chariot," but also whistled melodies and the humming bass lines of bees. This hole gets a little bigger with each stroke of my ladies' hoe. I'm changing something. I'm shaping the world with my thoughts. I had a thought to grow an outdoor crop—these Girls I call The Scouts—to have something more natural, something outside the fan cans, foil robot arms, and the artifice of the semi-closed system in the garage. I feel sorry for the garage Girls like I feel sorry for circus animals. Out here CO_2 comes from breath, the regulator goes *ba-bum, ba-bum* instead of a mechanical click. Another reason I decided to take this risk is because of the increasing heat. The AC is incredibly expensive and decidedly unfriendly—environmentally speaking—so I'm not running all the lights in the garage. I don't, it should be said, run the AC in my house. Only the one in the garage, for The Girls. I mentioned I'm their bitch? And I love them no less for it.

This spring has been so dry I have to coat my nostrils with ointment each day. Big swaths of forest are burning. The fires are so close that ash flurries from the tartar yellow sky, and there's debate in The Community about whether the extra carbon dioxide generated will compensate for the diminished light. There are warnings on the radio saying you should pack up your valuables and keep them in the car. But then where are you supposed to park a car full of your most valuable possessions?

Nobody knows what effect such a change will have on The Girls. I don't even want to know. I just want to dig with my dog in the sun and watch my chickens scratch the dirt. "This is exactly what I had in mind," I say to Vito, and lick my salty lips. I could pretty much just dig this place up forever. Bottom is wherever and whenever you stop digging. Baldasare Forestiere understood that. Now, there's a guy who knew how to dig. He was a second-born Italian son with no hope of inheriting land, so he came to America. He got a job digging the New York City subway system. He learned about pressure and airflow. But he still dreamed of oranges, and so he came to California. He bought a piece of land to plant an orange grove, but he was swindled and the land was all covered in hardpan, a concrete-y layer that roots can't break through. Did my boy Baldasare give up? No, he did not. He dug under the hardpan to where the soil was softer. He planted his orange trees under the hardpan. Alone. With hand tools. Not only did his oranges grow, but they had the added benefit of being easily harvested, as the tops of the trees squatted like bushes at ground level. Did my boy Baldasare stop there? No, he did not. After he dug himself an underground house with an underground claw-foot tub and underground mulberry tree imported from his homeland, he had a thought. Prohibition had driven drinking underground. He would take this literally and dig an underground speakeasy/B&B. Just before he finished, he died of a hernia. His guts didn't hold. He never married. That's probably not surprising.

Much of his work was unceremoniously filled in to accommodate the 99 freeway. What's left of his dream is an easily missed roadside attraction in Fresno. It's called, appropriately, the Forestiere Gardens. His empty wheelbarrow is on display with a shovel leaning on it, rusty and still. Was he a failure or a success? I still can't tell, but I've never forgotten the guy and I especially remember him now. Maybe even understand him. The appeal of digging is you can't be bad at it, nor can you really excel at it. But you can stick with it. The sticking with it is all there is.

For outdoor planting, some people use large white growbags, which make it easy to move the plants in case of an emergency. Unfortunately, they're so bright that they can cause an emergency. They're easily spotted from a helicopter—like with the naked eye—which is why some people build up little hillocks of camouflage around them. I have nowhere to move my plants should disaster strike, so being able to move them wouldn't be enough of an advantage to risk the brightness of the bags. So

I'm going to commit to putting The Scouts in the ground. Sort of. I'm cutting the bottoms out of five regular old thirty-two-gallon trash cans with my handy circular saw and nuzzling them into the holes I've lined with gopher wire. The open bottom will allow the taproot to burrow down to the water table and keep maintenance to a minimum. That's the idea anyway. The trash can contains Roots Organic soil, another popular ganja growers brand, so that the dense, resistant clay is kept from The Scouts' tender, searching feet.

I'm striving to keep it simple, which is probably an oxymoron. If I'm striving, I'm not really keeping it simple. What will happen if I didn't try to push these Girls? What if I just provide the basics and watch what happens? What if The Scouts don't have to produce the donkey schlong nugs the market values? What if The Scouts need no ambition but to bloom? What if they are allowed to be as she who smokes them? As in, not as concerned with maximum productivity so much as maximum awareness of the moment? I push the garage Girls so hard. I want to see what gentle does.

Outdoor can be pushed—nutes can be maximized, light can be manipulated. Playing God is possible and common. Most growers do two outdoor rounds: The early round is called light depo, short for light deprivation, where tarps are pulled over the plants at precisely seven each evening, and removed again at precisely seven each morning. This provides the twelve hours on/twelve hours off light schedule that tricks The Girls into blooming while not requiring the insane carbon footprint of indoor. It also means the outdoor growing season can bring two harvests. Many growers just do those two rounds and spend the rest of the year in Hawaii or Costa Rica. That sounds awesome, no? I'm sure light depo works out great if you have a partner who could occasionally have your back, in case there was one day where you couldn't pull tarps. Because all it takes is one day where you don't pull tarps for your Girls to stop blooming and revert to vegging. It's hard to get them to flip back again, like they don't trust the light anymore, and the final yields are never as good. Light tells them what to do and when to do it like some kind of mighty pointing Godfinger, except there's no God doing the pointing, just another renegade entrepreneur.

A prescription allows the growing of six blooming or twelve vegging plants. Out here, there are only five. I feel like this indicates a demure patient who is neither pushing, nor even really approaching any proscribed limits. Certainly not blowing it up. *No, no, Officer. I'm just quietly cultivating for personal use. Obviously. I'm not even growing one full prescription.* I think this somehow keeps the garage garden safe. Like a baby who believes she disappears during peek-a-boo, I am somehow under the impression that my logic is good, and that access to my exorbitant electric bill wouldn't, in addition to this little patch, now be sufficient for a subpoena. On its own, the electric bill isn't enough, but with some nice helicopter shots of this patch—it becomes clear that the risk-reward ratio hasn't been considered as carefully as my need for new activities. Busy is the murderess of lonely, and the Internet is really slow around here.

CRAZY DAISY

I AM WRITING A SONG ABOUT FLOATING WHEN SPROUT CALLS. "I MISS Feather!"

The sound of her little voice catches me off guard. It clenches up my ears, nose, and throat a minute before the softening kicks in. "I miss you too, munchkin."

"Papamee see you garden?"

"Um. See my garden? Like at my house?"

"We see Vito!"

"Papamee come to Feather's house?"

I can hear Judah prompting her in the background. I say yes, they can come over and see Vito and the garden because I haven't figured out my new thing of the day yet and I guess this will be it.

It's been a month since our breakup and this is my opportunity to be a Big Person, which means I can understand theoretically that he is an excellent human, just not my true companion human, and that's no reason to reject his little child. The child factor really does fuck me up. "Sure, of course you're more than welcome to come over, see the gardens, drink some iced tea."

"We'll meet you at your house?" Judah says, taking the phone.

His car looks strange there in front of my house, strange because of its former familiarity. It's funny, the way borders are drawn. It kind of makes sense when the border is natural, a river or a mountain range, but when it's just politics and property, like with us or the Dakotas, it's hard because the map bears no resemblance to the territory.

I take them down to the garden. I explain too many things. I'm nervous. I want to show off, but I don't have to. My land blossoms in full effect. The raised beds he built for me are overflowing with cucumber vines and tomatoes. The outer leaves of Red Russian kale are bigger than his head. I use it to make chips. The kale is the only thing in this garden from the seeds I planted at his house in February, but it's the most insanely vigorous thing in here. Temperature-resistant, pest-resistant—the chewing bugs that have made inroads elsewhere, before my liberal sprinkling of diatomaceous earth, have left the kale untouched. "So what's that, like hundred-dollar kale?" he says, and I laugh because he's got a point.

"Closer to three." When you factor in the seed trays, domes, the seeds themselves, the soil, the building of the beds, the compost tea, the deer fence, the diatomaceous earth, et cetera, et cetera, trying to go onavore (a combination of *onanist* and *omnivore* that describes an urge toward dietary self-reliance) is like growing pot—you are really going to wind up in the hole your first year. Equipment and inexperience are both very costly. There is a border of tougher medicinal plants around the inside of the deer fencing that didn't need the luxury of raised beds. All sown just a month ago, and already beginning to creep up out of the earth. "Sunflowers are here, and passionflower, and comfrey, nasturtiums to make spicy green burritos from the leaves . . ." The naming of things gives me something to say. I'm trying to show him that everything has turned out just fine. That I'm just fine. That I've done the thing we talked about doing together, alone.

He turns over a couple of leaves and sees no pests, no chewed holes. "It's so clean."

"Compost tea," I say. "That stuff is magic." I show them the berries and the potato patch, whose first green bracts are pushing through the mix of straw and soil. "Five kinds of organic potatoes."

Vito sits quietly watching. He is usually at my ankles, but he's keeping his distance, watching, guarding, taking in the whole. Wild sweet peas dot deep pink along the road. There is a festive profusion everywhere, the concupiscent push of late spring, flowers not yet giving way to fruit.

"We see chickens now!"

Sprout takes my hand and we skip along the road, then up the hill to the chicken coop. I look back and catch Judah staring at my ass. "Are those new jeans?" he asks. *You know they are*, I think, but say only, "Yeah."

"Did Ed build that door for you?"

"No, I did it myself."

Maybe he's mocking me, because Ed surely would have done a better job, but I don't care. I take a child's pride in it. Sprout is familiarizing herself with the chickens. They are filling out now, beginning to look less scrawny and more like hens.

"What's up with that one?" He's talking about Lilybird, who makes a strangled clucking noise at him.

"She's the boss."

"How'd that happen?"

"She just came that way."

"How are The Girls?" he asks.

"The ganja, the hens, or me?"

"The plants, I meant. But all of you, sure. I told you you'd be fine. Look at all this. It's everything you said it was going to be. And better."

"I don't know if I would say *better*. That's a lot of kale for one person."

I'm glad when Sprout asks, "How come you no clean you grass?" She's pointing at the eviscerated animal fluff that Vito has spread around the lawn.

"Because it looks like clouds, and sometimes I like to think the sky is on the ground. It makes me think anything is possible for a minute." Judah looks at the ground when I say it, because he probably thinks I'm talking about him, like I think something is still possible and that this visit has something to do with us and is not a way to pass one of his custody days and briefly the song "You're So Vain" flits through my head and out again because Sprout is asking me to turn on the crazy daisy. I bought the crazy daisy sprinkler in a fit of post breakup whimsy. It's a daisy head at the end of a green tube so when you turn the water on it flails around in random patterns squirting all over the place. I agree: It's about time we put on the crazy daisy.

I am bent over, taking off my shoes and Sprout says, "Crazy daisy!" and laughs, pointing at the tattoo of a daisy growing out of the crack of my ass to remind me that all beauty comes from shit. Judah's eyes linger on that daisy like the target it once was. If I'm not mistaken, his eyes are still lingering when my own flash up. He is looking at me like a woman he's not fucking. He's looking at me like he looks at Cedara. He is perhaps taking in the shrunken expanse of my waist, my new fragility, my visible bones, my lack of muffin top. He knows I see him, but nothing is embarrassing in the face of the crazy daisy, there is only enthusiasm and cold liquid joy. Sprout is shrieking and we run in short circles leaping over the sprinkler. Judah stands against the house and sulks. He looks mostly like a sad clown, the way he doesn't quite know what to do with his hands. I swing Sprout over the water, dangle her upside down, laugh more than necessary to show that sulking sad clown fuck that I am better off without him. There is a weird correlation between my urge to throw rocks at him and energy that I am devoting to playing with his daughter. The more he sulks, the more exuberantly I laugh, the higher my leaps bound around and over the crazy daisy. The more manic my laughter, the more manic Sprout's giggles become, and conversely, the deeper Judah sinks into his sulk. Emotional physics.

Sprout sees her father slouched against the bare unfinished siding and screams for him, "Papa come crazy daisy!" But he is not going to let his guard down like that, lest I get the wrong idea.

"You play with Feather," he says, and crosses his arms across his chest. I continue without her. I grab the crazy daisy by its green plastic neck and I squirt it at him, laughing like it's all in good fun, like I don't just want to shoot him with something and this is what's at hand. It's ridiculous, this assault by crazy daisy, and she does get him to pick her up and jump through the flailing stream of water with her, I mean, he's wet already, so why not? His jaw is set firm and grim, like to prove he didn't feel the flash, like his being here is normal, because we're friends and friends play to-gether, like it's better for all of us if we choose that thread and weave with it. Both of the people here right now are visitors. On the other hand, I could have spent the rest of my life with them. Go figure. Everything is as random as the crazy daisy's path, it seems, so I just keep jumping through it while Judah takes Sprout inside because she's thirsty.

HERMIED GIRLS

CEDARA ARRIVES. SHE'S DRESSED IN ONE OF HER COSTUMES—A NETTED cloche hat and coral lipstick applied crayonishly. "Why all dressed up?" I ask.

"Had a chiropractor appointment." She fiddles with the sheer black veil. "Found out what happened with that Scooter thing—when you thought he came here? He's been seeing some girl named Heather and he accidentally called you. He got your number confused with hers in his phone."

"He was at my house. Outside my gate. He lost the mirror of his car. I have it in my kitchen. He called about thirty times. There are voicemails. I don't think he thought I was someone else."

She shrugs off my simmer. "Well, Judah didn't say anything to him. He doesn't talk about you."

"Aren't those zucchini blossoms crazy?" I say, dousing them with the hose.

The potatoes stretch new bracts to be buried. The strawberries spread. New radishes are ready to harvest. I douse it all with the hose and listen to the suckling roots. It's quiet like that. "You're manifesting the Divine Feminine like crazy. Look at this garden! This whole place. Chickens, dog, the veggies, The Girls—your vision is reality, girl. You birthed this!" she says.

"I've been working really hard."

"You're so skinny. You're like skinnier than me. Are you eating? Do I need to be concerned?"

"I've been busy."

"You have to eat."

I pick a purple radish, wipe it on my jeans. "I eat."

I show her the dozen varieties of heirloom sweet peas blossoming on the deck, all of which smell like pastels with varying levels of powder. They will bloom for way less time than it took to cultivate them. Maybe this is the trouble with maturity. Blooms are short, cultivation is long. The time between maturity and compost is negligible.

"What we're doing at our place is more of a long-term project that will feed us into the future. You can't really do that with a rental," she says as Zeus's Corolla lands in the driveway. He has the combination to my lock. It was a demonstration of trust. Community. Openness. All that.

There are two new kayaks strapped to the top of his car. Zeus has recently harvested. He probably had a surplus of buds after taking care of his patients, which he probably exchanged for a donation to his farm. Still, it's ganja money—and if federal interest arises, any cash on hand will be seized. Instead of getting a watertight broken fridge free on Craigslist and burying it in their backyard, most people that I've encountered spend it. That's part of what creates the grower lifestyle: Live for today. That's what makes it so hard to get out, and that's what will make legalization and the accompanying price drop so critical for places like Nuggettown. The kayaks on top of Zeus's car were bought for cash at the local mom-and-pop kayak shop. I would suggest that shop depends on pot money. This huge cash flow and the huge amount of sales tax it brings in are perhaps relegated to other vague columns on the city council's spreadsheet. When legalization eventually happens, Nuggettown will likely be blindsided by the sudden drop in "tourism."

I show them my outdoor patch.

"Why only five?" Zeus asks.

"I'm trying to be subtle."

He rubs his hat. "Won't really be worth your time. Especially in this spot."

Cedara looks up at the dense canopy. "Is there enough light?"

"Is there ever?" It's mostly a rhetorical question, so I add, "It should come right through that channel by September," and I point at a slender aisle of sky, like I've actually sat down to calculate this like I'm Gali-fucking-leo. Or Co-fucking-pernicus. Trying to sort out an accurate trajectory for the sun would take away from valuable narcotic digging time. "This is the most discreet spot."

"It's definitely hidden," Zeus says.

"What I lose in yield, I'll gain in peace of mind. I mean, I'm bound to get *something* off of them, right?"

"You hope," he says, still rubbing his hat. I am hoping a genie pops out of there and lets me wish for abundance, but instead a chopper passes overhead and I lean against the house, not like I'm hiding, but with my arms cooly crossed, like I'm five kinds of fine with it. "That's a fire chopper. No worries," Zeus says. "If it's CAMP or cops it won't say anything on it. If one like that comes by, the first thing you need to do is take off all your clothes and run into the garden."

I look for a trace of smirk but don't find one. He adds, "If you're naked, the pictures they take from the helicopter won't be admissible in court."

"How do you know that?"

"You didn't know that?" Cedara says.

"Everybody knows that," Zeus says.

"Have you seen Vito herd?" It's almost seven and the hens are inching closer to the shed. They generally put themselves in at this time, but Vito loves to set stragglers straight. As I scratch Vito behind the ears and tell him "Put the chickens in the house," it occurs to me that I should use a different word for the flock he protects than for the meat I feed him.

Most of the chickens went to Sprout's mom's beau, a real homesteader who is so far off the grid he didn't have enough electricity to run the brooding lamp. I raised his chicks in exchange for his old nesting boxes. Vito gets six of the seven remaining pullets in the henhouse in under ten minutes. Creatures that stick together are easy to herd.

"What's up with her?" Cedara asks, about Lilybird, who is making her way in on her own time. It's true, she's odd. She's always been, that's why she's my favorite.

"She's always the last one in."

"But what's up with that sound she's making?" Cedara asks.

Lilybird is developing a loud, croaky cry that the others do not have. It's possible that Lilybird is not a hen at all, despite the best efforts of the chick sexers at the Murray McMurray Hatchery. But there's also a weirder option, which I enjoy.

Apparently every group of hens requires a leader. In the absence of a rooster, one of the hens will fill in the gap. She'll become a sort of gender hybrid. She'll lead and protect like a rooster would, even developing a mutated cock-a-doodle-doo—and she'll lay eggs too; an überfrau of poultry. This doesn't happen the other way around. If you have a whole bunch of roosters, what you get is not adaptation; what you get is fights until you have one cock.

Lilybird hides in an anorexic cedar. Vito throws his paws against it over and over like he has done this before except he hasn't, like he knows how to do this beyond all knowledge of knowing until Lilybird can't keep up the charade of firm footing anymore, or the ruse that her wings are better for flying than eating, and Vito catches her in the air (so gently) with his teeth, pins her to the ground and crouches just hard enough to immobilize her, as she squawks her freaky cry. He looks at me, calm and certain, as if to say, *Here's the last one.*

"Did you teach him that?" Cedara asks.

"No, he just does it."

As I approach he rises a bit, just enough to let me scoop her up. She still makes the same vibrations she did as a chick. Even as she settles in my arms, there's the insomniac buzzing of a creature that knows it's born prey. Like she can never really relax. Like she's just not safe. Totally possible that I'm projecting my ass off here. Still, chickens defy me to think that we are the only critters aware of our mortality.

Cedara leaves to go take the group empowerment call for her "gifting circle," which seems to me like a Ponzi scheme just for women. "It's five thousand dollars to get in, but it's all about women empowering women. Women have had babies, started businesses, recorded albums—all because of the gifting circle. It's about proving your capacity for commitment," Cedara says. This is probably one of the reasons I won't be joining. "It's totally legal!" she adds as she saunters to the biodiesel Mercedes some guy gave her for free. She leaves behind a wafting wake of French fries.

"That woman is powerful." Zeus sighs, cracking open a Session lager, a beer contained in a chubby little bottle with a feminine font and word puzzles under the bright red lid. He often has a case of Session lager in his car.

We go inside to check out my room.

"What the fuck is this?" Zeus wants to know.

"My nute cabinet."

"This is not what I told you to get."

I am now into my seventh week of flowering. There is only one week left. This is Zeus's third visit.

"This stuff was cheaper."

On unzipping it's clear that he's got nothing to complain about. Tonight the room smells like a bright green sword rubbed with a warrior's panties after fucking on a bed of pine needles beside a Celtic peat fire. The smell of success.

It's impossible to tell the difference now between the laundry orphans and the plants he gave me. Liz's Sour Diesel plants are the only individuals that can still be easily spotted. The SD plants are leggier than the Kush Girls and the buds aren't as dense. "Man, I wish they weren't in here," Zeus says. "I love seeing a full room of Kush, all that energy. I can't believe Lil Dick thought he could keep those Kush Girls down. Only an asshole would think he could control this. I mean, look at them—you don't even know what you're doing and look at them." He has a sparkle in his eye that I rarely see when he talks about Cedara.

Still, he complains about the size of my nuggets. He tells me it's because I didn't cut back enough. "Too much fimming and not enough early low cuts." Fimming is FIM pruning; the letters stand for "fuck, I missed." This kind of pruning, in another garden, would just be called pinching off. I've pinched off a lot of emerging leaves near the base to create more colas, the branches on which big buds bloom. Zeus shakes his head. This is not what he told me to do. He says, "Each Girl only has so much to give. Even when everything goes perfect, her max is her max. It's just that her max is also a secret that even she doesn't know. So you can have hundreds of little nugs or cut back and have four main, cheap to trim colas. You have a lot here, but it's all over the place. Your Girls lack focus."

"How would you like it if I complained about the size of your nuggets?"

He rubs his rough hemp toque again, all exasperated like a sitcom husband. "Girl . . ."

We start bigleafing, pinching off the fan leaves that are keeping the flowers from the light. "Oh. No," Zeus says.

"Oh no, mites? Please not mites again."

"No. Maybe worse." He points to a node that is not like the others, a sort of sac.

"What's that?"

"Male parts. Hermies." He points to a set of green gonads peeping from a node.

Hermies mean my Girls are producing male flowers, which means they have figured out that no green knight is coming. If they want to re-produce without getting cut, they're going to have to pollinate them-selves.

"Why would that happen?"

"Stress. That's what brought your resin up, but it looks like you took it too far."

I wish this conversation would stop landing so metaphorically.

"Why only a few of them? Why would only like three plants hermie? They're clones." I'm panicking.

"Do I look like a botanist?"

"More like a baller. Is that from stress too?"

"As is the grower, so go The Girls."

"Has anyone tested them?" I ask. "I bet they're a stronger smoke."

"No seeds. There can be no seeds in those bags. Doesn't matter what it smokes like if there're seeds in the bag."

Zeus pulls out his dope scope, a 30× magnifier that allows a clear view of the tiny trichomes that look like the penises in the *Kama Sutra* or enoki mushrooms. This is the shape that resin takes as it emerges on the flowers. Right now they're clear, next they'll get cloudy, then they'll turn amber. When about half of them are amber, we'll harvest. "You gotta get rid of those male buds. All of them. Any pollen hits the female flowers, your crop's gonna have seeds and I won't be able to help you." I pinch off the sacs and think about what Darwin wrote: "It is not the strongest species that survive, nor the most intelligent, but the ones most responsive to change."

NIBLET, THE JILTS, OR POSSIBLY TISSUE

"READY?" LIZ ASKS.

"So ready."

"Let's start."

Willa's guitar has blond wood and mother-of-pearl, and she's adorned it with gold stars. It's sized for a teenage girl. Liz's is super-regular, round and warm like an agrarian fetish in repose—uncut new strings sprouting from the neck, buzzing as she tunes. I have no guitar. Only three sheets of paper and the urge to wail. I stand behind the mic, adjust until I match it, straight and tall. I stretch like The Girls into trellis and hum. I hum the first two lines of the song they've asked for first and Liz assesses it as the key of G. At the end of each line she accompanies me with a full chord that progresses, and what's happening is a song. Willa matches Liz's fingers on the fret, crinkled and unsteady, then taut and sure. We're laughing open-throated pony laughs because that sounded like a new song, or a baby's first steps. Clumsy, for now. We are not a trio of dumpees. We are a fucking girl band.

Liz wonders if G is a little too high. This is because I cracked on the bridge. This did not affect my volume. It's good to howl among friends—it's fresher than keening. I remember what I love about performing, I remember what I hate about it, and those things bounce off each other at close range until liftoff. This is the thing I was trying to get at in LA, the ecstatic growl I traded for headshots and hunger.

We do Willa's song "Dark Night" next, and I improvise harmonies quietly. Our eyes are all full when we finish. Willa's heart is all over the song; she says what my defiance won't. Liz's song is somewhere in between—it drives like a Camaro down an open dirt road. We are banding together.

Jake is a jerkoff, but has good taste in girlfriends—we all agree—and we're grateful to him for this opportunity to practice gratitude for real.

We just have to wait out the waves of vacuum suck and let them be like that bank drive-up window tube thing. We put our shitty situations in that tube like a check, then let the pneumatic suck take it away, and when it comes back there's a pink receipt and a dog biscuit inside.

We try Willa's song again because the whole thing is so close to coming together. We are having fun and taking ourselves seriously all at the same time. We understand the importance of this deep play and acknowledge how much we need this. We have no ambitions, no rock star dreams—we just want to sing our broken hearts out for drunk folks at the Golddigger. No permission needed. We'll just do it. Two growgirls and a waitress, all of us in our thirties. We went to college for this? Yes. Yes, we did. We would not seem like people you should admire or aspire to be in any way. But trust me, on this night, on this first practice of this unnamed band, you should.

JU LIES

A VISIT FROM UNCLE HARVEY

YESTERDAY WAS INDEPENDENCE DAY; TODAY I'M CELEBRATING INTERDE-pendence Day. The Girls, the hens, the veggies, Vito, and I are having our first harvest. In ganjaspeak, this means Uncle Harvey is coming—and to welcome him, I made lasagna. A *Cook's Illustrated* one with béchamel from scratch and three kinds of animal. And a veggie one with spinach and ricotta. My relative isolation is causing me to invest this workday with a dinner party feeling. Today there will be a party. Sure, it will be a party attended mostly by strangers vetted by Zeus, and managing this work session will be my new thing of the day, which is a little unnerving, but still, it's a little like a party, and parties are fun and I miss them and I'm delighted to be a hostess today.

There are also gummi bears and an assortment of beers. Trimming is one of the only jobs that you can do buzzed on whatever you like. Chairs and wire hangers have been borrowed, extra black plastic trays purchased, and two boxes of turkey bags are optimistically at the ready. You know those Reynolds Oven Bags you can cook a turkey in? They have a fragrant secret life curing weed.

The only things missing are balloons and streamers, perhaps a piñata. I put some music on but recognize that putting out the guacamole would be premature.

The final touch is the sign I will hang on the gate. Vito traipses behind me and watches with tilted head as I tape up a sign with a stick figure meditating and SHHH . . . MEDITATION WORKSHOP IN SESSION, PLEASE DO NOT DISTURB! written on it. There's a happy face on the stick figure for adorable emphasis. I am hoping this will not only explain the numerous strange cars but also keep anybody not here to work from approaching the door.

Willa arrives and we tape tarps to the carpet along all possible routes that trimmers might travel in my house today. Sticky fragments of leaf and bud are not a carpet's friend. Even if you get the physical piece out, the smelly resin lingers.

Eleven o'clock. It's not unusual for people in the weed world to be tardy. Liz arrives, so the band is here, at least. She steps up to the table and wipes her scissor blades with rubbing alcohol from one of the fingerbowls on the table, prepping for a showdown. The sheriff is in town, bitches, and she's here to trim some weed. Liz is at least twice as fast as everybody else who will sit at this table. Liz is a Fiskary gunslinger.

"We should start bucking," Liz says, selecting a tray. "Is there more light?"

"No."

"Why didn't you set up over there?" she asks, meaning the living room, where the small amount of light that gets inside this house lands in its entirety.

"Because somebody could see us there before they would even knock on the door." Liz makes an effort not to roll her eyes. These are the worries of amateurs. If someone is that close to the door, it doesn't matter if we're in the living room or the dining room, but it would certainly matter in terms of the day's quality of life.

"You should go cut down so we can buck." At a trim scene, Liz is all business. After the plants are cut down in the bloom room, they are placed in a bin and brought to the trim table. The next step in manicuring weed is bucking. This is when the branches are stripped of their remaining fan leaves (those big handlike leaves that you think of when you think of pot) in order to provide the trimmer with clear access to the bud. I have no idea why it's called bucking.

In the garage, a canopy of leaves has joined to bridge the two tables. A pith helmet would not be out of order. It's a jungle in here. Success. The laundry orphans have thoroughly mingled with the OG Kush from Zeus. I think about how their where-are-they-now would read. They're very busy being awesome, thanks for asking. They're really stunning, glistening and humming. Prosperity on a stick. I know it's time to cut them down, I know The Girls in the veg room are ready to bloom, but it's one thing to know this and another thing to cut.

"I just wanted to say thank you," I whisper to The Girls, scissors dangling from my fingers. "None of us are what we were two months ago. The best, quite possibly, is yet to come. You will meet brains and mingle. You will probably, some of you, watch *Family Guy* and *Weeds*. Some of you will inspire cuddlefuckery a little looser and wetter than it would have been without you, while still others will ignite the taste of Cheetos or uncover the miracle of a caramel-dipped saltine. Some of you will remind a mind to sit on the lawn and do nothing, or take a hot bath, or pluck an eyebrow—perhaps even a tit whisker—with exquisite attention. Some of you will move a to-do list to the bottom of a pile or cause a hula hoop to come out of a garage or a melody to not just knock on the door, but be let in, despite the screaming world. You will bloom brains, balm pains. You will convince someone to hug, perhaps hump, a tree. You will make songs sung and supermarkets overwhelm. You are instruments of wonder, and don't you forget it. Dream on, little nuggets." I bow to them, then cut.

It's hard to know where to begin in the tangle of green. The grape scissors aren't really up to the job, and I struggle to sever a thick base. It feels like butchery the way I have to dig the blades into the fibrous trunk, twist them around until I split the stem, cut away the trellis and release the plant. I then hang her upside down, and snip at the V where each branch parts from the main stem. This V is the hook from which the plant will hang, so I can't just cut anywhere, I have to pay attention. That never stops.

ED GOT POPPED

IT'S ELEVEN FORTY-FIVE. I CALL ZEUS, WHO DOESN'T PICK UP. DITTO ED. Ditto Scooter. Ditto Judah and Cedara. I leave Ed a message: "Hey, I thought you were coming over to work today. We were supposed to start forty-five minutes ago. Where are you? Where is everybody? The Girls don't like to get stood up." I am too caught up in the tiny triumph of this first harvest to code my ganja talk with anything subtler.

"Seriously, nothing but world music?" Willa asks.

It's twelve thirty and only Willa, Liz, and I are here. I call Zeus again. "Hey, we need to get started—"

He picks up. "Don't call Ed. Don't call anybody. I'll be right over," he says, and hangs up.

The sight of Zeus's son, SaRah, in my growhouse freaks me out. I'm further freaked when he asks, "Can I trim nugget, Papa?"

"Sure, son. You see the scissors on the table?" I cut myself at least once every time I handle a pair of grape scissors. But SaRah, a connoisseur-grade wielder of sharp objects, is a way better trimmer than me. He selects a tray and takes a branch from the buck bin.

"Um . . . ," I say, uselessly.

Zeus: "Ed's been arrested."

SaRah is now the only one trimming. The only one breathing.

I want him to get SaRah the fuck out of here. *I have all the prescriptions I need to be state legal I have all the prescriptions I need to be state legal I have all the prescriptions I need to be state legal.* Ed should have too. "Didn't he have his scrips?"

"We were still working on that. But we already got a late start . . ." Ed was working at a new outdoor location for Zeus, who had been hired by a mystery investor who bought good growing land but didn't want to get his hands dirty. Now that something has gone wrong, the mystery investor will say he was renting the land and didn't know anything about any pot. If everything had gone well, the mystery investor and Zeus would have split the surplus after all prescriptions had been filled, and Ed would have been given a piece of what Zeus brought in—but now there's nothing but trouble, and that's all Ed's.

Stupid. We are all so stupid. "Is he okay?"

"Yeah, yeah, he'll lawyer up and he'll get probation probably."

"Probably?"

"You didn't call him today did you?"

"Yes." Nausea.

"Did you leave a message?"

"Uh-huh." Unsurfable wave of nausea.

"What did you say?" He adjusts his weight, stands even on both feet, like an antenna.

"I asked if he was coming to work today. I said The Girls didn't like to be stood up."

He rubs his hemp toque. "No more calls, okay?"

"But it's my trim. You're my consultant."

"Unforeseen circumstances. Nature of the beast."

Liz sighs. Willa asks to see SaRah's scissors.

"I'll see what I can do," Zeus says before he leaves. "Looks good though. Good to have more work than you can handle today. Think of it that way. Find the gratitude. Nature of the beast."

The beast, though, is different from The Girls. The beast is a man-made thing.

THE DOGS KEEP TRYING TO KILL SHEBA'S HOT PANTS

STRANGERS THAT ZEUS HAS ROUNDED UP ON MY BEHALF START ARRIVING and they say things like, "Your movie scared the shit out of me." I wish this had not been the tactic Zeus had used to round up trimmers on my behalf. My new crystal deodorant is not cutting it.

"Thanks, uh, sign in here, okay?" I say, indicating the sign-in sheet on which people will put the time they arrived next to their trim names, pseudonyms to protect themselves in case of a bust. Trim days are particularly vulnerable to busts. It's not too hard to estimate when you'll have a nice chunk of subculture in one locale. Trims generally occur around the sixty-fifth day of extra-high electricity use.

I am not cutting down fast enough, because I am greeting and catering and fucking with the gate and paying people out and getting them signed in and so there are lulls in the action where people get up from the table to smoke cigarettes and search my kitchen fruitlessly for bongs, and it's hard to get their asses back in the seats. The snacks have been moved from the table to make room for piles of plant, and the lasagnas are weeping in their pans. None of this resembles the dinner party atmosphere I was going for. I am expecting the sheriff to arrive at any minute, as he probably went through Ed's voicemail, or at least his call log, so he could write down all the numbers and then pick us off one by one. Shit. The bathroom is filling with rows of hanging nuggets. No one is allowed in there now. A scene like that is bound to fill the most innocent minds with thoughts of theft. It also fills me with a brand-new mix of pride and dread. People I have never met before, who quite naturally think it's a funny bit of trivia to be at The Girl from *The Blair Witch Project*'s first trim, are in my bedroom now that the guest bath is occupied. I put Willa on cut-down duty. The bin comes back cut without hooks. I take her into the room for a quick tutorial and her eyes well and I'm trying to be sympathetic because I really can't afford for her to take a break right now, because she's the only one I trust enough to let in the garage. We fill another bin, and when we return everyone is out on the deck. "Um, can you come back inside please? The neighbor's house is right up the hill and we've had a lot of in-and-out today." People who trim regularly are used to paranoid growers and improvised rules. If they want to keep a twenty-dollar-an-hour job where they can drink beer, smoke pot, and shoot the shit, then they know to obey. Even if it means bringing a tent and staying a week or more during outdoor season. Some growers will have trimmers meet in a parking lot and shuttle them in to the house, to keep the in-and-out down. I am thinking this would have been a great idea for me to have done today, and yet hemp-clad people loitering at the bowling alley before clownjamming into my car, might be more conspicuous than the in-and-out.

"Stop bucking and start managing," Scooter tells me, after ten minutes at the table. No hard feelings there. I need my buds groomed and he needs the twenty dollars an hour. He's right, but bucking is just so single action/single objective that it makes a nice respite. Nobody wants to think about Ed. We're all thinking about Ed. If tech communication is forbidden, you want to be somewhere you can get information by mouth, which is why people are Jiffy Popping in and out of my house. "Did you guys all see the sign-in sheet here?" They come in for about an hour, get the story, then leave. I call Zeus and leave a message: "Just wanted to let you know everything's okay. We have plenty of everything for the party!" Suspiciously, excessively, absurdly chipper. I am the opposite of cool.

"Dude. You got some hermies," Scooter says, holding freak seeds in the palm of his hand.

"Okay everybody, keep an eye out for seeds. If you see any, let me know. Really can't have seeds in the bags." I take them from him, put them in a brown paper lunch bag.

Scooter rolls a ball of fingerhash from the accumulated resin on his hands. "Nobody wants a girl with balls," he says, and swallows it.

A Mastiff named Sheba arrives wearing Hot Pants, a diaperish accessory meant to manage the menses of bitches in heat. The dog weighs more than me and has comparable flow. These Hot Pants, they keep coming off. Only Sheba's bedreaded mistress is unrepulsed. The dog is put outside. Now there is a full-fledged pack out there. At least one of them barks every fifteen minutes, which is unusual for a meditation workshop. My world music is getting on everyone's tits and the dogs keep trying to kill Sheba's Hot Pants, getting the blood on their muzzles. Vito lays on my feet because he has never been around this many people at once before. I brush trim from his snout. He is extra mellow. "Okay," I say to the trimmers at the table, "we're good now, no more people, okay?" Two admit they still have friends coming. I make a note to myself to trim on my own next time no matter how fucking long it takes.

"Please call them and tell them not to, okay?"

"You said . . ."

"The situation has changed. Nature of the beast," I say. Though I am still not interested in having anyone mad at me, I would like to have some idea of who the people are who now have the address of my growhouse and the knowledge that I live here alone. I am firm: "No more in-and-out until we're done. Anybody that has to leave soon should go now." My dinner party enthusiasm is gone like the lasagna. I have nothing left to feed newcomers anyway. Three people leave to pull tarps. I tell them not to come back. I have to stop again to pay them, and follow them out, noting makes, models, plates—notes I hope to never use. The front of my house looks like a low-rent used car lot.

Vito is curled in a far corner of the bedroom, with a ganja twig tucked under his paw. I replace it with a bully stick. He hasn't moved for some time, but he always straddles that line between mellow and lethargic. He bounds up when Jezebel arrives. Oh. Fuck. No.

ED WOULD LIKE TO BUCK

ED IS CLEARLY DISTRAUGHT, THOUGH NOT CLEARLY AS DISTRAUGHT AS ME, seeing as he's shown up. "Were you followed or anything?" He just stares, eyes red-rimmed. "Um, yeah, I'm fucking paranoid, okay?" I say, because duh.

"Judah and Zeus won't even talk to me. None of them will. They're too scared to even talk to me. I'm sorry. I shouldn't be here." He rolls the dehumidifier he promised to lend me into the bathroom. The tub is obscured by dangling nuggets. "Beginner's luck," he says. "It's how they get you hooked."

"I can't believe you remembered that," I say about the humidifier.

"I promised, didn't I?"

"Um, you didn't break out or anything, right?" He just looks at me and shakes his head.

He sits quietly in a corner near the table, near everyone, petting Jezebel and nursing a beer. Everything about him is swollen. He doesn't want to talk yet, and no one here will ask him to because none of us really want to know. He has no information, only the certainty of trouble. "They took a mugshot. I have a number again."

I cut down another binful and sit beside him. "Want to buck?"

He brightens a little. "Yeah, I wanna buck."

"Then shut up and buck," I say, and he smiles, pinches fan leaves, and joins the party. Liz glances, sighs, sinks back to Zen pebble in a river of clip. Vito comes along and licks Jezebel's face, then splays onto his back.

Willa joins us at the buck bin. "I'm really sorry," she says, between leaves.

"Yeah," Ed says, squatting back and studying the pile and stains on the carpet. "I was so careful," he says. "I cleared twenty-five feet around the generator. But still, today when I started it, it gave out a spark. Piece of shit. I told Zeus that piece of shit was going to be a problem in this drought, but he said it was all he had. Even the firemen said that break should have been enough. They were like, *Bad luck man. You know we have to call the sheriff, right?* Fucking helicopter dropping that fire gel all over my shit." I picture Ed like a newborn, covered in jelly and fear.

"They took all the scrips?"

"Guess." This means that any scrip that Ed was planning to use at that outdoor site is now invalid for the rest of the season, for everybody who has it. Which number is x. There's no registration system of who's got which scrip where, neither officially nor unofficially. It's like cops and robbers, or paintball: Everybody risks in varying degrees. If the grower you've given your scrip to, whose co-op you've joined, gets busted, you don't get your pound. If you get shady and give your scrip to multiple growers, you can end up with multiple pounds for no effort or expense beyond a visit to the pot doctor. Some patients do this as a way of hedging their bets. In reality, scrips are sometimes shared within communities of growers and posted in multiple locations without the patient knowing. The patient still only gets a pound from the grower they originally gave it to. In the meantime, it has become community property. Thanks Xerox! It's really that simple. It's really that tenuous. It's really that up to chance, this fourteen-billion-dollar-a-year business. Ed didn't have even this scabby paperwork together. If he did, the sheriff would have had to walk away. Unless of course he was feeling feisty or bored that day, in which he could decide to say the scrips were invalid because there were too many out-of-county patients. Though Prop 215 is a state issue, it's primarily enforced at the county level. Counties make up convoluted regulations that often violate the constitutional rights granted by the state, but by the time the issue gets adjudicated at the state level, the defendant has already served their time and paid their fines. We all play the odds, sketching the boundaries of deliberately vague laws and scattershot enforcement. Like the gold rush, it's a limited-time offer.

Ed said they took away all of his possessions, including his cell phone. He didn't see where they took it or what they did with it before they gave it back. "I think your check for making the window seat was still in my wallet too," he tells me.

"Dude, that was from three months ago." At least my checks still have my LA address on them. Small mercies are still merciful.

"Will we find more plants at this address?" they asked him.

"Not a lot more," he told them. "I'm only running four lights." So they leave the outdoor location that he was managing for Zeus, who was hired to farm it by folks who bought the land for just that. Everything was to be distributed at a percentage, with the person taking the most risk, Ed, being awarded the smallest percentage. The distribution of wealth in the ganja world happens at the family level, until some families interpret *family* in the Sicilian way. Even the most well-intentioned gentlemen can be assholes—just add money. Not to be sexist, but I find this rarely happens with women who grow. For growgirls, there is an instinct toward security and self-preservation that supersedes greed. Discuss?

So the sheriff takes Ed home, and, really, this is the part of the story that he can hardly get through. Getting arrested is one thing, but . . . "They fucking made fun of me. They unzipped the door and they were like *Oh man, you suck at this. You should really find another line of work.* Shit like *The grannies up here grow better bud than this.* They were like *This isn't even worth cutting down; way to punish you would be to leave it up.* And you know what? They were fucking right. Once again my shit was fucked. Fuck this shit. I want a crepe cart."

He takes another long pull on his beer so he has a good excuse for looking at the ceiling while the puddles in his eyes evaporate. "I even had a fire extinguisher in my truck. I just tried to do everything right, you know, tried to think of everything bad that could happen and make sure it didn't. I'm fucking tired of shitty luck, man, when assholes all around are just fucking fine."

"Hey, where's our manager? We need another bin," Liz says. Willa has finished bucking and with Liz's speed they are out of weed again. The pile in the bin has become the pile on the table has become nug-laden twigs dangling from wire hangers. I cut down more. When I get back Ed is in a chair with scissors in his hand. My number is in his call log three times today, then there are my calls to Zeus, his calls to Zeus, Zeus's calls to me, all of our calls to Scooter, The Community network present and vulnerable from Ed's one tiny device. Easy pickings one and all. That's what we are. One quick call to PG&E to verify the cost of our power bills and there but for the grace of God go I, into the county clink.

Zeus leaves his car at the locked gate. Just leaves it hanging there, so we are all surprised when he walks in the door, because the dogs don't bark at him.

Zeus hovers in the doorway. Ed is out of his chair immediately. Everyone inhales at once. "Why didn't you call me back, man? Why'd you leave me hanging like that?"

"Dude, you know why I didn't call you back. Same reason you're not supposed to call anybody. Same reason you shouldn't be here right now. You know the rules."

"I thought you were the king of The Community bullshit. Guess it's pretty clear that's another bunch of bullshit."

"Come on outside." Zeus hasn't crossed the threshold. He keeps one eye on the outside. He certainly hasn't picked up a pair of scissors. Ed's, however, are still in his hands.

"Scissors," I say, and he drops them on the table. Zeus doesn't even come back in to say good-bye before he leaves.

"How you like your fucking Community now?" Ed says, as he blasts back through the door, then adds, "I should go." No one argues with him, except Jezebel, who is cuddled with Vito on the couch. "Come on, girl," he says, squatting with his arms outstretched. She remains intertwined with Vito on the couch. There is nothing worse than being betrayed by your dog, except maybe being betrayed by your dog in front of a bunch of other people, up to and including the woman that you recently broke up with for the fortieth time who already thinks you are a douchebag.

"Is Zeus going to help you?" I ask, and it goes up too high at the end. Jezebel's blank stare keeps thudding. Vito goes to him and lays on his feet. He squats to pet him.

"You're a good boy. You're a real good boy." Then he abruptly turns to me, not the way he is with animals, but the way he is with people. He changes to his person person and glares. "What the fuck do you think? Zeus is for Zeus just like his cunt girlfriend, only give a fuck about themselves. So fucking free right? So fucking free to be self-centered assholes. Fucking Community. Fucking liars. Every asshole for their fucking self." Everyone at the table looks at each other with only their eyeballs, no movement of heads.

Ed's Tacoma goes too fast down the gravel drive. I choke on the cloud he leaves behind as I go to lock the gate. No more than three ins and outs on trim day, is the rule. I have lost count.

We don't finish until after two a.m. Late for a meditation workshop. Today cost double Zeus's estimate.

VITO AND A HAMMER

IT'S TOO LATE TO DISAPPEAR, TOO LATE TO GO OUT FOR A BEER. IT'S CORPSEY quiet now. I let the stereo run, then reconsider, because how would I hear the people coming to rob me? Vito is startled by things that aren't there and it's freaking me out. I study my mother's notecards on the fridge: *Trust in you. Tread lightly.* I didn't quite manage that one today. I open another beer and refuse to add up the number of people who know the exact secluded cul-de-sac where The Girl from *The Blair Witch Project* grows weed. Alone. At the end of the road.

I'm pretty sure that if I could get over the blind terror I would feel quite a sense of accomplishment. But I'm still not over the blind terror. Wait. What's in that bathroom right now? Weed. It needs to be a lot of weed for me to break even. Look at those adjustable shower curtain rods stretched sideways across the bathroom. Smell that kicking cloud that hovers without even opening the bathroom door. Round one. Done. It only makes sense to sample. I mean, I should know what I'm offering.

I put a bud in the microwave for ten seconds and then another ten until I think it is smokably dry. It's still a labor to keep it lit, but it is smooth and tastes like huffing Stanley Park in Vancouver in June, after a skunk has been by. Vito sticks close to me like he might need to be a crutch. Thoughts bounce inside my skull with too much bass. I am acutely aware of how I smell—like pine and myrrh and earth and balsam. It feels like I smell like this inside and out, like my shit will be green and smell like this. My socks smell like the book aisle of a thrift shop in the Pacific Northwest, particularly if it's near the aisle with old boots and wool sweaters. Pet Vito. I get the feeling he has something to say. He's so soft. I am lucky to have something so soft in my life. *You are,* he says with his blue eye, then nudges my wrist with his snout. My heart rattles my rib cage.

I seriously cannot believe people smoke this shit all the time. I just had a fifteen-minute eyeball convo with my puppy. Seriously, he didn't look away. I want him to know how much I appreciate him. How the rescue, the adoption, was mutual. He doesn't move, nor do I. We even turn our heads and keep our eyes locked. In the window glass too, we hold. I'm becoming one of those ladies. I make up names for him like Sweetpea Boo Boo Bear. I've lost all self-consciousness about being referred to as his mommy and accept it as a matter of course. The great thing about living isolated is that you stop comparing yourself to other people, run your freak flag up the pole daily. Wait. Did I just say that was the great thing about country living? I think I meant agoraphobia. That's the great thing about agoraphobia. I hope Buga's okay. I hope he has burrowed down to gold and now rules an ant kingdom like a god, wielding a golden scepter and drinking nectar from an acorn goblet. It would mean I gave him a better life than any Tupperware tote could. Or he's dead. I am grateful there is butter brittle ice cream left. I am too stoned to go out and walk Vito. Wait. I cannot afford to be afraid of something as basic as the dark. I think about Lil Dick for the first time since my first day here. The boys have switched from Kush to Sour Diesel officially, though not really. Lil Dick knows my car, that I remember. If he bothered with the license plate number, I would not be hard to find. New moon tonight. Meaning no moon. No. Vito and the moon are always there, even when I can't see them.

There are trim flecks stuck to Vito's gums. He pukes in my lap. It is possible that he ate a lot of trim. I open the bathroom door. A shrieking cave of dank green bats. When the great slam happens outside on the deck, I match it with the slamming of the door. *Just a deer. Just a deer?* Vito barely even stirs. It's up to me to protect us all. I think about leaving. If somebody is going to steal from me I'd really rather not be here. But if my car wasn't here, that would be more thief-enticing. Here I am. Like that hippie bumper sticker says, I should just be here now. I need a place to hide. Under the table. Yes. They'll never look here. There are too many windows in the bedroom, that curtainless sliding glass door. There are people who smoke this shit every day. Everything is amplified. I turn out all the lights and crawl to the door to see if anyone, or more than one, is out there on the deck. Or if it was really just a deer. Wait. I don't really want to know. New moon. Dark as fuck. Nothing moves. Things maybe just lurk. The hammer. I keep it by the bed like my mom made me swear. I crawl into the bedroom, stay low. Vito shits a stream and hangs his head. *It's okay, buddy, I can't even smell it over all that weed* I tell him with my eyeballs. I would clean it up but there's no way I'm turning on the lights. I don't want them to see me scared. They could rob me and just take it and go, but not if they see me. Then they'd have to "do something" even though I would say *Just take it take it* with my eyes shut tight. Wait for the light. Which is how I spend the night under the dining room table clutching Vito and a hammer.

PICK UP BRICKS

MUCH MEDICINE LINES THE BOTTOM OF THE TURKEY BAGS THAT I HAVE been opening and turning several times a day for the last three days. The rule: no nugs smaller than a thumbnail. I toss in a handful of smalls to boost the bags over the weight already required by the industry standard, the 457-gram Mendo pound, named for the generous people of Mendocino County, the second-largest jewel in the Emerald Triangle's tiara, after Humboldt, before Trinity.

Shake gathers at the bottom of my bags. I should sift it out. Instead I turn the bags upside down and make sure the shake is evenly distributed. I roll each bag like a festive yule log and lay it inside a heavy black plastic contractor bag, which I lay inside a corrugated cardboard box left over from my move. I surround the bags with bath towels, and under the top layer of towels I place six lavender and vanilla dryer sheets in the hopes that their smell will be the first waft to hit should I get pulled over. I worry about these too, that they'll pollute the Kush bouquet by the time I drive to Zeus's house. Once again the choice between product and peace of mind. I ask Zeus if I can bring two pounds at a time because the rumor is that's what I can legally drive. I have no idea if this is true. I am afloat here by chance and circumstance. I am aware of that. All the time. New gray hairs sprout clustered above my left temple, where sun blonde used to be.

I knock on Zeus's door and kick off my shoes under the prayer flags there. Zeus is on the phone. He holds a finger to his lips and looks into the box, gives a thumbs-up about the dryer sheets. Wacław always did that when he sent pot through the mail. Wacław knew a lot of things that would come in handy now. Zeus ends his call, looks me over, and writes *Madrona* on the bags. Finally, I get a hippie name. "It won't match up with anything on my phone. It means adaptable leggy red tree—you like it?" I nod. This shouldn't feel like dropping your toddler off at preschool, but I tuck in the ends of the turkey bags, making sure they're nice and snug— and also that the shake is still concealed. I turn back to look at them again before I go. "They'll be fine," Zeus says, and adds, casually, "How's the band coming?"

"We're playing the Golddigger Wednesday." I'm in a band. We have a gig. I'm choosing awesome, because the alternative wears orange jump-suits and they are not the new black.

"I'll call you when we're ready here. Could be tonight, could be to-morrow. Never know."

"Nature of the beast."

He calls the next afternoon. It's time to pick up my donation. I'm still not sure how much it's going to be. I'll basically just take Zeus's word for it, believe in the figures stacked in columns on a sheet ripped out of a spiral notebook. Pot is like lobster, in that market prices vary. It's not like lob-ster, in that it can't be profited from, it can only be given, donated.

When I arrive at Zeus's he throws me a somber bro-nod and gestures toward the couch. He brings two cups of maté and the tally sheet and sits on the French Regency couch opposite me. "Your shit was hermied bad. M'Onay said she had seeds like this . . ." He holds out both hands like a harvest goddess in a river of grain, or a dude recalling tits.

"So tell her I'll buy them back."

"It made both of us look bad. And she was psyched about a girl grower."

"Seriously, I'll buy them back."

"Hermied seeds grow hermied plants. She subtracted them and your shake. And the nugs were pretty small so . . ." I'll remain in the red.

"You grind it up to smoke it, right? Nobody smokes schlongy nugs whole."

"You want to argue with the market? Don't shoot the messenger, okay?"

Bitch-slapped by the invisible hand. Like everyone.

"Sorry. I know it's not your fault." *Humility is my friend.*

"I didn't take my whole commission." He hands me a brown paper bag. It's bigger than a lunch bag, smaller than a shopping bag. I open it, and inside is a brick-sized block of twenty-dollar bills. I roll the top of the bag back down and make it more like lunch. Like a ham and cheese on Wonder Bread with a Capri Sun like I might have taken to elementary school. I keep thinking about elementary school, innocence. What am I doing here? Why did I not just go to fucking law school? Where are The Girls in this equation? Where the tender tending? Severed. Like a head by a cartel, displayed on a post. I tuck the bag deep into my steaming armpit and walk around his living room with it stuck there like that, like it's not there, or like it's some sugar I borrowed. No, not sugar. I'm pretending it's not like anything with a ganjaspeak euphemism attached. It's hard not to think there's something sketchy about doing something that results in a house brick of cash. It's not like I haven't seen this much cash at one time before. Judah used to keep his in the freezer. Cold hard cash, next to the ice cream. Cool and comforting. My head pounds in a syncopated way. Each time I adjust to a new layer of this job, it excavates again, unearthing my new freak-out point.

"I think it's great with your band and all. I've kind of lost track of making music." His eyes are toffee, sweet and hard. "It's real easy to forget what you came up here to do."

"Living the dream?"

"You know."

"Learning."

I'm more unnerved driving with the bag of cash than I was with the nuggets. The nuggets I can defend. They are dried flowers, after all. I see nothing illicit in them anymore. But a bag of cash? A bag of cash illustrates just how dangerous the world is. How tenuously everything hangs. There is nothing behind these slips of paper anymore, no gold. Plastic credit cards, debit cards, those are meant to be abstractions, not meant to be something real. But this is cash, legal tender. There are two more prescriptions in my mailbox upon my return. I'm also a legal tender! The usual twenty minutes late of LA has translated to four months. Still, my friends came through for me. I have more than enough patients for a state-legal grow. What stands between me and an orange jumpsuit? These pieces of paper, these photo-copies. What stands between me and homelessness? The cash in this brown paper bag. A whole bunch of fragile little slivers of tree.

THE GENTLEMAN CALLER INCIDENT

"I can't wear this, it makes my boobs look saggy," says Liz, the only one of us to have fed through her tits.

"No problem." I reach into my bag of tricks and pull out a roll of duct tape.

"Push them up," I say.

"You are not going to put duct tape on her boobs," Willa says.

"Yes. Yes, I am."

"Does it work?" Liz asks. "What if I sweat and it falls off?"

"It won't, but it might sting a little when you take it off. And leave adhesive behind, which you can just wipe off with some rubbing alcohol, which will definitely sting some more."

Willa and Liz are skeptical.

"We're a girl band. We should have maximum cleavage. Think of yourself like an athlete taping up."

Liz's ellipticals have shifted into inverse pears. Thanks, duct tape. Way to bring it. Willa's not going to tape anything but concedes to a bit of lipgloss. A couple of friends come by to hear our rehearsal, and some neighbors come from upstairs not to complain, but to tell us we sound great. I slip into my blue salsa dress, take the curlers from my hair. We are not three dumped women in our thirties. We are girl band, hear us roar.

We walk to the Golddigger with an entourage of friends. An aging dude sings Rush covers, accompanies himself on keyboard. The 49er bar-tifacts will be gone when the place becomes a tanning salon, but tonight they reign in all their dusty glory. The side of the bar facing the street is wide open, and people here for the Summer Nights Street Fair—those who came by chartered bus for charm and turkey legs—are stopping to listen as a husband and wife sing about fairies and seeds. Scooter and Ed arrive. I reference them in what is planned as our a cappella finale, and I'm worried they might be offended. No. They will definitely be offended. I approach: "Thanks for coming you guys! And, just so you know, all these songs they were, you know, just written in good fun. Especially the last one. It's meant to be fun." Cedara and Zeus arrive with their friends A'Be and Pebbles—she makes pretty feather earrings, he's always a little stoned. The Golddigger, actually, is packed.

When the emcee says, "And now . . . Liz and Company!" I really do wish we had managed to agree on a name. Willa and I like Tissue, but Liz thinks it's gross. We considered The Jilts, but it seemed too sad, and The Jills just seemed too plain. Nobody was down with Niblet.

"Okay, we ready?" Liz's pick trembles against her fret.

"I think we're ready. Heather, are we ready? I think it's good, ready?" Willa says into the mic and we launch into her "Dark Night" . . . *Say that it isn't so, and maybe, I can let go* . . . We've been a band for only four weeks and we're remembering all the words. Triumph. Liz's song goes off without a hitch . . . *because the only thing you've ever given me is this ghost inside my heart.* . . . Everything Liz does seems effortless. It makes people forget to appreciate her when they really shouldn't. My song goes in and out of pitch. It sounds pretty bad but I'm very enthusiastic. I like to think this "sells" it. The girls put down their guitars and the emcee thinks she can put a fork in us, but we're not done. We have an a cappella finale planned. It's more of a musical theater number, complete with old-school Gershwiny introduction. This one is where I get so loud that quality doesn't even begin to cross my mind. When in doubt: louder. This is where every action of every douchebag flies out of our throats. Triple karmic vortex, bitches: *You say you wanna taste my cootah, even though you are a friend of Judah* . . . I like that line, it took a minute to find something that rhymed with Judah and also captured the backtracking that Scooter did after he showed up wasted at my house to find out if I wanted to "get nibbled." When we get to the end, flinging our arms over each other's shoulders to begin our chorus line kick, we belt it, we bleat it, we sing it: *Do you wanna get nibbled? Do you wanna get licked? Do you wanna take a pony ride on my magnificent stick? NOPE! I want a gentleman caller, not another raw boy who doesn't know the difference between a pussy and a toy* . . . The crowd goes wild. Whistles, claps, giggles, ululations. Cedara whispers vigorously, staring at Scooter and Ed who are not clapping, but vacating their barstools. Liz notes this, looks down. As we descend from the stage she tells the floor: "I think they're upset." She's gone from radiant rock star to shamed shouter in five seconds flat. Ed was never particularly good to her, so she's still eager to please.

I untie Vito from the horse hitch outside the bar. He has no comment except to lick my face. Scooter has a comment, though. I overhear: "She has no right. She's not even hot." Like volume and heat are equivalent. Like the amount of space a being occupies is necessarily contingent on its relationship to entropy. By which I mean: Fuck you dude.

EMPTY BEDS AND EMPTY BEDS

I COME HOME TO EMPTY BEDS AND EMPTY BEDS AND EMPTY BEDS. NUBBITY nub nub nothing for as far as the eye can see. The veggie garden has been decimated. Even the potato patch, which deer are supposed to find totally unappetizing, is gone. I was going to get a metal fence next year. Or never. I'm a renter, after all. The plastic deer fence now features a ragged slash. I first planted the seeds in February—that's five months of care to grow one day's deer snacks, not to mention the money. Vito sniffs madly, marking where the fence was torn and toppled. There were fat tomatoes forming. The Early Girls I planted, not heirlooms, but they would have been the first to ripen. I tied them to the bamboo stakes, so they could each have their place in the sun. The twist ties dangle on the splayed stakes.

Knees to the dirt, palms up, *why?* Again. I check myself. Pulse? Check. Hands? Check. Toes? Check. Voice? Ahhhhhhh. Check. Dog? Check. Bonus: The car is still running. I am lucky. Now the chicken poop that was going to nourish this garden is just chicken poop rather than a link in the permacultural chain. Now there's no more experiment in onavorism, seeing if a city girl could take care of herself, foodwise, at least. It turns out that this city girl cannot. Fail again. Fail better. Oh fuck no. I know I won't replant. I'm thinking it might be time to start cutting my losses and buying local from trained professionals. With the money I spent on this nubbed-out patch, I could have bought about three hundred pounds of locally grown heirloom tomatoes. Instead? A barren patch of sad.

CAKE AND SHAKE

I MAKE MY SUMMER CAKE: DUNCAN HINES BOX WHITE WITH CHAMBORD whipped cream and raspberries set like pavé rubies. Willa's birthday party starts outside by the creek—summer dresses, bare feet on lawn, a small-town potluck in the mountain air. Nurses, programmers, waiters, teachers—the party is full of no one who grows except Liz and me. Then Liz gets a text and stutters and leaves. Now I'm the only one hoping no one asks me what I do.

Just after we move inside for the eating of cake, a phantom tumbleweed rolls in, followed by the showdowny thud of six flip-flops landing on the deck outside Willa's door. The three of them are in triangle formation. Forks hang in midair as two worlds collide—growers, meet townfolk; townfolk, growers. Growers think they blend in because they only interact with their own. Pebbles and his dreaddy mane flank Zeus's left. Pebbles's presence means both Ed and Judah have declined this tour of duty. He orbits in the next concentric social circle out. Scooter holds down the right side, the top of his head touching the door frame from where I sit here on the floor. A chunk of birthday cake quivers on my fork, then plummets, to huddle with the rest of the slice. No one whistles like it's a spaghetti western, but I hear it in my head anyway.

"Happy birthday, Willa," Zeus says, arms hanging taut along his white ribbed beater. He gives the brim of his straw fedora a tug and looks to me. "Can we have a word?"

Which one? Which word would you like to have? Go? Away? I bring my plate with me as I wade through the eyeballs—the cake is delicious and a plastic fork is better than nothing, as defense goes. Willa flips the Aretha record and

"Respect" brings the party back to normal. *You know I got it.* Willa looks to me to ask if I need backup. I give her a shake, then a nod, thumbing up the musical selection. I step out the door along Aretha's sonic path, sit on the pretty white bench. The boys look at each other in the swelling silence before the commander begins. "You can't go around naming names and calling out people from this Community in public," Zeus says.

"What is this about?" I venture.

Scooter shakes with an irritated mix of disbelief and displeasure. "Um, your little performance the other night?"

"Inappropriate," Pebbles says.

"Not okay," Zeus adds, and it's a roundelay, not unlike schoolgirls singing "Row, Row, Row Your Boat."

"Can't do that."

"Naming names."

"Everybody knew who you meant."

"You are not anonymous."

"—oo are not. You have . . ."

"Have . . ."

". . . have a responsibility to The Community." Zeus completes the round then adds, "That's not why I encouraged you, so you could go around embarrassing yourself."

"Is that what I did?"

"You have no right," Scooter says, and I can see from the way he can barely contain himself that he called this meeting.

"I have no right to sing a song about what I like and what I don't?"

"You publicly embarrassed members of this Community."

"I thought I embarrassed myself."

"That too."

"I wasn't the only one up there."

"We've already discussed this with Liz. She realizes what you did was a breach of security. She assured me it won't happen again."

"Is that the definition of *community* we're working with here?" I can see my heartbeat through my rib cage when I look down. I continue anyway, "I thought freedom was one of the values of The Community, freedom of expression."

"For sure, but not when it creates trouble for the rest of us. You're being selfish."

"By singing a silly song about how men talk to women?"

Scooter can't take it anymore. "You quoted me. You were trying to embarrass me."

"I think you did a pretty good job of that on your own."

"Back at you," he says, in a way that suggests the schoolyard taunt about rubber and glue.

Willa comes out. "You guys want cake? There's plenty."

"Nah, but we'll have a beer." I'm not sure if Zeus is using the royal *we* here, or if he's ordering up a round because he thinks Willa is still at the Eggloo and not at her own fucking birthday party.

"Three?" she asks.

"They're inside," I say. "You can help yourselves."

"Sweet," Pebbles says, and follows Willa inside. He was a last-minute choice for henchman and hasn't taken to the role.

"We're not done here," Zeus says to me, and puts his hand on my knee as I begin to rise from the bench. I obey. I could swallow my pride here and keep the connection, or I could drive my nugs to San Francisco or LA and try to shop my surplus around on the dispensary market after filling my patients' prescriptions. Our interests are indeed tied, as Scooter is one of my patients.

"I need to pull my scrip from your room," Scooter says.

"That doesn't work for me." I have already paid to have him in my co-op. Like the incentives a car manufacturer might offer. "Do I get my money back?"

"No, but you get to show that you want to stay a part of The Community."

"I think we should find another word for this," I say, while Zeus gives Scooter the hand, then squats in front of me on the bench, putting both hands on my knees.

"You feel threatened," he says, and gives me the astringent eyes and everything tightens. I'm in what my grandmother might have called a pickle, though it is not delicious. If thoughts create reality, make a peaceful reality. Every muscle relaxes on the exhale.

"I'm sorry," I say. "I didn't mean to hurt anyone's feelings. I've just always been a city girl, and I'm used to no one giving a shit. I didn't think anyone would even come to hear us." My eyes drop anchor on Zeus's fingers, on my knees. "It was just meant to be funny, the song. I'm really sorry if that's not how it came off."

"It came off as aggressive," Scooter says.

"Don't cry," Zeus says.

Willa comes out with two beers. When she sees me crying she holds them tighter in her hands and sits on the bench beside me. Zeus gets up and leans against the wall with his arms crossed in front of him.

"We know it's not your fault," Scooter says to Willa.

"What's not my fault?"

"We know she wrote that song," Scooter said.

"Yeah, but we all sang it. It's not just her. We're a band." Now Willa looks like she's going to cry too. She's very sensitive to being excluded.

I take the beers from Willa, hand one to Zeus, and keep the other for myself. I come in peace. Willa remains, crossing her arms across her chest and looking positively huffy. "What's your problem with the song?"

"This doesn't involve you," Zeus says. "We have no problem with you and Liz." Willa stands, drops her arms to her sides, and gathers up some force of will that I didn't know she had in her—a cucumber cool assertion that Zeus will not deny. She's not eating his hippie chicken. She's volleying back like a pro, like a NorCal native. Like she never lived in Minnesota.

"Yeah, but you're at my birthday party, and this is my bandmate, and I don't remember inviting you." Willa leans in the door. "Hey, Pebbles, the guys are leaving." And so they do, and Aretha belts out "Chain of Fools" and Vito paws at a piece of dreadlock, left by the fridge like a follicular refugee.

THE SOUND OF BEING EATEN ALIVE

THE COOP IS EMPTY. THIS IS NOT POSSIBLE—THEY ALWAYS PUT THEMSELVES in at seven. Maybe they did, but something came in to wake them. I grab my trusty headlamp and ask Vito to bring me the chickens. He looks around, but seems bewildered. He is more concerned with staying by my side. I scramble in the needles, still in my strappy sandals, wondering where rattlesnakes sleep. It was a stifling day that has barely cooled. They'll be fine, I think. They're probably just roosting in some nearby trees. Better cover. I kind of think this means that I am overestimating a young pullet's ability to strategize, but I take some comfort in the idea that they are at least all together. Creatures that stick together are more difficult to pick off one by one. Lilybird is probably in some high branch, holding down the fort. Still, I tell Vito, "Come on buddy, find the chickens." He runs up the hill. He whines. I can't see him. Not even the reflection of his white-dipped tail. I think of bears, cougars. "Come on back, boy." I'm calling off the search.

There is no wind and it's so quiet that I think I have tinnitus. Or maybe it's just capillaries clobbering my ossicles. It's too quiet to tell.

Vito looks at me with a little disappointment, like he would prefer to finish the job of bringing in the chickens and can't understand why I won't let him. He stops at the end of the path to the door and won't come inside. I insist. Vito keeps watch at the sliding glass door while I curl up, dreams fueled by cake and beer.

My brain doesn't bother to make a sleepy narrative around the horrible screeching. No preamble, just the jolt. Vito's tail is frizzed high. I like to think he's not giving me a look that suggests *I told you so,* but I'd be wrong.

A streak of desperate poultry slashes past my ears. It is a scream, no anthropomorphizing here. It is a scream of pure chicken terror. My birds are not okay. Vito takes off in pursuit. "Stop!" I tell him, and he looks at me like I'm insane because he is a working dog goddammit and this is his job. I don't know what's chasing that chicken, but it is something with meaty murder on its mind. *Baaaaaaaaaaaaaaaaaaaaahk. Baaaaaaaaaaaaaaaaaaaa aaaaaaaaaaaaaahk.* No. Extra letters don't cut it. It stabs through interspecies boundaries. This is the last sound a creature makes. I can't hear any of the other birds. "Okay, Vito." I release him and he's off up the hill. The sound ascends, strangled, *buh-bah buh-bah*—like an airline hostess farewelling mixed with nails on a chalkboard.

Wearing only flip-flops, I crouch and stretch my eyes wide to try and see. There is a scramble toward the henhouse—predator, chicken, dog, me. I clap my hands loudly because that once worked with a bear. I'm in pursuit. The *baaAAAAAAAAAAAAAAAAAAAAAaaahk* carries long and high until it quits, ringing in my ears, reverberating in the gully. Now my pulse is definitely rattling my ossicles in a drum-and-bass remix of tinnitus. Vito makes his way back to me, his eyes saucery. Silence settles in. I calculate a lifetime of eaten chickens. But this time it's personal. I knew them fuzzy. One chicken down. It happens. I take one last look with the headlamp, but the birds are nowhere to be found. Wherever they are hiding, they know they are hiding, and they have few defenses available to them aside from remaining perfectly still. How shitty of us to have evolved them out of flight.

I go back to bed and one by one they are picked off in the night. Each one the same—the chase, the terror, and then the boomeranging echo muffled as it's swallowed by the trees. "At least leave me Lilybird, huh? At least Lilybird." It's a plea, a prayer maybe. Having not found the remaining birds, I go back to bed for the fourth time. When the next one is killed, it jolts me from my sleep, but I just pull the covers up to my ears. Vito barks at the sliding glass door. "Come, Vito," I say, and pat the bed twice. He buds up in the empty space next to me and I curl around him. The last one goes at dawn. I know it's Lilybird because the chase is agonizing. It goes on longer than any of the others. She did her best to protect her flock.

The next morning I find just a few feathers. Whatever ate them did a pretty complete job. At least they fed someone; they did what they were meant to do. Which is more than I can say for myself with any certainty. I find feathers that I am sure are Lilybird's right by the tree that she would escape Vito in. A little pile of her feathers are right below it, a sort of memorial. I put them in a baggie. There's a little gore at the tips. I will maybe ask A'Be to make a pair of earrings out of them. No. I probably won't. But I'll keep them anyway. Enough with the lessons about letting go. I want a few things to hold on to.

AUGUSTINE

TEN IS THE NUMBER OF COMPLETION

THE PUBLICIST FROM BACK IN THE DAY E-MAILS TO ASK IF I'M INTERESTED IN participating in some of the *Blair Witch* tenth anniversary celebrations, like a screening in LA. I'm enjoying hermit life, but it is getting a little claustrophobic up in this chrysalis.

The movie is like this thing I ate once at a stranger's potluck: It re-peats on me like cucumbers or chili. It seemed delicious at the time, but not now that I'm still tasting it a decade later. I thought The Great Purge and the move and, well, everything you've read about so far were going to change something about who I am. I believed I could become a different person. But a seed pretty much adheres to the fate indicated on the pack-age, with varying amounts of vitality and adaptation to conditions, unless, say, a deer cuts it off at the pass. I am still trying to figure out what's writ-ten on my particular seed pack. I am still trying to write it myself, which is turning out to be something of a fool's errand.

The publicist asks nicely and offers to pay for my gas. Okay. Done.

I enlist the help of Willa, who has never been to LA. I position it as an adventure. Then I add the part about bringing down some of the last crop for my LA-based patients and to maybe find a dispensary that would take me on so I wouldn't be so dependent on the will of Zeus. She balks at the whole transporting weed thing. "I'll vacuum pack it and put so many dryer sheets in the box we can be like *That smell, Officer? Why, we make lavender sachets!*"

"Uh-huh."

"If two people are shitting their pants, that cancels out all fear. That's just algebra, how two negatives become a positive."

Silence.

"Please? You're the single most innocent-looking person I know."

Nothing.

"I promise no detours across state lines and we can stop at a corn maze."

Silence.

"My Louise needs a Thelma."

"All right, all right, I'll go."

Since I've agreed to come for the screening, other requests have been added—would I answer a few questions for *Entertainment Weekly*? Uh, yeah, well, my where-are-they-now is a bit, um, you know. Post-veggies, post-chickens, talking about homesteading isn't exactly honest. Okay, I can say I moved to the country to do these things. I won't comment on degree of success. It's weird to talk to a reporter from inside my grow-house. *That's right. Farm. Red Russian kale. Heirloom tomatoes. Yes. Failing better. Thanks for asking.* "Are you married? Any kids?"

"Nope," I say, excessively cheerful.

"Don't you want that?" This is probably beyond the scope of a blurb in *Entertainment Weekly*.

"If it happens, that would be great."

On arrival in LA, I get pummelled by my old normal—crackling sunshine, giant billboards. I didn't realize there was no outdoor advertising in Nuggettown until just now, under the sky-sucking finger wag of all these shrill signs.

"It's weird," Willa says, watching people cross the street on their way to Runyon Canyon. "We've only been here a few minutes but I already feel fat and ugly."

My friends' house is majestic. Their subscription dinner sits atop the gatepost in an insulated bag, as it does every day. They have a nanny, gardener, pool guy, housekeeper. Their home has been prominently featured in a number of shows throughout the history of television. The initialed gate swings open . . .

". . . And poor. Yeah. Fat, ugly, and poor," Willa adds.

"I'll drive you past my old place. You'll feel much better." When I do, we won't be able to see it, as the block is cordoned off with crime scene tape. The abandoned liquor store on the corner will be just as I left it, except the roof sags more.

"How do you know these people again?" Willa asks, as we pass the Cadillac and Lexus in the drive. "I met her at a party thrown by someone I auditioned for once. Adriana was the only other smoker—she smoked Carltons like my grandmother used to. So we became friends. My mom told me later that Nanny smoked Kents. But by then we'd been friends for years and I was already her daughter's godmother. So, you know, by chance really. Same way everybody knows everybody."

We get out of the car and Adriana's dog pees all over Vito. Vito is so stunned that he doesn't even move away, even after the dog finishes. Vito just stares at me like he really hopes we're not staying here. Adriana hoses him down and he likes that even less. He and Willa are giving me the same look.

I don't know what to wear to the screening. My clothes have two main features: a permanent red dirt sheen and a slight scent of The Girls. These are impregnations no laundering can abort.

I try a shirt with jeans. I try a dress. I catch this fretting, this frenemy in the mirror. Oh yes, I remember this asshole. She was burnt to ash. You killed her and she thanked you for it. As if endings go like that, written in fluent voodoo in our own hand. I decide on the tunic and jeans.

It's been a long time since I've seen everyone, about ten years. There hasn't been much call to be in touch. Fellow actor Josh is there. He has giant bucks tattooed on his forearms. I ask if Mike is coming, to round out the trio. Mike is in New York. Couldn't make it. "You know, wife, kids," Josh says.

"Sure don't." Ha ha. Everyone is ten years older. Ten years softer, squintier, grayer. It isn't morbid though—it's gentle. There's a sparse crowd. Like really sparse. I needn't have worried about what to wear. I take a seat in the back row and sink into the thick cushy chair. Cushy. Kushy. Kush. Some things have changed.

And some haven't. Time collapses, and I remember what it felt like to shoot each scene, the things uncaptured. The oak leaves we sat on around the fire. Picking out my blue cap at the camping store. Buying marshmallows and Vienna sausage. My over-preparation for the role. I was ready to skin and eat a squirrel and had purchased a hunting knife just in case. Two guys, one girl—an ad out of a newspaper meant for young actors. When I got the role, friends warned that it sounded like a snuff film. The producer told me, "If we were gonna make a snuff film, don't you think we'd have a better cover?"

What strikes me now, from this seat, is the sweetness. There was so much earnestness and innocence from everyone involved. We all just wanted to make a movie. I mean, that sounds fun, right? I'm also struck by how funny the movie is. How ancient-looking the aesthetic. It makes me feel old in the best possible way. It makes me feel so tenderly for that girl—that little girl, she seems to me now. I am watching a movie, but I'm also seeing myself framed by the movie's premise: a girl that made a movie and then disappeared. This was a me that had her whole life in front of her and was totally unafraid to bring it. I wish I could tell her stuff. I wish I could tell her not to let anyone prevent her from enjoying the ride, and that she should never let anyone put her light under a bushel except herself, and only if she needs a nap. I would say, "Do you see how strong you are? You should. You should go to the mirror right now and see how strength is yours like blue eyes are."

By the time the confessional scene rolls around, I want to hug myself and give myself a high five all at once. I remember finding a quiet place to shoot that. I remember directing myself before I turned the camera on. *There is no doubt in your mind that you are going to die. There is no doubt in your mind that you killed Mike and Josh with your arrogance. You're a bad girl, and now you're going to die.*

I didn't think about how gross my seeping snot was going to look on a big screen. I just thought, *I'm a bad girl, and now I'm going to die.* I miss that about acting—total commitment to the moment, like a dog. I remember turning the camera off and thinking, *You did it.* Full throttle terror snot with no thought to beauty but the truth of it.

Everybody else was cashing checks and patting themselves on the back, but what's on the screen is us. Mike, Josh, and me. What we shot, what we improvised, what we made.

Isn't that just spoken like a true actress? That's what I don't miss about acting—the often narcissistic self-preservation that is the flip side of that much vulnerability.

As the houselights come up for the Q&A, it's like flipping on the fluorescent lights in a haunted house. Really? That's the movie Roger Ebert called one of the ten most influential movies of the twentieth century? Sitting on the panel, I'm looking at the largest number of new faces I've seen at one time in about a year.

When the moderator asks about what we've all been up to since *Blair Witch*, people say adrifty things like, "I've been doing quite a lot of, you know, projects."

I too have been doing quite a lot of, you know, projects. How much should I say? Hmm. If I say I'm a Northern California farmer, that pretty much says it without me incriminating myself. But then it also has an evasive air of shame around it, like what I think I'm doing is wrong. Being vocally hog-tied was one of my least favorite things about being an actress. Once, before going on *The Daily Show*, I was instructed by marketing executives to "young it down" as the things I was saying elsewhere were not appealing to the demographic likely to see the crapfest I was there to promote. Seriously? They wanted me to sound adolescent on the fucking *Daily Show*? When in doubt: Be fuckable and use small words, soundbite-sized, sweet, like Halloween candy. Keep up the tricks and there will be treats.

It's almost my turn. I write something in my head then edit a few times to make it as simple as possible. No shame. No apology. Deep breath. And then another. Here's what I've been up to in fourteen words: "I traveled the world and then I moved to the country to grow pot." Some people laugh because they think I'm joking, and then others laugh because they think I'm not. When I watch the video later, the smile on my face as I pass the mic is open and radiant. It's a facial expression of that old saw: The truth will set you free. Unless of course it lands you in jail.

ROLLING UP

WILLA, ADRIANA, CAT, AND I ARE EATING LUNCH AT VENICE BEACH. Willa is bewildered as she takes in Adriana's half-eaten burger patty sitting cold beside its abandoned bun.

"Why didn't she eat the bun?" Willa asks, as Adriana takes Cat to the beach to photograph her. We watch Cat pose. At five years old, she's already aware that she's beautiful, and that beauty is a way to be seen.

"Because carbs are the enemy," I explain.

"I don't even live in this country."

At the Venice Beach freak show we see a two-headed snake, a live dog with an extra leg, and a Feejee mermaid. The tiny dried up Feejee mermaid isn't what Cat has in mind when she thinks about becoming a mermaid. At all. It's disappointing in its reality, but it's at least reassuring in that it exists at all. Shit like that keeps hope alive.

As we walk farther, I'm handed a card for a medical marijuana dispensary. I look to the ladies, this odd assemblage of girls. "Do you mind if I pop in here for a minute?"

The place is in an alley, though the inside is cleanly Ikeaed. I present my patient ID card. They take down all my information. Because they are obligated to be a nonprofit, unlike Rite Aid, the more patients they have on the books, the bigger they can grow.

I eyeball the jar of OG Kush nugs. They aren't particularly glittery and are pretty loosely trimmed—and these are his display buds. As he's bagging up a strawberry sativa cross for me, I say, "Actually, I'm here as a vendor."

He's skeptical. We immediately drop into hippie chicken. The tumbleweed feeling settles. We eyelock the door on an imaginary side room.

"Where you grow?"

"Up north. My community is full of small-time family growers." Okay, so I'm making myself seem a little larger. Because immediately the thought flashes that if this works, then it's possible that he will come to my house to pick up my surplus and it will be beneficial to think me part of a small army. Wait. Dismiss that thought, stay in the eye hold. Breathe.

"I like your om pendant. It makes me think you might appreciate what I have to offer." I feel like a cartoon version of that character Natalie Portman played in that movie where she shaves her head. Serenity underlined by ferocity. This is what I like to think, anyway, as I say, "What any one of us grows is nicer than what's in that jar." *Nicer* is probably not the right word. I probably should have said *danker*.

"Do you have a sample?"

"No, I'm just down here scouting. For The Community. Looks like you have a busy place here." Now I'm channeling Cedara, and a beatific smile creeps onto my lips. "We're just kind of living the dream up there and The Girls show it. Pure feminine love goes in; pure feminine love comes out."

He looks solemn, reverent even. I just threw down the gauntlet of the Divine Feminine and it moves us beyond the cannabiz and onto a higher plane. This is not commerce. We are the keepers of the green flame, carriers of the vegetable torch. It's like we just did a secret handshake. The moment passes.

"How much do you pay?" I ask.

He tells me.

"Oh. I see. I couldn't bring it down here for that."

"We could pick up. For quantity. Can you arrange quantity?" In a flash I understand gambling addiction, which has always confused me. I'm hungry for higher stakes. This pounding heart.

"I'd have to discuss it with The Community, but most likely I could, yeah." I'm faltering. What the fuck am I doing here? I'm performing Cedara and some fictional bad-ass, because this is so not me, this attempt to roll like a divine G all up in his spot. When he asks my name I realize later that I should have said Madrona. What kind of OG name is Heather? That is really more of a soccer mom's name. That's a good girl's name.

"You all 215 clean?" Which means do we all have legitimate patients that we grow for and so what he would be taking is our surplus for his equally legitimate state-legal patients.

"Of course; 215, SB 420. We're all good." Senate Bill 420 is the aptly named bill that set up the prescription system. Can't say the California senate doesn't have a sense of humor. I take his card and in exchange I give him my real name, real number. I don't have one of those untraceable TracFones from the drug dealer prop box. Just a regular, wholly traceable one.

He will call me later. He will ask if I can put together a ten pack. I will nearbout shit m'pants when I Google him and his dispensary and learn they've recently been raided by the DEA. I will be tempted to throw my phone in the river and never replace it. I will get down on my knees and promise to find another line of work if I can just get safely through the year. I will find where too far is. But not today.

PATIENT DISTRIBUTIONS

I MAKE A PATIENT DELIVERY. IT'S FRIENDS OF MINE, AND AT THE STEPS OF their adorable house are some of the cacti and succulents I gave them before I moved. The plants are thriving. They never would have made it in the forest.

This couple, let's call him Cape and her Able, hung in there with the whole acting thing and now they own a house and have a beautiful daughter and guess what? A new one on the way! Congratulations! Cape is smoke-free too, in solidarity, so they didn't really need their prescriptions filled. They look awkward holding the bag. I'm pretty sure if you're used to buying eighths it looks like a shitload, but it's what they're owed as my patients. They look at Willa, a stranger in their house watching them accept this delivery. Vito steals their dog's toy. I don't like the way we look in the glare of all this normal.

"Just your friendly medicine woman, making a house call," I say, admiring a wall that's painted pretty yellow.

"You have a beautiful home," Willa says to a stuffed animal on the floor.

Able puts the turkey bag on the couch next to the dogs and we all move over to the dining room table, closer to the yellow wall and away from what I brought. My Girls. Cape pours wine for us and water for Able and we all watch their daughter on the full-color baby monitor. "That's our girl!" Cape says. "Can you believe it?"

Maybe what I'm living is not the dream, or even *a* dream. It's probably not my dream. That's the problem though—I can't tell.

THUS SPOKE THE TUTU

THERE'S A BAG OF DOG BISCUITS ON MY DOORSTEP WHEN I GET BACK FROM LA. The recipe is clipped to a note that says something like, "To Vito from Sassy, Some homemade treats for you! Let's play ball sometime soon!

Arf!" There's a paw sketched where the signature would be. Clearly a gift from Lotte up the hill, which in other circumstances would be charming. I would love to have them over for dinner. I really would. Instead, I'm wondering what time she dropped them off and if the fans were on. Six months ago this would have sent me into a tailspin, but my scrips are in order and if she called the sheriff, he would be here now. Or he'll be back later. I'm learning not to solve problems that don't exist yet. Also, I'm just kind of getting used to this.

I've decided to go to Burning Man. Everyone in The Community is going. I won't be camping with them. I still don't feel great about the whole Judah thing, and I don't think hallucinogens, high temperatures, and dust will really help that. So I'm going by myself. Just me and a tent and a bunch of homemade tutus. The only one not going is Ed, who will be everybody's designated plant sitter since he's required to stick around for legal reasons. People have rallied and provided back-dated scrips that he would have had eventually. He's already got his room back up and running. The overall consensus is *that's the price you pay sometimes*. Nobody said the dream came cheap, just that it was possible.

Burning Man is one of those things I've always been curious about, so I figure I owe it to myself to go since the drive to Black Rock City from Nuggettown isn't terrible and the sag and jiggle are nigh. I need to get to scantily clad events while the gettin's good. The loss of the veggies and the chickens makes the decision to go easier. I'm no longer a farmer with a duty to my land. I'm just a dog-owning pot grower with a sitter for both.

The new round looks scrappy. The mushroom compost that *The Bible* recommended is too heavy despite amending, maybe too salty despite leaching, maybe just wrong. There's trouble at the root, and their leaves curl under from burning. I consider transplanting them again in the soil that I was told to use. You know, the soil that worked last time. I can't tell what would be better for them, to stay in subpar soil, or to go through the stress of transplanting again, now that they're all wrapped up in trellis.

The Scouts look good with young buds puffing out, but the light I thought was going to hit them in September is here now. Which means it will be gone soon. Which means there will be little fuel for ripening.

Zeus was right about that too. On the upside, I am finally learning that I know nothing. Maybe that's all I'm learning. But maybe that's all I need to know.

You know the best part about making tutus? They are not alive. It is not a conversation that I'm having with this tulle or these silk flowers or this hot glue. Preparation is more elaborate than just costumes, since the playa which hosts Burning Man is as inhospitable as the moon and almost as vast. I need a bike. But I don't have a bike rack on my car, so I buy a tiny bike off Craigslist that will fit inside. I believe my tent will provide enough shade, and I can always just hang out in my car with all the doors open. I have twenty-five gallons of water, three cases of Clif Bars, two huge tubs of baby wipes, a case of beer, the normal camping stuff—my captain's chair, a cooler, dried fruits, sunscreen, sunglasses. And the Burning Man imperative: a new pink cowgirl hat, a bra and pantaloon set adorned with googly eyes, a purple and green daisy costume inspired by my tattoo—complete with an elaborate bamboo headdress—and my special burn night ensemble, a bright orange tutu covered in silk orchids with a reflector tape waistband and a white faux-fur top with a secret gap under my boobs for emergency fondling. This costume has a headpiece too, because why not. Burning Man is supposed to be about radical self-expression. My raddest self likes pretty.

CAMP SOLITARY CHERRY

IT'S DARK BY THE TIME I REACH THE RANGER WHO CHECKS THAT I HAVE A ticket and sufficient water and no gatecrashers under a blanket. He asks which camp I'm headed toward. "I don't have a camp. I'm here by myself. It's my first time." I'm sure I look pretty proud of myself.

He leans into my open window and sighs. "Tell the greeter that you're totally stupid and you have no idea what you're doing here." The Indian taco I ate outside Gerlach repeats on me. I bite my lip. I look more like a furloughed soccer mom than a libertine.

I do as I'm told and the greeter says, "Welcome home!" and then I ring a bell to announce my newness and make a playa angel, which is like a snow angel that doesn't melt.

I pull into the first available camp spot. It doesn't look like a camp spot, just like an empty spot at a large and quiet tailgate party. I wasn't expecting it to be so quiet or so dark. I can see the halo of the inner circle glowing in the distance, with the Man, a wooden effigy sort of thing that recalls the *Blair Witch* stickman, towering above it. I feel like I'm not there yet. I feel that a lot. It seems desolate until transportation in the form of an oversized eighties boombox drives by.

"Do you need more light?" The shadow speaks.

"Thanks." And so there is light, held by a dreaddy biker giant tattooed everywhere but his face. He's massive and in any other context I would shrink from him, woman alone. But tonight he hovers over me holding the lantern as I pitch my tent.

"Need help with that?" he asks.

"No, I've got it. Done this a million times," I say, though I have not done it a million times. Maybe a hundred. I load the tent with Tupperware totes full of tutus. His name is Lincoln.

"This your first time here?" he asks.

"Yup," I say.

"What are the odds of two people coming for the first time alone camping right next to each other?"

"This is the first place to pull in."

"True."

"Well," I say, "I guess that makes it Camp Solitary Cherry. The gathering place for solo playa virgins. Ta-da. We're a camp now!"

"Did you bring a shade structure?" he asks.

"No. You?"

"No." He looks forlorn. "Days are brutal."

"Have you been out there yet?" I gesture toward the Man's glow.

"I went a little last night."

"Is it overwhelming?"

"Kind of." His melancholy fearface reminds me gently of Harry, from *Harry and the Hendersons*. I offer him a chocolate chip Clif Bar.

"E?" He offers me a little orange tab with a squirrel pressed in it.

"Okay. Thanks." When in doubt, default to yes. Let the gifting begin.

I am allowed to push the gas pedal on a sculpture until fire whooshes out. I like this very much. We play on swings, ride on a pirate ship, watch fire dancers, drink at a vampire bar, dangle from a birdcage, wander a maze, gaze up at a giant metal couple, dance in an empty dome, sit quiet in a temple made of trash. We are mesmerized by the lit-up clothes and bicycles and take a break under an illuminated blue willow called Arbor Vitae with a message written on each leaf from the people who created it and those who just stopped by. Also there are mirrored leaves to reflect the viewer. You're part of it too now, see? We don't say much, but we stick close together. We move toward the edge of the playa to climb out of the pool and get more omniscient. We head toward Babylon, a ten-story tower constructed from steel that cost nearly a million dollars and was built in four days as a tribute to a Greek guy who helped build Las Vegas. It doesn't spit fire or anything; you interact with it by walking up the stairs, a lot like any skyscraper. It's a jutting, right-angled departure from the playa's lightmelt. Its presence here is unlikely.

After climbing the ten stories to the top of Babylon, we appreciate the quiet. My teeth begin to chatter from the E and the cold, and Lincoln drapes his heavy leather jacket over my shoulders. It almost hits my knees. Even with the E flooding my every synapse with seratonin, I don't really want to kiss him. I'm at the brink of overwhelm already. Keep diving? Just float? I'm overthinking this. At least when you're an actress and you kiss a stranger, you have a story around it to carry you. There's no story here. Just this random guy who probably figures we'll have sex before the week is up, because when it comes to radical self-expression, reckless fucking would seem to be synonymous with courage. Given our druthers, I guess, we humans aspire to be like bonobos, our happiest primate cousins who will fingerbang as soon as wave. *Be the bonobo be the bonobo be the bonobo.* Why shouldn't I be able to make out with anybody? Why shouldn't I be able to love everybody? Like I said, I'm overthinking this.

I sit up to cool my flaming brain and Lincoln pulls me down to kiss. E makes things pretty matter-of-fact, so I look him gently in the eyes and say, "I don't want to kiss you right now." Because it's true. He stretches up, revealing a tattoo that says "Beer" in gothic script across his belly.

BODY GLITTER, SPONGE BATHS, AND THE PUSSY DIALECTIC

THE NEXT DAY, CAMP SOLITARY CHERRY IS OUT AND ABOUT. LINCOLN'S bike has ape-hanger handlebars that he welded himself. A man calls to us, "Will you have my abortion?" I say sure, and he chops the head off a plastic baby with a cleaver to reveal a cherry Jell-O shot inside. "Suck it," he says, and I do.

We take a left at the stilt walker that looks a bit like Edgar Allan Poe and there's Body Glitter Camp. "You want to go in?" I ask Lincoln.

"I think I'll wait here. Watch the stuff." Despite what you might assume from his inky and be-dreadded bulk, this is a bit much for him.

Inside, people are rubbing a thick paste of glitter all over each other. I take off my pink slip dress and bring it to Lincoln. Um, yes, these are my breasts. I put it in the backpack that he's watching for me. I'm good with material trusting.

I slide on the goo that covers the bottom of the baby pool and squishes between my toes. I bend my knees to stay steady in the gush of hands and glitter. Everything is slippery. A man holds up a green squirt bottle and says, "May I?"

"Yes." I want his strange hands on me.

He passes the bottle to me, and I say, "May I?"

And he says yes too and we laugh, and more people join in. My breasts are particularly well glittered.

I've never had so many hands on me at once. Well, okay, in my mind I have here and there, but never so many actual pulsing fingers filled with so much goo. I'm a departing cruise ship, confetti launching from the deck of every pore.

I run back out to Lincoln. "Go, go, you totally gotta go!" I tell him, taking up the luggage. He hesitates. "I dare you." I hold the bags like a mom at an amusement park, if such a mom were mostly nude.

Lincoln returns with arms spread wide, the better to catch the sun. We high-five. "Camp Solitary Cherry! Woo!"

Glitter is all fun and games until you realize there are whole days left ahead of you with no running water. When we get back to camp, Lincoln asks if I want a sponge bath. Camp Solitary Cherry is right in view of the line of cars coming in, and baby wipes are not up to the job. "Okay, I say. But you first." He hands me the sponge and stands in the plastic tub with his eyes closed and his arms outstretched. The late light ignites his red glitter. Everything slows down and the wringing of the sponge gets loud. His tattoos are revealed again. He points to each one and tells the stories that they mark about his kids and ex-wives. "This is nice," I say. The sponge tickles his armpit as I hold up his arm and he laughs.

"I feel like a baby," he says. "In a good way." The playa has a way of making things basic. No sense in feeling awkward because we're bound to keep going 'til the glitter is gone.

My turn. He slows at the pink elastic border of my underwear, lingers in the space between hip and thigh. There's a lot of glitter stuck there. I don't feel like a baby, just self-conscious. *Turn.* Some people stare from their car windows as they drive in, like Camp Solitary Cherry presents *Dirty/Clean*, a performance about intimacy. *Turn*, I tell myself again, and I do. I just accept this tenderhearted moment, his care. "This is nice," I repeat.

"What should we do now?" he asks, when we're bathed and changed and back in our respective captain's chairs.

I think about it and I turn again, like I need to put the tenderness of an inappropriate man into a context I can understand. And besides, when am I ever again going to be in a situation where I get to say, "We're going to my car so you can lick my pussy."

"I thought you'd never ask."

Horizontal now, my pussy has the floor and says, *I'm not really into it.*

Me: *Come on, be the bonobo.*

Pussy: *I'm your pussy. Is that not enough?*

Me: *Why fight me on this?*

Pussy: *Because I keep the door to your core.*

Me: *What are you? My pussy or the Oracle of fucking Delphi?*

Pussy: *Don't build your house on unstable dichotomies, my dear.*

Me: *You really are dry. I don't understand who's more free, the bonobo or the dove.*

Pussy: *Free?*

Me: *Doves mate for life, monogamous. Bonobos will rub each other off as a how do you do—no big whoop—and really they seem pretty happy. Or maybe I just don't know what a dove smile looks like.*

Pussy: *If a dove tried to be a bonobo, it would not be peaceful. If a bonobo tried to be a dove, it would be hard to have hope for such a creature.*

Me: *Pussy?*

Pussy: *Yes, Heather?*

Me: *Why are you talking like Glinda the Good Witch from* The Wizard of Oz?

Pussy: *Why are you letting that man lick me?*

Me: *Well played, Pussy.*

Lincoln says, "Are you okay?"

"I don't want to do this anymore."

"Yeah, I kind of got that."

"Sorry. I've got a lot on my mind."

"Yeah. Seems like it."

"I'm an amateur when it comes to sluttery."

"It's not slutty to enjoy your body. To let someone pleasure you."

"I hope to come back a bonobo. But I'm more like a pigeon."

This is weird enough to get him out of my car. Which is good, because part of me feels like I owe him a hand job.

I come out too and we crack beers and it's not weird until a chubby guy in his early twenties from a neighboring camp comes over and asks, "Are you The Girl from *The Blair Witch Project?*"

And I say, "No, sir, I'm a woman now."

And he looks confused but says anyway, "Can I take a picture with you?"

And before I can answer, he asks Lincoln, "Can you take a picture of us?"

Which Lincoln does. Nice guy. After the picture is taken the other guy asks me what I'm up to now.

Beyond naked in a purple tutu, daisy bra, and spiral bamboo headdress, I say, "I grow pot."

He is perplexed. Can't tell if I'm lying or not. Maybe it's another playa costume. I don't clarify.

"Aren't you gonna make any more movies?"

"Nope."

"But you really made a name for yourself."

"I was born with it. No making needed." He looks at me like I'm an asshole, which is not far off. I correct. "I don't mean to sound like an asshole. Thanks for liking the movie." Now I just sound lame. I preferred sounding like an asshole, to be honest.

"Um, can I get my camera back?" he asks Lincoln. "It was nice meeting you."

"Okay. Yeah. You too."

"Where do you know him from?" Lincoln asks.

"Nowhere. He thought I was someone else."

Lincoln heads out in the morning. "Not staying for the burn?" I ask.

"Nah. I think I've had enough. Your people here today?"

The Community is due to arrive.

"I guess you could call them that."

"It was nice camping with you."

"You too. Thanks for the sausage and the sponge bath." I'm definitely blushing as I clarify sausage. "You know, from the grill."

WHITEOUT

I HEAD TOWARD CYPHERTOWN, WHERE ZEUS, CEDARA, A'BE, PEBBLES, and Judah are camping. Cedara, at least, is expecting me. My motivation to move toward something familiar is enough to get me there, at the edge of the playa, despite the inadequacy of my tiny bike. When I arrive, I ask various people if they know where Zeus and Cedara are.

"No, but can I platonically kiss you?" He is bare-chested in shorts and flip-flops and a cowboy hat.

"Sure."

He does.

"That was nice. Now can I kiss you romantically?"

"Uh-huh." My mouth just goes with it and holy shit bonobo toes hello. When I open my eyes I see Zeus laughing and shaking his head in the background.

Zeus joins the drum circle Judah is already playing in. Judah watches Zeus's hands spank the djembe so he can fill in the countertime. This prevents eye contact but in no way diminishes how much of an asstard I feel like for being here. I followed him to Nuggettown. I followed him to Cyphertown. Have I no dignity? Don't answer that.

Cedara and I go exploring. I notice again that my free expression looks a lot like everyone else's. If we could be anything, it turns out, most American women between twenty-one and thirty-five would be themselves at seven, but orphaned and with cash. Shirtcockers, men with T-shirts but no pants, pass the Geisha Lounge, where sake is dispensed from a watercooler. Beside the watercooler is a fur-lined tent. The motto of this camp is "Be your own geisha." The wind is picking up and a whiteout is beginning. Cedara wants to get back to Cyphertown. I wrap my scarf around my face and learn that all the people who said sunglasses were no substitute for goggles were correct as I attempt to pilot my midget bike while choking on dust and knees. Free sake, you're not my ally. Cedara has a normal person's bike, so I lag behind. If I lag behind ten feet, she disappears. I can't see my hand in front of my face, but instead of blackness, everything is white. I am incapable of pushing this kids' bike any farther through the soft ground. My legs are shaking. I can't see anyone and my scarf keeps falling off of my face, letting the dust pummel my eyes, nose, throat. I kneel beside my bike and can't see anyone or anything except the googly eyes on my pantaloons and the absurdity of my bike. The calla lilies on the handlebars stick their tubular tongues out at me. Cedara finds me. I'm making crymud again. "Are you okay?" she asks. I am still suffocating, even with my head so low, below my heart, where it belongs, but not low enough to escape the dust. There is no low enough to escape the dust.

People stop and ask Cedara, "Is she okay?"

"Yeah, she'll be okay," she says and they disappear again. "Just get back on your bike," she says to me.

Rangers manifest from the chalky fog. "Is she okay?" they ask Cedara, and I am glad she is my representative because she fits in here and remains at ease and surrounds me with her goddessy authority. I want to scream but if I start I'm afraid I won't be able to stop. Cedara rubs my back like a mother. She is not sure what to do. She is a controlled person, for all her openness. She doesn't make messy displays like this. "Let's go back to your car and get your stuff. You can come and stay at our camp tonight."

The storm passes, but my camp is destroyed. My tent is torn. There is dust in every single space including the ones between my eyelashes. I am stunned by my nose hairs. I pile everything into my car, which makes it nearly impossible to breathe in there. Inside the car Cedara says, "You remind me of my mother, always throwing herself off cliffs and wondering how she got broken."

The overriding feeling from Judah is *What the fuck is she doing here?* But I am way past the point where I am concerned about weirdness or that I'm insane or crashing their party. I am all of these things. I am weirdly, insanely (though by now the insanity is manifesting as catatonia) crashing their party. I want to keep sitting under their shade structure. It's made of panda paper—not really paper but plastic, black and white, deflect and absorb, yin and yang. The white side is facing the sky and the black side is turned in, resulting in the coolest shade I've sat in all week.

While I kind of nap in my captain's chair, Cedara tells Zeus what happened. That crowds gathered. That medics came. That it went on for two hours. Two hours? I don't think it did. Did it? "All by herself, out by the entrance." She is incredulous, voice full of pity.

SOMETHING LIKE A FOX

EVERYBODY CHANGES INTO THEIR BURN CLOTHES. I PUT ON THE OUTFIT with the reflector tape and the orange tutu and the orchid headdress and the white fur tube top with the slit in the middle, though I no longer anticipate any fondling emergencies. Amid their earth tones and natural fabrics it's clear that even here I've overdone it.

I wished I wasn't here even before A'Be and Pebbles woke up and dispensed the liquid acid. There is pot, obviously, and a bag of molly for finger dipping. I didn't even know that LSD came in liquid form. "It's pure," A'Be says, and who doesn't appreciate a bit of purity? It's in the kind of vial a perfume sample might come in.

Judah joins another group for the burn because I'm not supposed to be here. There isn't much space for shame since the acid has kicked in and the putting of one foot in front of the other is so full, it's all-consuming. Pushing a million molecules with each step. Breathing in the recycled air of thousands.

The Man has a spectacular fall, caused by a structural failure. He wasn't supposed to go down like that. The theme is American dream. People rush toward The Man and I'm just still and thinking *be at ease* and getting even stiller in the middle of all this flaming chaos. When I raise my chin I feel it rushing through me, like Sigourney Weaver in *Ghostbusters*, so in retrospect, the LSD had definitely kicked in by then.

When I turn back around, the group is gone. I wander. There is nowhere I need to be, nowhere I am expected, and I am tripping balls. I am disoriented, but everything is clear and perfect. I am lost, so I can't get lost. I move from the flaming center toward the quieter edges. There used to be a tourism ad campaign for Canada: "The world next door." I'm in neurochemical Canada.

Most people seem to be in groups or pairs, sitting around fires. The campfire of a bunch of goth kids seems appealing and there is an empty chair. "Can I sit in that chair?" I might have asked. I can't remember. I asked in my head, but I don't know if the words escaped me. I am out of place here in my ivory coat and orange tutu. I just stare at the fire. I remember the ranger: "You're totally stupid and you have no idea what you're doing here." After some incomprehensible passage of time I rise and thank them for letting me sit in the chair. I'm a child posing. A child who understands that posing is how she gets seen. In this ridiculous costume. I keep walking and a pirate ship passes, carrying passengers from the fringes to the center. Most of the camps are underpopulated and dark and it looks like a refugee camp when you take the light away. Maybe one year they'll just lock it up and make it an alternalife internment camp. I hope the end is a long ways off because the motion of dust and tulle and legs and boots feels so steady. But the end comes, as it does. And I'm back at Cyphertown. No one is there except Judah, who is wearing a hat that looks something like a fox and a shirt striped like Bert or Ernie. He barely acknowledges me. I sit and feel self-conscious but my body refuses to join me. It's preoccupied with rest.

I quietly chuck Molotov spitballs at him. They are of course invisible. Judah is the butterfly that made the hurricane. It takes me a minute to remember his middle name. At least the goth kids had a fire. "Where's everybody else?" I venture.

"I don't know."

"How was your burn?"

"Good."

"I almost didn't come here because I thought it would be weird."

"It's fine, but it's definitely weird."

I want to fuck him and punch him in the face, pour every sizzling thing inside me out onto that stupid fucking hat. This guy changed my life? It's hard to know which choices are irrevocable, at the time.

I want to kiss him on the forehead, then on both eyes and cheeks and ears and everywhere he took me in, hold him for a minute, rub his back. This guy changed my life. I don't want to know which choices are irrevocable, at the time.

SEPTEMBER MOURN

TOILET BABIES

THE FIRST THING I DO IS PICK UP VITO. HIS TAIL DOES THE PROPELLER OF joy when he sees me. I bend to rub behind his ears and the dense white fur under his chin that grows denser as his snout extends from puppyhood to dogness. He's growing up. In him it's obvious. "So how was it?" Ed asks. "A bunch of assholes spending a shitload of money to convince themselves there's something righteous about being a self-indulgent asshole?"

"Ask me later."

"You look kind of like your room right now. Mites ate the shit out of everything."

"Did you spray?"

"I don't think that would have made much difference."

I go to run my hand through my hair, but it gets stuck in the grease and dust. Me and mine are sucked to husk. The Girls are as astonishing in their defeat as the mites are in their triumph. Spider mites have established an entire civilization in my garage. They have built webby roads between the plants, they have created egg sac nurseries under leaves, they have spun skyscrapers around colas, established homesteads in the nooks within the buds. They themselves are nearly invisible, like humans in a satellite picture of earth. They have utterly transformed the garden. No doubt they are very proud of themselves and their chronic growth economy. Little Rockefeller mites investing nectar into hardworking entrepreneur mites. Do they marry? How do they care for their elderly? Is there some equivalent of Florida in the growroom nation?

The Girls were vulnerable and I knew it, and like with the chickens, I left anyway. I thought what I wanted mattered more because I thought I was bigger. They surge under the damage. They produce more sugar, because it's their way of shitting their pants. They sacrifice the tips and curl down the edges of leaves but keep most points of attachment intact. None of these Girls is singing her own song and telling The Community to fuck off. Well, actually, two or three of them are fighters. I wish I would have known. I would have cloned them. Turned them into mothers. That's the tough thing about cloning. Sometimes a plant vegges like a champ, but then you bloom them and they underperform. You also get some veg stragglers that rock the bloom room in a way you couldn't have guessed. Maybe it's because I'm still new at this, but I can never tell, and you can't take clones once the plants have started blooming. It's too late. They've moved on. You can't look back. I mean you can, you can go ahead and take a clone from a flowering plant, and it will probably root but then you have to wait for it to revert back to vegging and in the end, it won't be as strong. So really, for maximum thriving, you might as well not look back.

I'm seven weeks in, so there is nothing I can spray on the buds this far into blooming. Anything toxic I apply now would remain in the flowers and potentially hurt someone. There is only one thing left to do. Gas them. I have to raise the carbon dioxide level in the room to catastrophic levels. This will not harm the plants, but is supposed to eradicate the mites. Sure, it could suffocate Vito and me, but it's still warm enough to sleep outside. On the upside, CO_2 doesn't stink and is not explosive. I turn off the lights so the plants won't use any of the gas, letting it remain at murderous levels. Also, The Girls look like they could use some light rest, though I could be projecting. The Girls in the veg room, however, are my best yet. Being a growgirl means you're always about to try again, whether you're ready or not.

ARE YOU GROWING IN THAT HOUSE?

WHEN I DROP OFF MY RENT CHECK, A CLUTCH OF RASTAFARIANS FROM Wisconsin are signing a lease on a thirty-five-hundred-dollar-a-month house on ten acres.

"Don't hesitate to call about repairs," says the lady behind the desk. "We have a handyman—and he's cool."

It looks like the upcoming presidential election might make things a lot safer around here, if the new influx of economic refugees arriving daily to try their hand at the ganja trade is any indication. A price drop is coming, but nobody's talking about it yet. What we all have in common is still no plan B, made vivid by the recent economic downturn. California is still the land of speculators and pioneers. Can't go any farther west, young man.

The property manager, a swarthy guy in his late forties, beckons to me. "Hey, can I see you in my office for a minute?" A lump pops up in my throat and slides like a chicken down a boa. I take a seat in his tiny office. He shuts the door. The lump is in my chest now, headed toward my guts.

"Are you growing in that house?"

I could lie. No, I couldn't. He could come and check and I would obviously have to let him. He could let himself in. He did already when he replaced the screen, back in March. He knows. He's asking like a cat would ask a mouse if it's delicious. His black eyes are steady across the desk. I can't afford to get kicked out of that house right now, what with the condition of the garage at the moment. I would leave in the red. "Oh yeah, I had some Red Russian kale going, Rainbow chard but the deer ate it."

"That's not what I meant."

My armpits are already moist and I am grateful to my black tank top for its absorption without discoloration.

"You mean medical?" I say.

He nods.

"I've got all my paperwork."

He nods again.

Panic turns my diction pedantic: "Any alterations to the house will be imperceptible when I move out." I'm not sure I believe this. I realize I am wiping my palms on my thighs until they show up at my knees. I steady them there. Pause them. Center. Focus. Breathe. Only through your nose. No mouth breathing. Hold his gaze. Hippie chicken commences. It's on. It's how I know he's a grower too, before he asks, "What strains you got?"

"OG Kush. A little Sour D, which I'm not too crazy about."

"Yeah. Can be larfy."

"Yeah. It can."

Hippie chicken impasse. We're both good at this.

"Got any Kush clones?" he asks. And I think, *You have got to be fucking kidding.* I go ahead and breathe through my mouth again.

"How many you need?"

"How many you got?"

"I could spare a tray in a month or so."

"Sounds good."

He stands. Extends his hand across the desk. "No sense lying about it. Only adds to the stress."

"I can see that," I say, shaking his hand.

"Nothing wrong with it."

"Not morally anyway."

"Nothing wrong with it," he repeats.

THE CUMULUS WOMAN DOES NOT FIX

THE VOLUNTEER COORDINATOR FOR HOSPICE IS A CUMULUS CLOUD OF A woman with sensible shoes and a soft voice. She plays a rheumy-eyed version of hippie chicken via Sally Struthers circa 1987, two a.m.

"I'm really glad to possibly have the opportunity to give back," I tell her, because it's true and because volunteering for hospice is a way for me to pull my head out of my ass and do some good. "I'm new here and I really feel like I want to give something back." She stares at Vito. "Should I not have brought my dog?" That should have been rephrased as a statement.

"People don't usually bring their dogs," she says, leading me to her office. "You won't be able to bring him when you serve."

"Sorry. I've just gotten used to taking him everywhere." I consider becoming more devoutly agoraphobic instead of explaining that it's for reasons of this puppy that I'm here at all.

Last winter my grandfather died of cancer. It had spread from his lungs to his liver and his brain. We were estranged for most of my life, but became close when he got sick. He was Pop-Pop, Walt, or El Chiefo, depending on how ornery he felt that day. He was dying, but he still had all the piss and vinegar of the guy who smacked my mom around and cheated on Nanny. Still, we talked for hours at a time about love and electricity and alternative cures. And dying. And reincarnation. I told him he could absolutely not come back as my kid, but he could come back as my dog. I went to see him when he was in hospice, where he didn't want morphine. In our chats he told me that he wanted to know if dying was as painful as living. He didn't think it could be. I kissed his bare head, held his hand bones, massaged his curled toes, looked away when he wet himself.

"You like chocolate? I lurve chocolate." He was getting a sponge bath from a Haitian aide with skin like pure cacao. The family collectively cringed. Pop-Pop found it hilarious. The chuckles brought on a spasm of pain. His baby bird head bounced on the pillow. Cringe again. Look away again.

The Haitian man just nodded. "Old people say whatever. I'm used to it."

"So when you getting that dog?" Pop-Pop asked.

"When I move to the country."

"What was the name of that place again?"

"Nuggettown."

"That's a stupid name for a town."

"Thanks."

"When's your birthday again?"

"Saturday."

"How many more days is that?"

"Three."

"When's Christmas?"

"Three more after that."

"Got it."

He waited the three days and went ahead and died on my birthday.

Two days later, Vito was born in Nuggettown. This is the real reason I didn't want a puppy. This is why, despite his smallness, I feel protected. Volunteering at hospice is my way of returning the favor.

The cumulus woman explains the position: "Mostly our patient-care volunteers give breaks to the caregiver so they can go run errands, get groceries, take care of themselves for a few hours. Mostly you would listen as people review their life stories and maybe prepare a light meal here and there."

"I make an excellent grilled cheese."

"Do you have any experience with caregiving?"

"Oh yes. Lots," I say without adding *primarily failures*. I talk instead about the role that hospice has played in the passing of my grandma, my uncle, Pop-Pop. She asks about my support system and my self-care and I talk about my great parents, wonderful friends, hot baths, patience, meditation, equanimity. What is it they say? Something like *fake it till you make it?* Yes. A little bit of that.

"To be honest," the Cloud Woman says, "I'm a little concerned about your level of enthusiasm. End-of-life care tends to be a little less . . . exuberant."

"I see."

"Quietly respectful."

"I can totally do that. I can definitely be quietly respectful." This might not be true.

"Training begins Monday. Does that work for you?"

"Yes!" and I catch my bubbles, mete them out. "Yes. Thank you so much for giving me this opportunity to be of service." So this is what first gear feels like.

It's pretty much all retirees at the training so nobody asks me what I do. In this room, I'm a whippersnapper. We open with a guided meditation: "Press your hand into the sternum. Breathe into it. Don't try to protect your heart. Let it all come through. The complete lack of control. The fear of the unknown. Insecurity. Self-doubt. The loss of love. The loss of your mate, your parents, your children. Nothing to push away, much to let through. Feel your heart expanding into space, the pain just floating there. Fear and loss suspended in compassionate space. Now take your hands away and fold them in your lap. Feel the sensitivity in your chest as though it were a vent into your heart, and draw each breath into that warmth and love. Breathe in and out of the heart. Breathe gently into your heart."

The first speaker has on a long cotton skirt with an elastic waistband and a white blouse. In a magazine, the layout might be called "Amish Pride." She talks about listening. Repeated like a mantra is "Listen, don't fix." The speaker says how we are all mostly terrible listeners and how we need to be especially good at it to do this job well. We need to get rid of holding on to what we want to say next, get rid of judgment. "If you listen," she says, "you'll probably find there is nothing to fix. Acceptance is love. Forgiveness is love. This is at the core of listening. You'll find that listening takes care of most problems before they start."

At the end of the day, we schedule our appointments for drug testing. *Umsaywha?* Of course I don't notice that one of the ladies that presented at the training is behind me in the health food store when I say, "I'm a pot patient who needs to pass a drug test. Do you guys have that tea that I can drink?" The hospice lady just looks down at her seitan and carob.

I drink so much of the tea that I can't really leave the house. It's like an internal baptism. I pass the drug test, failing better. I am going to work with the dying, like Mother Teresa, or—yeah, that's all I got.

FRONTING

I bring my scrappy nuggets to Zeus's house.

"I don't think I'm gonna get COD on this. I'm not sure M'Onay is gonna want it. Not only is it dry-trimmed, but it's all so small. You're gonna have to front it."

There is a sad-ass turkey bag in each of our laps.

"You're lucky it still smells good," he adds.

I don't tell him about the sachet I conjured with pine needles, soil, and a tortilla, to give the scent and moisture levels in the bags a sense of legitimacy. At least the gassing of the mites was effective. Though, if you look with a dope scope there are occasional corpses amid the shake at the bottom of the bags. Hope no vegans smoke my shit.

"How'd that mushroom compost work out for you? Save you money in the end? Was what you got from *The Bible* more useful than what I was trying to tell you?"

The answers to all of these questions are in the bags.

"Are those outdoor plants gonna make it up for you?"

I hang my head.

"Not enough light?"

"Not enough light."

"At least you're learning something."

"Yeah. How to endure humiliation."

"Nah. How to have humility. You wanna tack shame onto it, make it humiliation, that's up to you. But why bother?"

"Got your Buddha pants on today."

"Better throw down wisdom, 'cause you're not gonna see much money."

"On the upside, no brick of cash anxiety this time."

"Still writing songs?"

"Not so much."

"Livin' the dream'll keep you busy." He knows.

"True dat," I say.

We don't even try to fist bump.

OKTOBERFEST

FOXES AND VULTURES

I DIDN'T KNOW ABOUT THE FOXES. LARRY DOWN THE ROAD TELLS ME WHEN I ask about the vultures.

"Went after the neighbor's chickens. He shot 'em." The vultures circle, eating the foxes that presumably ate my chickens too. Their heads are bald so they don't get dirty dipping into corpses. Vultures eat death for breakfast.

I went to the home of a hospice patient this morning. The social worker called a few hours later to say they appreciated my enthusiasm, but since the guy was dying and not planning a tea party, they decided to try someone else. Okay, the social worker didn't say that, but I got the point.

In other news, it's harvest season for the outdoor crops and the air all over Nuggettown is redolent with skunky riches. The scent flutters every prayer flag, babbles over every bamboo fence. Trimmers arrive from parts unknown. I saw one walking around town with a pair of grape scissors peeping from his shirt pocket, signaling his availability.

Over at Big Lonely, The Scouts couldn't be healthier, except they're starved for light. The light they needed landed last month, so they're leggy, larfy, and too fragile. Zeus was entirely correct, and I am nothing like Copernicus.

With all of the competition after harvest time, it won't be worth it to trim them, though what's there is organic, which is nearly impossible to achieve indoors. But outdoor weed's abundance and low overhead makes it less valuable than indoor. It gets less artificial stress, so it doesn't get so resinous. Despite the lack of bag appeal, sun-ripened, bee-nuzzled organic outdoor is what everyone looking for the cleanest medicine should be smoking.

Meanwhile, I'm trying to resuscitate my clones. There's always a time when the clones begin to root that it looks like they're dying. This is not that. They are burnt, thin, spindly. I overfed them early on and didn't flush in time. It's another result of my tendency to overdo everything—too many nutrients, too much water, too much heat, too much light. Too much, too soon. Let's see if we all can recover. Or maybe, like the hospice couple, these clones would like to try someone who has more respect for fragile things. Unfortunately for the clones, it's me or the compost heap.

So now Vito and I are sitting here in the veg room giving CO_2 CPR. *May my expiration be your inspiration* . . . It's humbling to realize my fate is in their hands. I've made many phone calls, tried various sources. No one has extra clones on hand. I have to convince these Girls to take the next step. I give each plant a gentle tug, and those that had nothing anchoring them are thrown away. Though only four show visible roots, there are more that didn't give up to the tug. There is something there, even if I can't see it yet.

On the upside, the garage is full of grace and sugar. The week four water fast I tried was definitely a risk, but one that paid off amazingly well. It might stunt them in the end a bit, but it definitely brought the resin up. They were thirsty, and when they were quenched, it turned to resinous sugar overnight. The fast was like my summer—you wilt a little like you might not make it. You look, at the very least, unwell. But just continue to put out sticky, receptive calyxes. Pollen may come, pollen may not, but you may find yourself becoming a beautiful, valuable dank-ass little nugget in the process. Why did I take a risk when everything looks so good? I'm a growgirl.

WIG NIGHT

TODAY I WENT SHOPPING FOR A HALLOWEEN COSTUME WITH WILLA AND her friend Jen. I'm going to be cherry pie. Yeah. I don't know how long I'll hold on to the spirit of recklessness that lets me think this is a good idea. Willa is going to be a black widow. I thought I was above slutty Halloween costumes, but I'll be thirty-five in December and I am going to want these pictures later. Probably sooner. We agree to wear our new wigs out tonight to the local saloon. "You've never had a wig night?" Jen is incredulous. She has wig nights all the time.

Willa gets a text, announces: "The Germans are coming."

"Who?"

"My friend Uwe."

"Uwe?"

"And his friend."

"Huh. How do you know him?"

"He was seeing a girl up here. We got dumped at the same time."

"Is that how you meet all your friends?"

When the gentlemen blow through those saloon doors I immediately notice the one wearing those glasses that are the exclusive provenance of architects and Germans. This is Uwe. A brain cowboy, all confidence and no swagger. Everything about him is solid and handsome and bright. He sees Willa and comes toward our table. We are staring at each other, not unlike when I met Vito at the pound.

"Nice to meet you," he says.

"How do you say that in German?"

"*Nett sie kennenzulernen.* Literally it means, 'Nice to learn you.'"

"I think I like that better. I think it would be nice to learn you too."

"What is your job?"

"I grow pot." He is so unperturbed that I wonder if Willa told him in advance. I wonder what else she's told him. I would turn to her and ask but I like looking at him.

"I would love to hear this when I am in my twenties. I was a total stoner. Ask Franz."

His compatriot nods and pats him on the back. I hope my wig is on straight.

"And now?"

"I do computers."

"What do you do to them?"

"It is complex. You can say I specialize in search."

"I specialize in search."

"Yes, I specialize in search."

"Me too. How long have you been here?"

"I have been in California for three years." And the way he says *Calee-forneea* is just enough like Arnold Schwarzenegger to distract me as he orders a round of shots.

"None for me," Willa says. "I'm going home." Willa has her waitressing shift the next morning. Working weekends saves her from debasement. "You're in good hands," she tells the Germans. And for me: "I knew you'd be able to entertain them."

I learn that East German girls looked like boys because we only saw the athletes who were doped by the government from puberty. I learn that he doesn't freely smile because when he was in high school, a girl had a swastika carved into her cheek and said some neo-Nazis did it. "I was head of youth government of my state and I made anti-hate crime march that was very successful. The skinheads were upset and so they come for me, for to punch off my teeth with . . ." He gestures across his fingers.

"Brass knuckles?"

"Yes. This is what you call this. And I have braces that come off six months before this. Later, this girl says she does this to make herself attention." The story comes easily, despite the syntax. Everything about him comes easily.

Among the limited media that would have been part of both our childhoods there is *The A-Team* and *The NeverEnding Story*. The drunker we get, the more we rely on singing one of these two themes to bridge the cultural gap. He has been here for three years and has only been speaking English for that long. But he knows Russian, if that helps.

I am primarily a beer and wine gal, and the new thing of the day is that I don't wear whiskey well. At all. There is a reason I'm primarily a beer and wine gal.

By closing time, I am neither elegant nor sexy nor charming nor even really ambulatory. I am a raw, wet, wig-wearing version of me that is truly unappetizing. The hill on which his friends live is neverending, like the story, like my talking.

"I just keep falling down you know and getting back up again. Here. There. Everywhere." I demonstrate involuntarily.

"Here. Let me help you." I would like to say he gives me his hand, but he gives me both, hoisting me up from under my armpits. It makes me weep. Sloppy, you are not my friend.

"I don't usually have help like that."

"Just lean on me, okay?" This makes me weep harder. It makes me weep so hard, further walking is impossible, as all my energy is devoted to the weeping.

"For real? Are you for real?" I ask.

He takes it as a rhetorical question and puts his arm around my waist.

He holds me tighter as my ankle bends off the curb. The high-heeled Victorian boots seemed just right at seven thirty, what with the wig and all. He holds me up like a surrogate skeleton. Maybe it's good to get all the preemptive scaring out of the way. Would you like to see the worst I have to offer? Now you can make an educated decision about seeing me again sometime. I think it's only fair. I flatter myself that this was a conscious decision. It was not. Oh retrospect, you little minx.

Eventually, we crest the hill. I'm flaccid and rubbery.

"You could stay here too," he says. "They have some rooms."

"I have to go home and walk my dog."

"It's two thirty in the morning."

"Then he really needs to be walked."

"I will make sure you go home okay."

"You don't have to. I can do it on my own." Feasible, but daunting.

"I know. But I would like this."

He wrangles one of the town's two cabs.

MY PLACE

As the cab's meter passes the forty-dollar mark, he says, "You live so far from town?"

"I live in the forest. So far from everything."

At my request, the cab drops us at the intersection of Kingsnake and Red Dirt Road. The fans are on and it's obvious I live alone. It's impossible to be drunk enough to forget that.

We pass the two houses and my heels aren't handling the gravel much better than the hill.

"It is still so far? I cannot see anything. I cannot see even my hand in front of my face."

"Just keep putting one foot in front of the other. There's no cliffs or anything. The worst that can happen is you walk into a tree."

"Do you have the black bears ever here?"

"They're heavy, so we'd probably hear them coming."

I can very nearly hear his follicles seize up.

Vito greets us both with helicopter tail. As he rolls onto his back between our feet, I see that Uwe has passed the Vito test. My house is a mess. The dishes in the sink could be carbon dated.

"I am also messy," he says. "I like it. It means you are real."

"Are you?"

"Yes?"

"I think so."

"I don't understand this."

"What's the German word for *sincere*?"

"*Aufrichtig.*"

"*Aufreeshteesh*. I like that. It sounds soft. Are you *aufreeshteesh*?"

"Yes."

He pulls my one remaining copy of *The Little Prince* off the bookshelf.

I tell him about my Little Prince collection and how I bought one in every country where I could find a translation. My ex took them all, which sucked because I was buying them for my kids one day. "Would you like to have kids someday?" I venture.

"Yes, I would."

"I was just wondering. Because I know I would. And I thought since I'm being kind of gross anyway I might as well throw that in. Give you the full scare."

"I am not scared."

Vito rings the bell I've hung from the door so he can let me know when he wants to go out. I grab my headlamp, though it is not the most flattering accessory, and try to get it on without mussing my wig. Uwe offers to put it on himself. We only need the one. We walk down my road and back. Uwe takes my hand. We are just the right matching heights to hold hands effortlessly. We take our time walking because it means we get to keep holding hands, and Vito is sure not complaining. He walks right between us, under where our hands hang down.

"I cannot believe you live here in this forest only yourself."

"Me either sometimes. Do you want to see my garden?"

"Okay."

I open the door, unzip the plastic.

"They are beautiful," he says, and I am explaining the various gadgets when he runs wheezing out of the garage.

"Are you okay?"

"I was afraid of this, but I was wanting to spend more time with you."

"Of what?"

"I am allergic to your plants. I was not sure how much allergic."

"Is that even possible?"

"Yes. I was heavy smoker in my twenties and now I cannot smell even it. My body has enough with it."

"Are you gonna be okay?"

"Yes. I will be fine. But you will know this is my medicine." He holds up an inhaler for me to examine. "And I will keep it in this pocket. You see this."

"Yes."

"So if I cannot breathe, you will give it to me."

"Of course. You want a Claritin or something?"

"Thank you. If you have this."

"Why don't we sit outside?"

"You're bivering," he says.

"What?" He crosses his arms and trembles.

"Oh. Shivering. Yeah. Kind of."

"Let's go inside."

"Is it okay for you to stay?"

"It is okay for me. I can stay on this couch. This is okay for you."

"Well . . ."

"This is okay."

"The bedroom is farther from the garage. It'll be safer. For your breathing."

"I will only hold you through the night. Can I hold you through the night?" It's the first question that lands softly like a question and not Teutonically like a hammer.

He repeats: "Can I hold you through the night?"

"Nobody has ever asked me that before."

"So this is okay?"

"Yes. This is more than okay. Let me just take my wig off."

We are two people who haven't had and held recently. He gives me what he has for me, and takes mine in return. Just this. Just gentle.

"What should I know about you?" I ask, because I can feel my clenched bits giving way.

"You should know I'm a workaholic."

"I love having time to myself! What do you like most about yourself?"

"My ability to solve complex problems."

"I'm full of complex problems!"

What if this is the last first time? I am hovering over him for longer than I should be because I'm thinking this. We look into each other's eyes in that way that won't always happen if we become a couple. In that way that says, *you, yes you*.

GRACE AND SUGAR

THE CLONES ARE STILL NOT THRIVING, BUT FRAGILE ROOTS EMERGE FROM the plugs, and so today is the day I pot them, veg them, trust.

The Girls in the garage are my best yet—the best I've ever seen, actually. Each gemmy nugget is flawless. As goes the grower, so go The Girls.

I have just over four more months left if I stick with the original one-year plan. That includes what's in the bloom room now plus one more round, so four rounds total. That won't be enough to save anything to be able to go anywhere else. That will leave me with pretty much nothing. Breaking a little better than even, unless something freakish and spectacular happens. I could also end up in the pounding red if something bad freakish and spectacular happens. This is not a business for the faint of heart. It is a good business, however, for teaching one to be a little less faint of heart. Liz's advice that first day was absolutely right: Worry isn't going to change a goddamned thing. Zeus was right too: Nobody makes money their first year. The crossroads looks the same from here as it did this time last year. The contrast with Uwe the overachiever isn't exactly helping either. But there was a dog today scared on the road and he needed a ride and I had the time to give it. I wasn't working, I wasn't rushing anywhere. I was only enjoying the wide open day, and so I gave the dog, a border collie named Monty, a ride home. My life is a big old aberration from the norm right now, maybe an accumulation of mistakes. Like a bird, I have no career, and really, at this point, very little ambition. And I have never been happier. The only time that slides is when I think about my future place in the world. Growing pot isn't my calling. I know it's temporary, and I still don't know what comes next. I know that I'm as unemployable as when I started, and I'm still not quite sure what that makes me. A loser? A slacker? A good-for-nothing lazybones? Maybe all of the above. Mistakes have been made into a present.

While I transplant the clones, Uwe is driving back from Palo Alto to see me. Vito and I go out to the road to meet him. He stops his Passat in the middle of the road and we hold each other for a saturatingly long time.

I bought a German dictionary yesterday. *Verwundbar* means vulnerable. *Unglaublich fantastich* means pretty fucking amazing.

When I chose Lucy in 1999, I was torn between her—a midsize four-wheel-drive—and a VW Passat sedan. At the time, I was acutely aware that I just wasn't the Passat yet. I wanted to be, but you couldn't sleep in the Passat; you couldn't live in it if shit hit the fan. Lucy's kind of sluggish, but she has not yet met terrain she couldn't handle. The Passat's ride was almost too precise, fragile. Such precision was going to need retuning all the time. The seats were kind of hard. They obligated me to sit up straight. The Passat was elegant and wouldn't wear dings well. Lucy carries them quite naturally, I think. And now here's this Passat parked in front of my house. Lucy has about 150,000 miles on her. At some point things are bound to change, whether I choose or not.

SUN AND MOON

HE'S BROUGHT VEGETABLES FROM HIS GARDEN: SUN AND MOON WATER-melons, eggplant, squash. I show him where my garden used to be, the cedar beds that now host each round's discarded soil. While he rolls out dough for a potato loaf, I present him with the chef's costume I bought for him when he said he was coming back for Halloween. I got it from the kitchen store, so it feels legit, because he's less than enthusiastic about this holiday that didn't exist in East Germany and whose journey from honor-ing the dead to costumes and candy I am hard-pressed to explain in a way that makes his face move. I pin the #1 CHERRY PIE blue ribbon from my costume to his new white jacket, fluff the hat, dust some of the flour from the counter on his face.

"This is the first time I am celebrating Halloween."

"This is the first time I've had a theme costume with somebody."

He puts the loaf into the oven and takes another puff off his inhaler.

"Are you trying to fatten me up? Like the witch in 'Hansel and Gretel'?"

"My job, it is so abstract. This opportunity to make food for you means very much to me. Yes, it does give me great pleasure to feed you." He shows me how to knead the dough.

He made three—that's right, three—meals yesterday. Starting with breakfast in bed. He's a vegetarian like Buga, but with a strong focus on carbohydrates, and I'm pretty sure I've gained five pounds in the last forty-eight hours. I've got the urge to let myself go in the way that means my reptilian brain can take a load off, like not everything requires vigilance. This letting go might also mean a muffin top, the emergence of the flab of love. Think of fairy tales—is the woman accompanying the baker ever anything less than plump? Even if Uwe turns out to be someone who doesn't have my back, he is at least someone who will fatten my back so it will be better cushioned. And he is someone who needs to be reminded to put his toes in the grass, give a dog a lift. This feels like a winning combination. If both people are willing to keep telling the tale, maybe love-at-first-sight stories can stay true.

When I get out of the shower, there's a heart drawn in the steam on the mirror.

He works outside at a card table under the now flaming maple because he can't really breathe inside my house.

We pack up our costumes and head over to Willa's. Uwe goes out to get some snacks while Willa and I get ready. Other friends join: a sailor, a man-lady with abundant chest hair. Uwe is sitting in a chair eating potato salad when I come out in my costume. He blushes. I sit in his lap. He's gone mute. I will probably always be too much. Instead of fighting it, I'm learning to live with it. I hope that loved ones will join me in this. I am glad to be cherry pie with sparkly fake eyelashes. I feel potent as my Girls. We take pictures then head to town. Trying to dance without my wig falling off is both fun and challenging, and we dance all night. Uwe and I just bounce from place to place—wherever there's music. No language box, no language at all, just bodies in space. He's a really good dancer. I have never dated a really good dancer. I have dated men who mostly sulked in the face of dance. Everybody else falls away and it's only us. I reapply flour on his cheeks from a bag I've tucked into his apron and straighten his blue ribbon. He swats me on the ass with his wooden spoon. We know to hold the space before the early kisses. That space that quakes and won't always. We know to keep dancing until everything closes. Then we dance at my house, and he just huffs on his inhaler.

In the morning, when I get out of the shower, the heart on the mirror reappears.

After he leaves, I find a sign under my pillow that reads, "Sweat dreams."

NOVEMBER IS A MONTH OF SPRING IN THE SOUTHERN HEMISPHERE

KINDA PUFFY

I ARRIVE AT CEDARA'S BIRTHDAY PARTY, WHICH BLENDS SEAMLESSLY WITH Zeus's ongoing outdoor trim: A couple of tents. Some extra cars. A buffet of foods my parents have never eaten.

The people here have been trimming in captivity for about a week now. During outdoor season, trimmers are usually required to stay until the job is done in order to keep the in-and-out to a minimum. They're generally paid by the pound rather than the hour, and there are plenty of perks to keep them placid and focused during their stay. Zeus is manning the quality-assurance table. He sends a trimmer back to her seat with an unsatisfactorily groomed cola. Turkey bags abound. Trimmers check in, weigh in, and Zeus tallies numbers in a notebook. The bag of outdoor that I've brought to show him looks pitiful beside what's on the table, like a bunch of shake. I am embarrassed to even have it in my hand. "You're not doing your outdoor any favors by showing these together," Zeus says, motioning to the indoor sample I've also brought. "Unless you're trying to give an illustration of what people want and what they don't. Do they all look like this?" He's pointing at my indoor sample, a solitary nugget twinkling inside a pesto jar.

"Yeah. They all look like that."

"For real?"

"Yeah."

"You still thinking about getting out after a year?"

I shrug. This thought hasn't butted up against a day yet.

"You can't get out now. You're just getting good. At indoor, anyway. You'll lose on your investment if you get out after a year."

He is correct.

"I can probably do something with your indoor, but I mean—" He gestures to the table, then to my Scout sack.

"It smokes great," I try, weakly.

"Why don't you make tincture with it? I don't think you've got enough crystals there for hash." Some people make hash from their trim, shake, and subpar buds. This would be a whole new process to learn, involving icy washing machines and net bags, and I'm still sticking with just one new thing a day.

Cedara wafts down from upstairs. She used to be a trimmer, but she's been promoted to pot wife. Never has the class difference been so obvious.

"Oh my goddess, look at you! Is there something you want to tell me?" she asks, but it's not clear what she means until she puts her hand on my belly. "You look kinda puffy and you're radiating mama energy like crazy." She assumes I've gotten knocked up with pot wifeesque velocity.

"Um, my new boyfriend likes to bake?"

"Oh. Well, it's very womanly and you're tall enough to wear it well, like an Amazon!"

It's true that Uwe's potato loaves are already evolving from a muffin top into a tire. A thing on which to travel for great distances, I like to think. But I probably shouldn't be changing this much, this quickly. This is the downside to going balls to the wall all the time. It makes what Cedara said to me at Burning Man feel true. "Are you still thinking about getting out after a year?" Cedara asks.

"To do what? There were more than half a million jobs lost last month. What the hell else am I gonna do?"

"Pray," she says.

"Are you pregnant already?" Scooter asks. His approach gives Cedara leave to flit away.

"No. Okay? I'm just eating too much bread. Okay? My boyfriend makes three meals a day when he's here. He loves to cook. All right?"

"You still getting out after a year?"

"I don't know. I still have nothing to put on my résumé."

"Yeah, I've got about a year left up here. Gonna save and focus on my music."

A year is one of those easy pillows. A slippery unit of limitation. The revulsion and attraction of a straight job is always there, humming its lullaby on that gray rock beside the siren's volcanic one. A question as simple as *What do you do?* leaves you justified in your urge to flee, so you stay submerged in your own small circle.

"How's the saving going so far?" I ask. It's sarcastic, but he just laughs. I don't mean to be defensive. I know why they're all asking about my one-year plan. They haven't seen anybody get out. At least not recently. This isn't just a job, it's a lifestyle. It's a set of ideas around which you justify who you are and what you do. This is what everybody in the mainstream culture does too, it's just that the set of ideas in The Community is more specific and adhered to by a smaller number of people. Because of the risk involved, the ideas form an ideology, around which The Community coheres. We/they have to believe it's good and right because it requires so much devotion, so much sacrifice. You don't test your ideas out in the larger world, because you stop participating in the larger, mainstream world. You don't get to shoot the shit with your machinist neighbor over beers, because you have firmly established yourself as a neutral nonentity to anyone who doesn't do what you do. Ideas grow feral into culture. If you saw it as a cult, The Girls would be the charismatic leader. It helps steel me to get out, thinking this way.

I sit on the couch nursing a Sierra, one of the only people here in clothes not fastened with knots. The Community has shifted. I don't know most of the people here. Then Judah shows up.

"You have to check out this idea I had for the show today," he tells me. He's so enthused that he's forgotten we're not usually this friendly with each other. He's been talking about writing the show since we met. He thought maybe we could write it together. It's the carrot he dangles in front of himself, gleaming hermetic orange. By never actually writing it, it stays pure. I understand this all too well. Now that Obama has been elected, there's a sense that things are going to change. Zeus, for example, is considering midwifery.

"I have a ton of scene ideas," Judah says and tells me one about Ed going savage and raiding people's vegetable patches at night.

"Ed as a vegetarian werewolf," I say.

"Who says *fuck* a lot."

"Huh. Have you written an episode yet?"

"I can't do that on my own."

"That's what you've always said and it's just not true." I remember when Willa said to me: *You usually only like people who need you.*

"How many scene ideas do you have now?"

"Probably hundreds."

The words *golden ghetto* cross my mind. The real challenge of this year will not be getting good, but getting out.

One certain thing: I am not getting in that hot tub tonight.

The men are inside and the women are outside talking in a circle on the deck. Judah comes out and begins massaging them one by one. Classic hot tub prelude. He begins with Lily. Lily is an audible recipient to Judah's ministrations, so audible that it stops conversation. She moans again and he says, "That's my girl."

She abruptly lifts her head and says, "I'm not your girl" and glances at me, making sure I heard. I did. He moves on to Vidalia—yes, like the onion—who sits between Lily and me. That would make me next in the circle, and I don't want him to rub my shoulders. I don't want to moan for him. I tell him with my eyes, like Vito taught me. After rubbing Vidalia halfheartedly, Judah goes back inside. To divert attention, I pull out the jar with my indoor nug in it. But only one other woman out here is a grower, and growgirls are rarely as interested in product as they are in process. The jar echoes puny, but is the pinnacle of my skills.

I don't want to be here anymore. I've been invited out of kindness, or habit, or because they're not quite sure what to do with me. I click my heels three times when no one's looking and think there's no place like home and I still don't know what I mean by that. That's just movie shit and I'm still here.

You can veg a plant for as long as you like, but flowering only lasts a limited time. When a bud is ripe it's time to harvest, trim up, move on.

"I'm going home," I tell Cedara, and when I get there I find a link Uwe has sent me to a video called *A Short Love Story in Stop Motion*. It's about a girl and a boy who meet each other and fall in a love they keep. "So this is what it feels like to have something to lose," I tell Vito, as I bawl my eyes out in the jewel box garage. How did I end up in the gap between lives again? But then I settle, sitting quietly on the table, petting Vito, amidst The Girls. I'm not between anything. I'm just ready to harvest.

JUST BEA

After meeting Willa for a beer, I'm excited to be going home. The mighty German furnace is back again. He greets me with the now customary body meld and we take Vito for a walk.

"After you are leaving, I have this iChat message from Bea," he says. She's his ex who lives here, the twenty-four-year-old who made the necklace that he carefully takes off when he showers, then carefully puts back on. The necklace that is the first thing I see when I wake up as the outside spoon. I untangle my hand from his and put it in my coat pocket. "This does not make me happy," he says, "but I want to be honest with you. She sees that I have Nuggettown in my location and she thinks that I have some new girlfriend here. She says this is because she is psychically connected to me, that she can just feel this."

I am weary of hippie manipulations. His iChat said Nuggettown— this hardly makes her Dionne fucking Warwick. I know, I know, Dionne was only the spokesperson, not a Psychic Friend herself. My hands tighten into something resembling fists. I'm probably not breathing enough. I look up at all the many stars, the many other worlds. It doesn't help.

He goes for my hand again, but I want to listen first before I relent. "She said she was sad. And I said, 'You broke up with me,' and she said, 'I know, but it still makes me sad.'"

Great. Everybody's being honest. Which means everything will hang awkwardly 'til kingdom come. I don't want to hear about his sad young ex-girlfriend. My hands are definitely fists now, but safely tucked in my pockets because I'm not sure who I'd aim them at.

He continues: "I told her, 'You are the one who wanted to see other people.'"

I briefly contemplate asking to see this iChat, instead of the continuing reenactment. I want to see the actual transcript of this reunion that happened the first time I stepped out the door without him.

"I know how you are seeing this . . ." Women dread hearing this phrase, or something like it, almost as much as men dread *We need to talk*.

I look up again and this time my clenched hands soften. "So how did you feel?" I ask, finally.

"Angry that I must to deal with this instead of doing my work so I can spend more time with you."

And maybe it was because I'd already melted those fists a little on my own, or maybe it was the *aufrichtig* and *verwundbar* permeating him, but this time when he went for my hand, I let him have it. Not in the I-slapped-him sense, but rather I let my fingers find their way between his again. "I want to be with you. No one else," he says.

"Good. Me neither."

"Was this our first fight?" he asks, because right now it's hard to tell.

"I don't know. I was okay until the part about the psychic connection." My hands again tingle with the bitchslap urge. "What I mean is yeah, I think that might have been our first fight."

"I think we do pretty good."

"I'm afraid sometimes."

"I am afraid too."

"Okay. Maybe two fears can cancel each other out and we can just be good to each other." He holds me in that enveloping way that is steady and bright. He does this all night, every night. He said that other women he was with couldn't stand it, that they wanted space. What I need is a growroom, snug and full of light.

"I'm definitely making you a new necklace."

NUGS OF LOVE

TODAY IS THE TRIUMPHANT RETURN OF UNCLE HARVEY. THIS TIME THERE won't be exquisite *Cook's Illustrated* multi-animal lasagnas. I just head over to Grocery Outlet two hours ahead of time. There's beer and Swedish Fish, Terra chips and Annie's frozen pizzas. There's a German edition of *The Little Prince* inside my mailbox.

My room is abloom with glittering riches I have not previously seen in mine or any other. They swell and sweat a little more each day. They are showgirls—brilliant and bright and flaunting it. Happy shall be the patients who smoke these loving nugs!

To step in my growroom is to step into Eden, or that place where Wonder Woman was supposed to have come from that was populated solely with very tall, very strong, very beautiful warrior women. I cry a little, but mostly because I touched my eye with a finger full of resin.

I hire Liz, her new boyfriend, Tuck, who resembles Ed a lot, and Willa. I keep it on the DL because the shit looks so good. Because the nugs are so big and dense and sugary, it will take less than half the time of the first round to trim. I don't know what brought them perfection this time. The week four water fast was an accidental discovery that seems to work wonders. Something about being brought to the wilt point really makes a Girl bounce back hard. Did the hospice training teach me to listen better? Maybe. But I know I can do everything exactly the same next time and have a different result, kind of like a couple can have two vastly different kids.

Liz and Tuck ask me about my plans for Thanksgiving and I tell them I'm staying home because I can't afford to leave. Willa just looks at me and resists shaking her head because we're going to the same dinner at a friend's house. I don't want to lie to Liz, but I don't know shit about her boyfriend or who he knows, who he talks to. Paranoid? Cautious. Or, if you prefer—security-conscious.

Tuck examines my hollow stems. "Shit," he says. "You got every last bit of juice into these buds." He shakes his head as if to spread mad props and holds a bud up to the light while talking about endocannabinoids: "You have any idea how many CB1 receptors there are in your brain? They are fucking everywhere, man. Every part. You eat fish or take some flax seed oil like those omega threes and sixes? All that shit hits up those same parts of your brain as weed does. Your body makes its own kind of cannabis to make you feel good, to forget stuff that made you feel shitty in the past. Helps you put the past behind you. That was in *Scientific American*, man. Swear to God. How can you make illegal something that your brain makes all by itself? So fucking stupid, man. Anyway, that's part of why it's good medicine for anxiety, cause it makes you not react to things that scared you before. Keeps you rolling with what is, you know?" This cracks us up because we're all succumbing to the transdermal finger stone that makes a trim scene giddy.

"Do you think the brain made those because people smoked, or did we have them already and that's why we started smoking?" I ask.

"Look at these plants," he says. "They are some powerful shit. If you ask me, they did it. Like you know the things that make energy in your cells? They used to be a separate thing, like they don't share your DNA actually? Think about all the things inside you. Hella other beings. Like your guts? Fuck. Billions of bacterias and all kinds of shit. You are not just you, dude. You are never just you. But these plants don't need us nearly as much as we need them. We're just like, some little bird that shits out a seed. That's pretty much what we are to them."

After everyone leaves, and I sit with Vito in the bathroom among all those sugared flowers, I'm grateful that this little bird has a very full belly.

PALO ALTO

Uwe made himself scarce for the trim. He comes back by the weekend, but is losing his shit allergically with the cut Girls curing. "You are in between rounds," Uwe says. "This would be a great time to come and see my place."

"And just leave all that in the bathroom?"

"We can go in my car and I will bring you back. If your car is here, anybody that will come to take this will think you are here."

I appreciate this indulgence of my paranoia. We load Vito into the car and go to his place.

On the way, he wants to take me to lunch at this Indian place he knows in Berkeley. We take the exit I once took with Judah to finish the road-head I'd started when a minivan pulled up. I am glad when we drive past that particular restaurant. But the one we're going to is closed so we head back. "I had a feeling we'd end up here," I say, but don't explain. The all-you-can-eat buffet is a dollar more now. I am happy that Uwe and I are eating together at this particular Indian restaurant.

When we arrive at Uwe's house, the first thing Vito does is take a shit on the carpet. I take off my shoes and wait—is that Camembert? It is not. It is my shoes. We are not quite suited to civilization, Vito and I.

Uwe shows me his backyard food garden. I ask if it was planted with Bea, a student of agriculture. He's offended. "I did this myself. She did not help me. This is my garden."

"So you did it to impress her?"

"I did it because I want to eat food I growed myself. It is not a show. It is a garden."

"Touché. Sorry."

"It's okay. It's just you."

"That kind of makes it worse."

"I like that you're not so sweet," he says.

I can tell he means this as a compliment. It's hard to be more than in-termittently at ease with being loved.

DECEMBRRR

FIRE AND ICE

Vito and I just had another conversation:
  Mr. V: [Rings bell]
  Me: No.
  Mr. V: [Rings bell]
  Me: No.
  1, 2, 3, 4, 5 . . .
  Mr. V: [Rings bell louder and longer]
  Me: [Out of the chair and opening the door]

Vito pops out for a second, as if he just rang it to prove he could get me to open the door, and to prove to himself that the super-fantastic snow is still there. He's never experienced it before, so he likes to check periodically to make sure it still exists. Once he is convinced again, he comes back in, drinks some water, lies down, drops head to paws, and sighs.

Willa calls to see if I want to be evacuated before I get completely snowed in. I don't. "You might not be able to get out tomorrow if it keeps up," she says.

"I know. It's okay."

Solitude is solid food. Until Bone Lonesome rears its head and you're all like, um, who's got a hand? 'Cuz I can totally hold it! Until compromise—that filthy bitch—steps in and you can't get your own shit done because of laundry. I don't tell her this, because I'm feeling a little word averse. The spoken kind, anyway. The snow is making everything quietish.

Uwe's Mac Mini is on the mantel, where my candles used to be. His dirty clothes are on the office floor, to be washed and folded. My red velvet chaise longue has been shifted to accommodate the card table he works on. I catch the bile in the back of my throat and pick up the blue T-shirt with the dreamship on it off the floor and put it on. It smells like him, a soothing merge, though possibly unhygienic.

Sun touches the deck from two to two fifteen. I stand in it. I don't want it to pass unnoticed.

Vito and I walk to the mailbox. It qualifies as an event. There's nothing in it, but it still qualifies as an event. I check for Buga. The whole world is quiet as him today. He should be able to survive in these conditions, but I don't know if he can go it alone. Russian tortoises usually hibernate in groups, in a sprawling underground development. I think about the time he disappeared at Judah's and came back with a tan. That's right. A tan.

I miss him. I grieve him, actually. This soft day fills and empties without any fiery gestures on my part. I want the changes that are coming, but I also want to acknowledge the loss. My life here has been a good one, and yeah, I'm scared shitless about how the hell I'm going to make a living. But I want to know my neighbors, I want to make something that I can share widely. I don't want to bring harm to Uwe. I don't want to be a good liar.

The other great thing about winter and snow, aside from cozy fires, ruddy cheeks, snow angels, lower air-conditioning costs for The Girls, and the fact that the most dangerous animals are hibernating, is that I am unlikely to be robbed in the snow. These are subpar conditions for a getaway car, or a cop car. The release of this anxiety makes me realize its chronic low-grade din; it reverberates a ting-tang aftertaste like a clapper that just stopped flinging an alarm.

I'm grateful to The Girls for this experience of winter. When my body is tired, I rest. When my body is hungry, I eat. For my parents, this isn't possible, as it isn't for most people. I don't have words for this beyond *that sucks*. I don't have to try to dig my car out. I don't have to scrape the windshield and slosh to work through salty gray slush. I don't have to do these things today. I will at some point. But not today. It's weird to feel honored by what shouldn't be a privilege but so is.

The new Girls are not in the garage yet. They're still in the veg room. They're from the clones that struggled, but they're snapping out of it.

I'm making Uwe a new necklace and writing him a song for Christmas. *When you walked through those saloon doors, my jaw dropped right down to the floor. Behind those sexy German glasses was the man to kick all other's asses . . .* It comes while I'm stringing the beads. I add blue and green beads amid the brown ones because he reminds me of water. Water feels good after all that fire.

I have grown really adept at doing nothing.

I love this dark cocoon.

Even the snow has stopped falling.

Blow out the candles.

Turn out the lights.

I put *The Little Prince* under my pillow. Both of them: German and English, side by side.

Vito once again rings the bell.

"Hey, don't be a dick," I yell to him. "It's dreamtime."

TENDER ED

ED CALLS TO TELL ME THAT NOT ONLY WILL HE BE LATE, BUT, "I HAVE something important I have to talk to you about." That's never good. So now I am sitting here figuring there's some glitch in the plan to have him babysit The Girls while I go home for Christmas. It's enough of a risk as it is, seeing as he's indisputably on the sheriff's radar. When he finally pulls up, I go outside.

"What's going on? What's the important thing?" Vito and Jezebel frolic like the siblings they are.

"I think I might have somebody to take stuff down to LA, but they're gonna need me to put together quantity. Can I count on you?"

"Zeus said he's got me covered this time, but for the next one, yeah. You know this person?"

"Friend of a friend."

"What else?" I ask, because that's not enough. Which is why the whole Guy-from-Venice thing fell through. There are too many stories of medicine "lost" in transit. Transportation is the grayest area in terms of the law, and so there's still black market–level risk involved. Zeus's position in The Community comes from having reliable, legal connections who have all their ducks in a row.

"Probably won't work out. Probably end up begging fucking Zeus again."

"How's the court stuff coming?"

"Probation fucking bullshit. They took those postdated scrips, but forced me to plead guilty anyway or they would just make shit harder on me."

"You know they have no case if you've got those scrips, right?"

"You know I have no money to pay a lawyer, right?"

"Right."

"Probably won't see you much anymore, huh?"

"I don't know. I don't know what I'm doing yet."

"You say that, but you know."

"Glad you're so sure for me."

"You were never gonna be here long. You got possibilities. You should get out while you can. Before you get too used to it."

"I don't know how you get used to it."

"Hope. Same way a black guy becomes president."

"American dream, bitches."

"Choking on the fumes is more like it," he says.

We go inside so I can show him where I've left instructions about The Girls.

"I'm gonna just veg them in the flower room until I get back because they could use a little vigor," I say. "That should make it easier too."

"Jesus Christ, your nute list reads like *War and Peace*. Those breakers any more stable?"

"No. But the AC probably won't come on much, so there's that. What's the latest on the crepe cart?"

"Still looking into it. I want one with a double surface, but you can only get those in France."

"Why don't you just buy two singles and rig something?"

"I want the real thing, like they have in France." His tone is final.

"Thanks for watching Vito too."

"Jezzie'll be happy to have him. I think she's bored with me."

"Not easy keeping the ladies happy."

"You don't have to tell me."

"So, same day rate for the week?"

His head holds at the bottom of the nod. "Same."

HOME FOR THE HOLIDAYS

AT THE AIRPORT, MY PARENTS HUG MY BETTER-INSULATED BONES AND LIKE Uwe already.

"He's fattening you up," my mom says.

"Yes. He is."

"It's good. You're softer," my dad adds.

I am.

We arrive at their new condo, which is in a wooded area. "We really liked your place," they tell me. Their new condo is a partial replica of the house I grew up in, but in a location that recalls my current one. I've become a bright absence in my family. It makes it convenient for me to forget my effects. While I've been throwing myself off cliffs, or rather, having adventures, my family has continued. Everyone in my family but me has childhood friendships intact. I may have been on the cover of *Newsweek* at twenty-five, but who's that for? I'm largely seen as someone who cares about no one but herself, because I largely have been.

Under the framed cover of *Newsweek* autographed by me is a bookshelf that houses Taschen's *Movies of the 90s*. I know there is only one reason my father would buy this book, and so I turn to the index to find *The Blair Witch Project*. Next to a snot-dripping third of my face it says: "They neither look nor act like future stars, but more like we would imagine ordinary film students: they are not particularly attractive, they're not necessarily very nice, and they're ultimately a bit nerdy." Apt, Malte Hagener, lecturer in film history at Amsterdam University, who lives in Hamburg and Berlin, apt.

I was thirty-five by the time my parents picked me up from the airport. I became that alone. It's not worth mentioning really. It's just counting. People say that thirty-five begins the body's decline, the slide into pucker-town. What was once plump, puckers and folds. This invisible threshold is cushioned with supermarket birthday sponge cake. The frosting is gritty and oversweet, like it's trying too hard.

My parents say, like they've previously discussed it, "Please don't talk about work in front of anyone at the party, okay?" *Work*, they're calling it now.

"Well, what should I say? Surely you've told people something." Uh-huh. That I have a farm. Later, when I decide to write this book, my dad will tell people that I moved to Nuggettown as an investigative re-porter, which I will consider endearing. He's finding a version he's proud of. Me too.

SANTA DROPS SOME FRANKLINS

My family has a Christmas Eve party every year. It's always fun, and it's pretty much the only time I see those cousins related by both blood and friendship. There's lots to do to get ready for the party. I'll help my dad with his answers for Holiday Jeopardy, but I also have to shop for gifts. I want to get everybody gifts too big to bring on the plane. It's my version of worth it.

"What do you guys need?"

"We don't need anything. We're just happy that you're safe."

"What do you want then?"

"A flat screen," my dad says. "HD."

So my mom and I drive to Best Buy while my dad picks up the hoagie trays from Slack's. Neither of us knows anything about TVs, but I don't think it matters because they're all so big and so clear that it's really splitting hairs.

"Do you want our product protection plan? For a year it covers—"

"No."

"But you would have—"

"No."

"Debit or credit?"

"Cash."

"Um, okay."

As I throw down a stack of Franklins (travel light!), my mom looks around the cavernous store like she's just walked the dog without poop bags. We don't get the biggest and most expensive, because blowing it up is how you call attention to yourself. I know that much, at least, though I'm not sure this knowledge means anything here. When I had the timing belt on my car replaced and paid with cash, the guy at the auto shop said, "What are you, some kind of drug dealer?" And we laughed because obviously I was just a nice lady who—what? Doesn't have a bank account? Sleeps on a mattress full of twenties like it's 1899 and she's just off the boat from Palermo? I explained that I was conducting an experiment in onavorism, beyond organic, beyond local, to find out if a former city girl could live for a year on cash and seeds alone. Apparently, she cannot.

"Oh, okay," he said, like it wiped his eyes of badness. Words are good like that.

Not until you start paying with cash do you realize that nobody makes a purchase of more than five hundred dollars with it unless they're part of an illicit economy. The cashier watches me count it out. Santa, I assume, either makes his own shit or pays cash, like me. "I'm part of the Santa economy," I explain, with no small amount of swagger. My garage and I are currently in different jurisdictions, and Obama's election has given me some unwarranted confidence. I'm rolling like a rough approximation of a G.

HOLIDAY JEOPARDY

THE DONAHUE CHRISTMAS EVE PARTY IS ONE THING IN MY LIFE THAT SUGgests continuity. Guests arrive, mostly aunts and uncles by blood and long friendship. Friends of my brother and sister come, many with families now. I mostly resist showing pictures of Vito. I get that it's not the same.

I can tell who my mom has told everything to because they don't ask any questions about what clearly has been a massive change in my life. Aunt

Chachi, my mom's friend from childhood, says, "I hear you got a farm up there. I would never in a million years have pegged you for a farmer."

"Yeah, well—I was really ready for a change." I am guessing that my mom has told her around seventy-five percent truth from the way she doesn't ask any follow-up questions, not because she's not curious but because she knows she's not supposed to.

"I can't even imagine what you'll be up to next year," Aunt Chachi says, and holds her glass to mine. This is the advantage of having done unexpected things most of my life. Taking up flamenco? Uh-huh. Backpacking through West Africa for three months? Okay then. Hitchhiking through the Balkans after shooting a crap movie in Bulgaria and ending up at the Trumpet Festival in Guča? Don't mind if I do. And now you're a farmer? My unsettled oddness used to be tempered with *Ah well, you've got your whole life ahead of you*. But nobody says that anymore.

Very nearly everybody I grew up with is here. It's one of the reasons I hate seeing that *Newsweek* cover on the wall. It feels weird for my parents to have an autographed picture of me.

Dad continues to tell people proudly that I bought them the TV for Christmas, somehow traded for tomatoes. I can tell he hasn't really thought it through. Evidently a heritable trait. I pull him aside. "I would need some serious acreage to grow that many tomatoes."

"Right. Yeah. I see what you're saying."

"I could just be honest."

He looks at me like I suggested serving shit pâté on toast. I understand why my parents don't want me to talk about it. I understand, but I'm not ashamed. The Girls gave me some breathing room when I was suffocating. They gave me solitude, a cozy chrysalis to become in. They gave Santa that stack of Franklins to throw down at Best Buy.

My uncle Bob says, "So we hear you're growing some heirloom tomatoes up there in the mountains of Northern California."

"Yeah, organic. From seed."

"How high are you?"

"Um, just over two thousand feet."

"Uh-huh," he says, like that's not what he meant. "Didn't know

Northern California was known for its tomatoes," he says, with a wink and a twinge of *bwah-ha-ha*. I don't know what he's been told and what he only suspects thanks to good old logic, but I am really, really trying to respect my parents' wishes.

"Really?" I say. "Maybe it's because you have all those Jersey tomatoes here. I guess you guys don't get much California produce."

"Not enough, my dear, not nearly enough." And he pats me on the shoulder, muffles a guffaw, grabs another beer.

My dad dresses up in a Santa suit that Aunt Chachi brought over and plays Bad Santa, doing bawdy comedy for the grown-ups while handing out presents to the kids. He is completely different than when he visited Nuggettown. Here, with old friends, in their cozy new condo, he's in his element, brighter than a thouie. Mom shakes her booty with the high school friends she used to hang with at Dunkin' Donuts on Sixty-ninth Street. Their dog Meeko is eating cheese from the appetizer trays. My sister is newly in love and has wonderful friends around her. My brother has just announced his engagement to his longtime awesome girlfriend. After that, he tells the story of when they came to visit me at Judah's and there was a hippie jam session with everybody dancing around my theremin, making music with their motion. He demonstrates, "Like those air dolls at a car dealership," and everybody laughs.

Dad brings out his guitar and we have a singalong, the usual Christmas carols as well as all-occasion Donahue family classics like "Sarah," about a woman who works in a tailor shop, where all day long she "tucks and fits." In an earlier verse, she works in a shoe shine shop, where she "shines and spits." I loved singing this song as a kid. It's been in Dad's repertoire for decades.

After the singalong we move into Christmas Jeopardy. My dad has written most of it. I helped where I could, but this is really his deal. The board is wrapped like a gift with a string of Christmas lights around it. There are rows of index cards to show the categories and point values. He's made red and green Jell-O shots as prizes, though he himself doesn't drink, because his father sure did. One of the categories is "Three of a Kind," which has answers like, "A jolly elf named Kris, a potato chip in a can, and the sensation of peeing down your leg on a winter's night." To which one of my brother's friends answered, while dandling a daughter on his knee, "What is a Kringle, a Pringle, and a tingle?"

We throw down 'til the cops come. Seriously. The neighbors actually called the cops on my parents' party. My dad could not be prouder. From now on every year we'll say, "Remember when the cops came?"

UWE'S NEW GIRLFRIEND IS YOUNGER THAN ME

AS THE LAST OF THE GUESTS LEAVE, UWE CALLS WITH SKYPE. HE'S AT HIS parents' house in Germany, where it's already Christmas morning. He seems foreign and abstract through the computer screen. I can't smell him. He's an occasionally coherent bundle of pixels. I repeat myself, speak slowly, and keep my words small. It's a big adjustment after being enmeshed in the livelong tribe of mile-a-minute talkers all night. He says I also have an accent now. I sound like where I'm from for a minute. He got my present, the illustrated song. He says he loves it. He wants me to sing it for him and he wants to make sure nobody is in the room on his end—he would not want his mom to hear such lines as *We had a shot, then another. Breakfast in bed. I called my mother* . . . I open the box he's sent ahead and I love it. It's *The Little Prince* translated into ten different German dialects and a standard German version in Braille. He's giving me back what I lost. I love it and I tell him so.

He has his phone in front of him and the screen is still lit. It has a picture of me on the home screen that wasn't there when he left. In it, I'm twenty-seven and professionally decorated and presented at the premiere of *Taken*. "Is that who you're telling them your new girlfriend is?"

"I got it from the Internet," he says.

"I wish you had one of time we've spent together. You know—recently."

"This is you."

"Yeah, ten years ago."

"You are still so beautiful."

"But not quite so envy-making back on the block."

"I do not understand you."

With the families around and the inadequate connection and the raging accents freshened by time on home turf, I have this feeling of *Who is this person?* The same kind of thing happened with Judah. I find this happens with most of my relationships at one point or another, even with my family. Sometimes you just look at someone and get shocked by their otherness. The tweak into a quick chasm.

"How about one from our first day together when we went to the ladybug tree at the river?" I offer.

"I love this one." It's hard to let go of the past these days when some other version of you is just a click away. Harder still to be seen for what you're becoming when your past looms so large.

"That one doesn't exist. That one is a figment of light and pigment and extra-fine cloth. A premiere is like Halloween. Why not a picture of real Halloween?" He diverts the question by taking his laptop to the living room to introduce me to his family. Both families do some awkward nodding and waving. His mother is a soft-spoken woman who speaks a little English. She actually makes German sound gentle and full of swishy sounds like grass skirts make. His father is more reticent. He has a niece who shrieks at the top of her lungs. His sister is my age, which is three and a half years older than Uwe. She is blonde and blue-eyed and looks nothing at all like him.

I muster a few words I've been learning. *Nice to learn you. Merry Christmas. Thank you for to make this nice boy. Happy New Year. I am happy yes to make more German words.* The whole *Blair Witch* thing comes in handy as I don't have to explain to Uwe's parents what my job is. Between the language barrier and my past, I'm spared the classic question *What do you do?* I wonder if he's told them the story I gave my neighbors about savings and solitude.

He returns to a private room and says, "I have some news."

"Good or bad."

"We will find out."

He pauses. Not quite dramatically, but importantly. "The company who rents the house I live at will be being sold and they will no more need the house."

"You have to move?"

"Yes, and so I am thinking it is possible to move to San Francisco. Or maybe to Nuggettown. You will think about if you will like this."

"Let's talk about this in person when we're back, okay?"

"Okay, honey. I will help Mutsch make the knudel now."

He hasn't called me honey before.

"Okay, babe, I'm going to go to sleep now."

I haven't called him babe before.

"I am not a baby."

"Okay, Uwe. Have fun with your family."

"Sweet dreams," he says.

My parents are already asleep on the couch. Under the shared blanket they look like a chenilled set of Siamese twins. They snore in perfect counter-time.

JANUARY MEANS
CAMELLIAS IN JAPAN

ABUNDANCE CAN BE A PAIN IN THE ASS

VITO'S PURE JOY WHEN WE ARE REUNITED IS SOMETHING I AM HAPPY I CAN rely on. The Girls, however, are expressing some abandonment issues. I return from Pennsylvania to one hundred percent humidity and choking fecundity. I need to prune them back and get a dehumidifier in here stat. They're vigorous, but there's something a little off about them. Ed thinks it's because they were being vegged under bloom lamps.

"Maybe they've been in between too long," I suggest, though outdoor plants that run the full season veg for months.

"Okay, now you're just talking about you," he says.

They've finished stretching and the only thing left to do is bloom. I'll just have to raise the lights and hope for the best. Some buds will get more light, some will get less. This round is clearly about compromise.

I pay Ed, thank him, and start to cut. The humidity brings danger of mildew and rot, so I'm a little overeager. I'm hoping less foliage will help dry the room out. I cut the bottom third like I usually do, but then I try to shape them, give them some breathing room between branches, try to find some way back to four main colas. Cut too little and they choke on each other. Light can't get through and I'll have a bunch of larfy mini-nugs. Cut too much and you've crossed a sort of Rubicon where there will just be loss when it comes to the final yield. There's a fine line, and I can't always tell where it's at.

The volunteer coordinator from hospice calls to tell me she might have a patient for me. "How would you be with a dying vigil?"

"I'd welcome it." There's not really much talking that happens in dying vigils, so I won't have to moderate my talking, I can just sit there quietly and hold someone's hand.

"Are you sure?"

"Yes."

"We don't have a face sheet on the patient. She was referred by the nursing home when they took her feeding tube out. We've been trying to get in touch with the family but at the moment we don't know anything about her but her name. And she's aphasic, so she can't speak. So you know, just hold her hand and read to her from the Bible. Do you have a Bible?"

The Bible I have will perhaps not be appropriate.

COULD BE NEWSY

IN A FEW MORE DAYS I WILL HAVE TO DECIDE IF THE NEW CLONES ARE GOING into the veg room or to someone else. They're doing beautifully, my best ever. I wonder if this is some kind of sign that I should renew the lease and keep going. I suck at reading signs subtler than red octagons. I have never had so many clones. There's not enough room for all of them on the heat mat. And it doesn't seem to matter—the ones on the mat aren't rooting significantly faster than the ones that are not. Things happen when it's time. The more I do this, the more I see how little is up to me. I just show up, pay attention, pour the nutes, wave the watering wand. I think acknowledging this means I'm learning something.

The amount of greenage in the house right now is beyond my comfort zone. By definition, a plant has roots. Before it has roots, it's not a plant and shouldn't be counted against the total allowance. Not that I ever want to have the *Officer, that's a twig, sir, not a plant* debate. It's that kind of thing got my ass kicked in middle school. So I gather up the firmly rooted overflow and take a tray into the management office.

The manager takes the domed tray out of the bag. "Can I give you anything for these?" he asks.

"Good juju?"

"Yeah. I actually can't."

"Um. Okay."

"The owners of your house called."

I wish the tray wasn't sitting on the desk between us, looking all abundant like that. "They don't want to extend your lease. They want to move back in on March first. The husband got transferred again, though they're probably going to sell it. Probably be a short sale. You interested?"

"I don't have however much money they're asking, I'm sure."

"They'd like to send in an appraiser. A handyman. Some friends."

A familiar tin can tang singes the back of my throat. "My Girls are only four weeks in. They can't bring people by—?"

"Cut down, let this round go? They have to give you twenty-four hours' notice and they haven't been specific yet. Just that they want to get in soon. Can you rent a van or something? Put the plants in there and park it somewhere?" This is a fairly common practice in these situations.

"What do I do with the equipment?"

"Nothing anybody can say about equipment."

"There's a complete growroom inside their garage. With drywall, doors, its own ceiling. People don't do that for strawberries and lettuce."

"Nothing anybody can say about equipment. Look, technically, legally, you're in possession of the property, so they need your permission to be on the grounds. But you could find them calling the sheriff to settle a dispute like that."

"I have my scrips."

"All in-county?"

"No." To further confuse the medical marijuana laws, there is a seemingly unconstitutional local addition that says each co-op can only have one out-of-county prescription. I have more than one out-of-county yet in-state prescription. "Any other options?"

"Well, if they're smart, they'll go to great lengths to avoid knowing. If they suspect you're growing, and I don't see why they wouldn't—I mean that place is perfect for it—they probably won't show up themselves, which is probably why they're sending friends in for the inspection. If they know for sure that you're growing there—that's how they could get their house seized if you had trouble."

It would be embarrassing to throw up in his wastebasket, so I think of water fountains. Cool, refreshing, soothing, but not vivid enough to drown out the ninjaesque gentlemen with guns and shields that are now raiding my head. "You're so small you shouldn't need to worry. Unless somebody's interested in somebody you know. Or, you know, that whole Girl from *The Blair Witch Project* thing. Could be newsy."

NOTEBOOK NINE

FROM *INTOXICATION* BY RONALD K. SIEGEL, PH.D. (PAGE 149): "AND CAP-tive iguanas act as marijuana 'clocks' for Mexican Indians. The iguana is placed in the center of a circle of smokers. When it falls down under the influence, the participants know it is time to stop." I could use such an iguana.

Maybe terror is just another way of saying I don't have a well-organized to-do list. Maybe anxiety is just a superpower surge of energy for you to battle whatever's scaring the shit out of you until the fear is vanquished. If you don't use that energy for the battle, it will eat you alive. It helps me to think about it this way. Otherwise I think about spontaneous combustion. I can always trim. There's always trim work somewhere. But I am not a great trimmer.

My breathing is shallow and I'm pacing a lot, to no avail. The pacing doesn't help; must direct that energy toward completing the task at hand instead of succumbing to paralysis. What is the task at hand? I still have no career. I have a series of projects. Who makes it to thirty-five without a career? Birds, most dogs, the majority of monkeys, and a large percentage of trees. I see the ninth notebook I've filled over the past year lounging expectantly on the kitchen counter. The only thing I have done without fail throughout my life is write. I could write about trying to become a country girl and just leave the pot part out. Though people tend not to enjoy books about abject failure.

I peruse Craigslist and more and more houses are now specifically saying "no 215" right in the ad. The tide of the pot economy is turning. The tide of the entire economy is turning. Growing pot is getting safer as every other economic option grows more tenuous. More people will have nowhere to turn. More people will get in. Prices will drop. If legalization happens, prices will drop further and mom-and-pops won't be able to keep up with the corporations that will be able to grow on the kind of land-devouring scale that only corporations can. Then it will be up to the patient, the consumer. But who can afford to pay more just to subsidize a scrap of the American dream? Then again, who can afford not to?

Thanks to Uwe I have an invitation to a different dance, but what kind of sorry-ass excuse for an independent woman does that make me? It's because of some dude I met by chance that I got into this, and it's because of some dude I met by chance that I'll stop? That's one way of looking at it. Also: I keep following my heart. An organ known for sloppiness and staining. Also: steadiness and reliability. And really, is any of this less chancy than the particular sperm that made me winning the cervical marathon on that particular night? I'm chance's daughter as much as Jim and Joan's.

As I continue clicking, there's a house that I fall in love with. It's painted insane pastels—peach and lavender—and the inside is green and pink and the bathrooms evoke macaroni and cheese. It has a sunset view with a fenced garden and a mature little orchard. I send Uwe the link. He calls me immediately. "I'm coming up tomorrow. You will look at this with me?" There's a time to make choices, and there are times to let go and be led. It's possible I'm learning the difference. Or I'm tired.

SURRENDER DOROTHY, PART ONE

MY GRANDFATHER WAS GREATLY DIMINISHED BY THE TIME HE GOT TO hospice. He was days from dying when I saw him last, but not even that could prepare me for Dorothy. She looks like a person one-third her original size, as though her body didn't contract around her, but wilted. Her skin doesn't seem to fit. Wispy hair is spread out on the pillow. There's no movement to register that I've sat beside her bed. I feel like an intruder. I feel like I have no business being here. I feel like if she has family somewhere I would like to write them an angry letter.

The Darth Vaderish drone of her roommate's ventilator is so loud that I can't tell if Dorothy's breathing. Her chest doesn't appear to be moving. I take her hand and try to feel for a pulse on her wrist. I can't feel anything. Or there is something, irregular and faint, and then there isn't. My hand hovers over her nose and mouth in a gesture that strikes me as invasive, inappropriate, but I very much want to feel her breathing. I don't. "Dorothy?" I whisper, close to her ear. Nothing. I rub my hands together and hold her hand again, trying to warm it. That's when it happens. Like my hands became flesh defibrillator paddles. They bring a great cracking clutching breath as she chucks a sickle back at the reaper in the nick of time and with no small violence. I thought she would split apart, but only her eyelids did, and she looked at me like it was all my fault. I tell her my name is Heather, and she makes a groan that in other circumstances would unmistakably be disgust.

I take out the Bible, flip through at random and begin reading from Song of Songs. I don't really know the Bible very well (though I was once in a production of *Godspell*) so I didn't know that Song of Songs is essentially the Bible's version of erotica. When I read, "Let us get up early to the vineyards, let us see if the vine flourish, whether the tender grape appear and the pomegranates bud forth: there I will give you my love. And our bed is green," I think it might be obvious that this is my first assignment. Poor Dorothy. Due to her inability to speak, she is stuck with me. I should have revisited the training manual before I came in today, to find the best things to read to someone about to die. Note to self: Do that. Plan B: "Amazing Grace." In the training they said people generally like it if you sing that. "Would you like me to sing 'Amazing Grace' for you, Dorothy?" She gives a low, steady affirmative growl. Her *no* is more along grunting lines. In between I track the flicker of the milky spark that's somehow sticking to her bones. There is a laminated card beside her bed with nouns she can point to. But she can't really move her arms, so I point to things like the glass of water and listen for the long or short sound.

As I begin to sing, a woman outside the door starts screaming: "Flowers! Flowers!" There are also Alzheimer's patients here. Flowers are worth getting excited about. Especially in January. One of the nurses tells her it's okay and she'll show her where the flowers are, but the lady isn't having it.

She starts flailing her hands and continues chanting, angry now, "Flowers! FLOWERRRRRRRS!" I will take this over the drone of the ventilator that Dorothy's roommate is attached to.

I have sung "Amazing Grace" so many times in a row that I'm just humming it now, because there must be verses other than the one everyone knows, but I had never really thought about that until now. "Do you want me to keep singing to you, Dorothy?" Her *no* is a look I don't have words for. It could almost dial a phone.

A nurse in Tweety Bird scrubs comes by and asks if I'd like to take Dorothy out into the hall so she can look out at the trees. The trees look pretty fucking dead this time of year, but okay. Yes. One of them asks if she's my grandmother. I say, "No, I'm her hospice volunteer." No one here seems to know anything about her.

Dorothy prefers dark pink to pastel. I learn this by holding up sweatshirts of one and then the other and following the groans before the aide changed her clothes to go outside. These seem to be the only clothes she has here. I get the impression she didn't buy them. They are her only female marker at this stage, I think, until the aides change her. She has one breast. There's a deep scar where the other one used to be. The nurses bring in a contraption like one used to hoist a beached whale back into the sea. They lift Dorothy out of her bed and into a geri chair, which is like a slightly cozier gurney. It's no small thing for Dorothy to see trees.

THE HOUSE ON THE HILL

THE TECHNICOLOR HOUSE UNABASHEDLY FLIPS THE BIRD AT WINTER. EACH of the colors, inside and out, we are told, have been inspired by something that blooms in the garden. The house is painted the exact peach of the roses that bloom off the deck. But I won't discover this until summer. There is a sheriff's car parked across the street, from the next county over. There is a lovely little greenhouse, but between Uwe's allergies and that sheriff's cruiser, there will be only veggies here. Budding camellias line the front of the house. There are two already open, a double blossom fractured pink and white, another the deep solid pink of Dorothy's preferred sweatshirt.

When camellias die, the petals don't fall separately from the calyx. The whole flower falls off together. In Japan, this is said to represent the everlasting union of lovers.

The cherry, apple, peach, and fig trees are gathering light. There's a rose garden. Empty beds where the food could go. Full sun, even now, on this unseasonably warm day in January. No hot tub. No gully. A view of the horizon.

Uwe will take it. He will sign the lease. The lady at the management office asks if I'll be living there too, and there is a pause. They are both looking at me. "Not right now. I have a house." As soon as I say it, I feel the telltale clench. He takes my hand and kisses it. The clench ripples out, softens, disappears. Back in the car, he gives me the camellia he picked. A double-blossomed one.

FEBRUARY'S EXTRA *R*
SHOULD JUST LET GO

GOING GENTLE

I've never done indoor in February before. Expecting anything to thrive this time of year seems like hubris. I know nothing all over again, except to pay attention. It's been raining nonstop, and despite Ed's best efforts to make my room a closed system, there is really no such thing. The Girls are all blocked up in the wet air, but the room is so tight that when I add a dehumidifier it dries the plants near it to a crisp and does nothing at all for the plants at the back. Condensation drips from the ducting. The back and front of the room are stunted for two different reasons. I've got an arid zone and a rain forest in one tiny space.

On the upside, spider mites are mostly at rest until the weather gets hot again, so I'm on to powdery mildew. Fantastic. There will never be a *done* and there will never be a *well, I've got that covered.* Like any relationship, it's a constant conversation. The mindful management of flux. There is balance for a hot minute, but even just by noticing it you disrupt it and then you have to sort it out all over again. You never get to stop paying attention.

I've spent the last three days wracking my brain, trying to find a way to solve the humidity problem so that I can freak them out into maximum potency. I surrender. Let's all go gentle into that good night. I take the dehumidifier out of the room and turn off the supplemental CO_2. CO_2 is expensive, and with all this water in the air The Girls won't really be able to use it. They won't be considered as valuable as the last Girls, but maybe they'll be a truer sort of "kind bud."

I could go back to Uwe's house, but it's nice to sit between the tables, with Vito dozing under them, as he has his whole life while I've worked. It feels right to be between things in this literal way, with my Girls bridging their canopy above me. I feel like I'm straddling two completely different lives, but they're still mine. I'm the canopy too, absorbing light and sheltering. I would like to live here for a round each year, the way Persephone is supposed to descend for a time into the underworld according to the Greek myth of winter. I would like to have a season where I drink too much and wear tutus and grow pot and bring boys home and raise chickens and puppies and kale and watch vultures eat foxes, if I could go home at the end. But that's not going to happen in any kind of literal way. I'm enough of a grown girl to see that.

The little surge of loss I feel at not potting up the ripe clones takes me by surprise. Okay, yeah, I'm a little weepy. They'll veg somewhere, just not here. They're my best clones ever and I won't get to watch their story unfold. A lot of people would say the nugget is the whole point; I disagree, but appreciate how that makes pot growing one of the few places in American culture that something female is considered to have its highest value after maturity.

I'm going to miss my Girls. Sometimes I will miss them a lot. The Girls have been medicine for me, and like any medicine, they've both endangered and protected me. And I them. And so we grew.

THE MILKY SPARK

As soon as I am sitting in the chair beside her bed, she begins:

"Yoooooooo . . ."

Wait. She said *you*? Meaning me? Meaning she is fucking talking?

"Waaaaaaaaaan . . ."

"I want something. Okay. What do I want, Dorothy?"

"Meeeeeeeeee . . ."

She is beaming every last electron of her milky spark right through her tunneling pupil at me.

"Toooooooooo . . ."

And she stops. She stops with the speaking, but the beaming persists.

We both know there is only one thing left for her to do. Her hand is still in mine and every last bit of her that is her makes a needle tattooing this onto me.

Fuck her. Fuck her for making this memory I can't undo. I am mad at her. I am mad at this zombie who is fucking with me. I bet she didn't say that to the spiritual care volunteer who was here before I came in. Didn't give that lady her Yoda impression. The woman in sensible shoes and a yellow blouse with a Peter Pan collar buttoned to the neck who kept her nose in the Bible reading John because she couldn't bear to look at Dorothy for the fifteen minutes she committed to sitting here. Because to look at Dorothy is to see death. And I'd like to think I can take it, but oh how it is fucking me so deep I want to yelp but I can't because who would fucking believe me because she can't speak. It's horrifying. It's horror movie horrifying. And I should know. I'd like to think I'm doing some kind of Mother Teresa–esque noble service here but I am one selfish fuck. I want to understand what it means to die without actually doing it myself. Dorothy has called me out. Her hand is still in mine like a bird that has just crashed into a window.

"I think you're one tough-ass cookie, Dorothy." She grunts in the affirmative. I swear to God there is a smile that can't quite make it to her face and through it seeps the satisfaction that she has fucking freaked me out.

"I guess nobody takes this job without a little morbid curiosity. You called me out, Dorothy. You just freaking called me out. You know why I'm here, and you don't like it one bit, do you?"

She grunts in the affirmative and it is pushed through the smile that can only be felt and I cry because yeah, Dorothy is dying my worst imaginable death aside from being buried alive or drowning, and this is what it looks like. And yet she is still a tough enough cookie to want to fuck with me even if her eyeballs are sinking in her quicksand skull.

"Do you want me to sing 'Amazing Grace' again? Did you know there are actually seven verses? Sorry about repeating just the first one over and over again last time. I didn't know."

A short grunt and a light hand squeeze.

"John?"

A particularly short grunt and a failed attempt to turn her head.

"Yeah, I know. They're really fond of John over at hospice. Ditto 'Amazing Grace.' Do you want some water?"

Short grunt.

"Are you in pain?"

Silence. She closes her eyes.

"Are you afraid?"

She turns her head back toward me and opens her eyes again.

She's terrified of letting go. She has no idea what comes next.

PEARL EARRINGS (NOT LIKE THE NECKLACE)

IT'S VALENTINE'S DAY AND I HEAD OVER TO THE HOUSE THAT UWE AND I will share. Moths cling to the bright peach walls. They were looking for the moon, but they found the light Uwe left on for me instead. I've been loading up Lucy every time I come. There will be a rental truck day for the big things, and by that time maybe I will have gotten used to the idea of cohabitating with a human again.

I put my boxes on the shelves in the garage and notice a carved wooden box inside a larger open cardboard one. It's the kind of box that holds something special. I don't hesitate to open it. Inside are mementos from his relationship with Bea. On top is the necklace he was wearing when we met. I was wondering what he did with it and now I know. There's also a heart he drew with their initials in it, movie ticket stubs, museum visit stubs, and a print of the Little Prince, wielding his scepter. That's the thing that bugs me most, though I would like to throw the necklace in the river.

I am not the kind of person who hangs on to things like that. I am the kind of person who burns things like that. I will mention this, but not today. I choose to believe he kept this stuff here in this special box because he's a sentimental fool. I love that he's a sentimental fool. Sure, it will come up again, this box, when I'm feeling a little less like I've learned something. But for now I just want to go into that office and play the song I wrote for him and kiss his big ol' peony bud of a head.

Uwe doesn't hear me when I open his office door because he's writing code with headphones on. There's no way around it. I'm going to startle him. I do. His relief at seeing me is equal to the start. "I will help with to carry your boxes," he says, getting out of the chair.

"I already did it," I tell him and sit him back down, wrapping my arms around his big shoulders, my hands dangling on his belly, soft and warm like the dough he makes for the bread he bakes. I draw my head down close. Me on two feet, he in the chair with my chin on his head and my nose in his hair. He feels so full under my hands. The deep sweet inhale I make is like mothers do to babies, a cell-deep signal—this is yours: Love it.

I can't really hear what he's saying about the bug he's fixing, which annoys him a little. He likes to be appreciated for his technical prowess, which is prodigious, yeah yeah yeah, what I want more of is this scalpy musk. "Oh." He sees me huffing. "I didn't take a shower today." He seems apologetic.

"Good. You smell like home." He disagrees. He hates when he doesn't take a shower. He's German; he likes cleanliness and logic. He doesn't want to fuck my murk to ash; he wants to cuddle. He doesn't need to annihilate anything; he wants to make order. This is how he stokes his spark. I am not German. I like tangled things, unwarranted enthusiasm, and the smell of his scalp. But when the coding stops I'll be there to plant some chaos under each delicious follicle. Even the gray ones. Especially those.

"I wrote you a song. It's your Valentine's Day present." I play it. "I think that your lovely eyes are made of bears and chocolate. I just want to look in them and I never want to stop it."

He loves it, me.

"I have two things for you," he says. The first is in the bedroom closet. I close my eyes like he asks and sit down on the bed.

"Okay, open." He has made an incredibly kick-ass spraypainting that says HOME in bright orange and pale blue, outlined in black. It's true: He really was a street artist. It perfectly ties together the crazy colors of this house. We put it up in the living room and play "Home" by Edward Sharpe and the Magnetic Zeros. Our song. We dance around the living room.

I love it, him.

"And for Vito . . ." He pulls out a flat nylon disc that springs into a den. Vito immediately puts all of his toys in it and two of Uwe's socks. I never crated Vito as a puppy; it seemed cruel to me, too restrictive, like Buga's Tupperware habitat. I didn't realize that Vito might actually *want* a crate.

Uwe left the necklace I made him on the bathroom sink. I bring it to him.

"I forgot," he says, putting it on.

"I'm reminding you." And it's hard not to think about the box in the garage.

He hands me a black velvet pouch. "This is for you also." Inside is a pair of pearl earrings. "They are real," he says, "like you."

"I can tell." And I can, though I have little experience of pearls. You can't fake that kind of radiance. They're big as moonvine seeds, and I never would have picked them for myself. I think I'm more ruby—bright and hard and shiny at the cuts. Or opal—colorful and quick to shatter.

A pearl is something else entirely. It's not cut from rocks, but made through sentience, where grit meets diligence. They're not an accident of pressure and time; they're an act of attention and consent, this pearlescence. He thinks this of me and I'm starting to believe him.

"Be carefully," he says as I put them on. Sure, it's a little off, but since I like to overthink things, I take it as good advice. I want to be carefully. "Be carefully they do not fall out." The pearls dangle from white gold wires with nothing to anchor them. He's right. I don't want to lose them. I'll get something to keep them from sliding out of my lobes, not just leave it to fate. Not just say, if I lose them, *Well then, it wasn't meant to be.*

"They look good on you," he says, and adds, "I got the ones that hang down a little bit because of the way your ears are."

The way my ears are is torn and crooked. The second piercings are uneven and the first ones were torn into slits by the eighties. With these new earrings, you can't tell.

They're so light I can't tell if they're there or not unless I'm really still. So still I can feel my heartbeat. So still I can feel the weight of pearls.

THE SOFTEN AND CLENCH

THE OBAMA ADMINISTRATION DECLARED TODAY THAT THE JUSTICE DEPART-
ment will no longer raid medical marijuana dispensaries in states where
they are legal under state law. So basically anybody who's state legal will
not be persecuted or prosecuted. This means that more and more people
will come up here to grow, and the increased safety will mean increased
supply and any gray market remnants will be swept into white. No more
Lil Dick telling anyone what they can grow and where they can take their
surplus. Everything is more open now. It's been developing that way for a
while, but today's announcement gives the time line a jolt. Things have
changed over the last year. You can get a prescription for fifty dollars and
a record-free claim of PMS. There are new people who will take this economic leg up, this time to sort out where they fit in this America.

Zeus comes by with SaRah in tow and says he won't be able to help
out with my latest crop. "Good isn't good enough anymore. It's got to be
perfect. You're crispy up front and wet in the back." He spreads and examines the canopy, shakes his head. "Those crispy ones aren't gonna grow
anymore and those wet ones won't sugar up. You should just cut down,
give yourself enough time for demolition. Get this place back in shape.
You got a steamer? Ozone generator?"

"Yeah. You interested in buying the equipment when I'm done? I'd
rather not put the stuff on Craigslist."

"You should. 'Girl from *Blair Witch Project* sells indoor garden equipment from wooded location. Come see!' You'd probably get more for it."

"I'll pass."

"I'll make a few calls. See if anybody needs anything."

He tells me that Cedara's getting her own place. She didn't feel like
she got a big enough cut from him, so she wants her own show again. He
says it from my couch, staring at the woodstove with no fire in it. He's going to be her investor again, though he tells me, "She says she wants to
move on. Right now she's in Peru at an Ayahuasca retreat." Apparently
her cut was not terrible. He's alone with SaRah and The Girls. "I would
give her anything. I did."

"Somebody will give back to you next time," I tell him.

"If it's gonna last, there probably needs to be somebody wearing the pants."

"Tell that to the hermied Girls. Can't you do like one leg each in the pants?"

"There's a reason those races are funny. Nothing's equal for long."

"The laws of thermodynamics would back you up on that."

"How's that?"

"Nothing's equal, nothing's lost, everything's always shifting."

"True dat." He goes to bump my fist. That part goes well, but the fingersnap is a fail.

He wears a woven bucket hat and the holes in his lobes are empty.

While SaRah chases Vito and Kali with a stick, Zeus tells me of the rumors that Philip Morris has bought up thousands of acres in Mendo and Humboldt. Just waiting for legalization to happen. "And then what?" I ask.

"We'll be migrant farmers working for corporations. Slaves in the world we built." Everything about him seems as overturned as his bucket hat would suggest. A single dad with an uncertain future.

It won't be worth a dispensary owner's time to drive up here anymore. Driving is the one point in the chain where you will likely find trouble, and there will likely be a grower in their neighborhood who they already know. People like Zeus, who've had the privilege of a network, will have to go peddle their nugs like everybody else, for an ever decreasing price and ever more discerning buyers.

Growers will probably look to nonmedical states where there's still a thriving black market economy. California terroirs like Humboldt are strong national brands. Of course the nugget that lands in Utah with a Humboldt provenance could just as well come from Riverside unless there are rules akin to winemaking in place.

It's not because of this that when I think about setting up a new growhouse, I clench. It's because when I think about walking away, I soften. Beyond money and any thoughts about career or safety or fear, what I've got now is the soften and clench. I'm not as interested in leaning into the clench as I used to be. Although if you lean into it long enough . . .

Growing pot sure as hell made me clench, but the softness I feel welling in its wake is more expansive than any I've previously known.

One thing I will miss about this job is that it was really clear what I was supposed to be afraid of: getting caught. It's a deep and ever-present fear, but it's also pretty simple, and it keeps other vaguer and more slippery ones at bay. Like fear of commitment. Like fear of not being a girl anymore. Like fear that you have taken so many wrong turns you might not put things right again. On brighter days, I don't think of them as wrong turns. I think of them as strong, independent, interesting.

I offer Zeus a tray of clones. "I want them to go to a good home." He's bumming, and clones are good green hope. They're prosperity. They're first kisses and spring. Most of them are descendants of his laundry—that bag of branches Judah and I cut and plugged last April. Four generations later, they're going home.

He's losing weight. I know the drill. He loved her. That's all. It made everything he did make sense and now it doesn't. "I can't believe you're really getting out after a year," he says, like he's considering it himself. "I think you're gonna miss it."

"I think you're right."

He loads the clones into his Corolla and puts a blanket over them, tucking them in. SaRah doesn't want to stop throwing rocks at Vito, but Papa says it's time to go. Zeus pulls on the brim of his bucket hat and swoops up his son.

THE SUPERNOVA EFFECT

ONE TIME A FEW YEARS BACK I WAS BACKPACKING IN MALI WITH WACŁAW. We were in Dogon country at the time. The Dogon are a people who live along a cliff known as the Bandiagara Escarpment. I saw a supernova happen over his shoulder while we were eating spaghetti. He was mad at me because it was another peculiar and spectacular phenomenon that seemed to have just happened to me through no special talent or effort of my own, like with the movie. Anyway, seeing the supernova was something I remember a lot. Watching it flare before it disappeared is something I remember today because Dorothy is flat-out lively in her pink sweatshirt and her urge to hear John and all seven verses of "Amazing Grace" while looking at the picture of herself and her husband that has recently appeared, accompanied by an Instamatic snap of two kids in front of a Christmas tree. Is she hungry? No. Is she in pain? No. Is she totally fucking terrified? Not anymore.

I don't understand how she could be so much better. Her tongue is flaking apart. Her eyes are even deeper in her head. There's a black gap between her tear ducts and her eyeballs big enough to see into, but she's surging anyway. The speck is milky but the spark is bright.

I am listening to the skin of her eyelids. They're too small now for the balls they're supposed to cover. Even her eyelids can't understand why she's still hanging on. They want to sink back away into the earth or the ooze or whatever primordial thing would bring relief. She's alone. Except for me, a stranger holding her hand. It's hard to watch someone die slowly, even if they're not in pain. I signed up for making someone a sandwich while their family caregiver went to the grocery store or the hairdresser or something. I didn't expect a six-week meditation on dying alone.

"Dorothy," I home in on her irises, then pupils. "I thought we might read something different today." I hold up a copy of *The Little Prince*. "Would you like that?" Long affirmative growl. I read the whole book with my hand resting on hers between pages. I read for a long time before we get to the end: " 'He said to me: "I'm glad you found what was the matter with your engine. Now you'll be able to fly again . . ."

' "How did you know?" I was just coming to tell him that I had been successful beyond all hope! He didn't answer my question: all he said was "I'm leaving today, too." And then, sadly, "It's much further . . . It's much more difficult." ' "

I usually sandwich her hands between mine to warm them, but this time it's impossible. No matter how many times I take my hands away and rub them together to heat them again, in seconds they're cold. And not just cold: There's a pull, like when a supernova hits the brink and shifts into collapse. The force of the pull is strong enough to draw the heat out of me. It freaks me out a little, the numb cold tingle creeping up my arm, like she could take me with her, just suck the life out of me—collapse the whole world if she wanted to. I continue reading: " 'But he said to me, "Tonight, it'll be a year. My star will be just above the place where I fell last year . . ." ' "

It's almost seven and the lights will be coming on in the growroom soon. " 'But he didn't answer my question. All he said was "The important thing is what can't be seen . . ." ' "

I have to do the final flush, getting all of the fertilizers out the soil so the buds will be sweet. Uwe is back from the Bay today. We were going to eat together and I'm already late. "I'm going to go now, Dorothy." Often she has no reply to this, but today she gives a shuddery groan. And I think to myself, *Please just let go.* But what can I say? *It's going to be okay? You love Jesus, so he'll totally take you to heaven?* I can't say any of that. I don't believe any of that. I can't say anything. I remember in the training they told us again and again: *Listen, don't fix.* I can hold her hand and so I do. I start to cry. I start to grieve this woman whose life I know so little about, except how it's ending, which maybe tells me everything. A wife, a mother, and a death like this. I bend close and whisper in her ear, "I will never forget you, tough cookie." She looks at me and I like to think she's glad I'm crying, that it comforts her to know she'll be remembered. I add, "Thanks for letting me be here." And there's nothing of the clench. Everything is soft down to the bones.

GROOMING NUGGETS

I HAD TO CUT DOWN EARLY TO MAKE TIME FOR DEMOLITION, WHICH WILL take less than half the time it took to build. Only about thirty percent of The Girls' trichomes were amber, so this particular batch of OG Kush will give the patient more of a cerebral "up" stone, as opposed to the deep couch lock of riper buds. I can't say that I'm entirely sorry about this. For things grown in winter, they look pretty good. Light, though. Sometimes if you cut too much, you lose too much. There's a point where you need to stop and keep. I kind of get it.

I've hired Willa to help me trim. We're doing a dry trim. I cut down alone and hung them in the office where the nursery used to be. We're listening to my backlog of *This American Life* podcasts, hearing the story of a guy who, by chance, got into cryogenics, and despite only the best of intentions, left corpses, one of them a child, rotting into each other in the Southern California sun when the refrigeration gave out while he was away once.

"I'm glad I met you," Willa says. For her Nordic genes, this is effusive. The shift in this house is felt all around.

"I guess we got gifted by the triple karmic vortex."

"I can't believe you're just moving in with Uwe."

"I guess I keep getting gifted by the triple karmic vortex."

"You just say yes to everything."

"That's kind of my thing."

"You should learn to say no sometimes."

"It's not too late. You can have all this equipment. I could be your consultant!"

"You're the worst advertisement for this job."

"Nothing worth doing is easy."

"I like my life."

"I didn't say you didn't."

"It's easy, but it's still worth doing."

"You're the person I'd most like to trade places with."

"You wouldn't like my life if it was yours."

"I've never had a friend who volunteered to help me pack before."

"How about a friend who volunteered to drive pot to LA with you?"

"No. Never had one of those either. Have you ever had a friend who steam-cleaned your regurgitated nori?"

"No. Never."

And it's right about now that I finally become a good trimmer. I let the opposite motions happen, stop trying so hard and let my hands work independently, doing only what's needed. The clipping hand clips, and the turning hand rotates and we get through the work in a day.

Some Hindus say a guardian lives in the cannabis leaf. And yeah, I kind of buy it.

AND THERE ARE SOME THINGS
I WOULD NOT TAKE BACK

With Zeus unable to move my stuff, that guy I met in Venice getting busted by the DEA, and my terror of driving it anywhere, I see if maybe Judah might help me out.

"Hey, any chance you'd like to share a six pack with me?"

"What do you got?"

"Well, I thought after moving that cushy couch today, a cold beer would be nice."

"Yeah, I could join you for that. Meet me at Bean Bugs in thirty?"

I'm not expecting him to show up with Sprout, dropped off fresh from the farm. She runs to me. "Feather!" I swoop her up and she puts her hands on my cheeks and shrieks again, "Feather!" and when I put her down there is egg all over the sleeve of my black wool coat. "From the chickens!" Sprout laughs. And yes, it's from the chickens I raised for Sprout's mom's homesteading beau. I got an egg from those chickens, in the end.

We sit down in the coffee shop, Sprout on my lap. I slip the bud sample into his bag on the floor. He takes it into the bathroom for examination.

"It smells amazing," he says.

"They're not so abundant, but they're big and dense."

If I hadn't cut so much back, if I'd been able to add a bit of a water fast in week five or six, they would have been my best round yet. Then again, if those things worked, something else might've gone wrong.

"I have no back pain anymore," he says. "I thought you'd like to know."

"You must be living a very different life then."

"After eighteen years of pain . . . I've opened up a lot these past six months."

"I'm really happy for you," I say, and mean it.

"Market's shifting monthly now."

"A lot has changed."

"Have you told your dad what you do yet?"

"Nah." His dad thinks he's a kitchen consultant, and a relative fail-ure. He has this whole glittering world in his garage that he can't share with anybody who doesn't already know. And the odd woman who wouldn't be seduced by Formica. Judah knows he is seductive with his leather-pants eyes and his secret weapon in the garage. It's hot to see a man wield that much feminine power, for him to respect that this is what shapes his world, his community, his home. For all their quirks and crazi-ness, the growers I've known have more connection to the land, their families, each other, and every kind of matter—mountains, rivers, pup-pies, plants—than anybody else I know. And they're happier for it. Every last one of them.

"I love your hair. I want to take it home to Papa's house," Sprout says and laughs.

I flop it onto her head. "Okay, you can have it."

She climbs off my lap and goes toward the door, pulling me along by the hair.

"It's a trick!" she says. "I bring you too!"

"I think I can help you out," Judah says. "Come by my place, door's open. Leave it in the dryer."

I don't know if *dryer* was supposed to stand for something else, so I just put it in the dryer. I'm glad to see the table I decorated for Sprout is still there. I touch the O like the last time I was here. I'm glad to see something I brought here stayed.

Liz is there, cleaning his house. She's carved out a niche cleaning growhouses for the pot wife–less, because they know she'll be discreet. "How've you been?" I ask.

"Good. You?"

"How's Tuck?" Her boyfriend.

"Good."

"Levi?" Her son.

"He's real good."

"Playing out at all? Writing songs?"

"I've been pretty busy." She gestures to the dust on Judah's table. "Heard you got out."

"Yeah. Looks like it."

"That's crazy. What you gonna do?"

"I don't know exactly."

"Heard you're moving in with that German guy."

"Yeah, Uwe."

"Heard he's got some computer job or something?"

"He's a programmer."

"That's different."

"I guess so."

"He want you out?"

"Not really, actually. I think he kind of liked it, except for the part that he's deathly allergic."

"To weed?"

"Yeah."

"Seriously?"

"Yeah."

This is the first real laugh we've shared since that night we played the Golddigger.

Later I hear sirens outside my house, and though it's probably a fire truck, what I think is that this whole thing was a setup and the sheriff has retrieved the bags from Judah's dryer, and is now about to pull up and cuff me. It doesn't happen. Judah was really just willing to help me. We really just did what we could for each other.

SURRENDER DOROTHY, PART TWO

I WENT TO THE NURSING HOME TODAY, BUT DOROTHY IS DEAD.

One hundred eight people die every minute. Two hundred fifty-five are born.

Newness is not just for the young. New things happen all the time, to everybody. *New* is just another word for change.

I come home to Uwe and cry and cry and cry. And he holds me, not as a sandbag tethers a hot-air balloon, but like someone who can listen and not fix, like someone who loves.

I had trays of seedlings at Judah's house this time last year. I ended up losing them all. Well, except that freakish kale. I didn't understand about frost. How swift and final it could be. Especially to the newly emerged. The Latin root of *prosperity* means to emerge. Probably good to keep that in mind, what I've learned about frost. You need the freezer, but it's smaller than the fridge. I don't know what I mean by this yet. It's just that Dorothy is dead and nobody bothered to let me know. They forgot. Or they just didn't have time. Everybody forgot about her at the end. Except you know about her now. So there's that.

I'm planting a new tray of seeds. Freckles lettuce, sweet peas, chocolate mint. Definitely Red Russian kale.

CHLOROPHYLL

I PASS THE WHITE STAKE AT THE END OF THE ROAD, PASS THE TWO HOUSES, round the bend through the open gate and the house opens up to me for the last time. Today is not leap day; it's just the end of February. Leap day is not a day at all this year. Maybe I couldn't handle a catalyst like that more than once every four years. Maybe I need to be president of myself for a full term, see what campaign promises I can actually keep.

The light has been taken down in the hallway. The fixture is on the low wall that divides the living room from the dining room. Looks like the owners finally sent their people in. I guess I could be mad, but I'm so fucking relieved they only came now, when the house is in better shape than when I moved in. Zeus sent workers to take the equipment away. He says he'll give me something for it later. There is no way I could store it at the new house with that sheriff's cruiser across the street. And really, I don't want to. I still think fresh starts are possible. Or freshish. My rent got paid, and I ate some sushi, but I didn't really make any money—just like Zeus predicted.

The property management dude arrives to take pictures of the house. Vito greets him with a wag and roll, and the dude says, "You raised a great dog."

"Thanks."

"The Sufis say a dog reveals the heart of its master."

"That's about the best compliment you could give me. What's good for him has been good for me. With the exception of kibble."

"Damn," he says, snapping shots. "Looks better than when you moved in. I can't even smell anything."

I point to my trusty steam cleaner and the odor annihilator, a Big Blue industrial ozonator. "The clean team." He confirms that the owners sent a handyman in. They're trying to come up with ways to hold on to my deposit. He asks what I have on hand, if I'm left holding any turkey bags. I tell him I've already taken care of it. He says too bad, he would like to have seen it. The only thing that could really hold up the refund of my deposit is the red stain on the carpet from housebreaking Vito on Moroccan kilims. I'm not sad we've left a mark on the place.

"You really quitting?" he asks.

"Again. It seems I'm something of a quitter. Congratulate me."

He doesn't.

"You do end up giving up a lot for them," he says instead.

"Or maybe you're just really in it together."

"Back to the culture of obedience?"

"There was plenty of obedience required here."

"You feel different? After living out here? Doing this?"

"I haven't changed much. Just learned to live with myself."

"What are you going to do now?"

"Drink a little liquid chlorophyll each day so I don't have to use chemmy deodorants. It works. True story. Viva plants!"

"It's hard times out there," he says. "Real hard right now."

"Yeah, I don't know. Who knows?"

"Well, good luck to you," he says, and goes, and I'm standing in an empty place again. The soften and clench are fluctuating madly.

I mean, look, nobody is immune to the global economy, but guess who doesn't need a bailout? The pot industry. It's a literal growth sector. Plus, it's satisfying labor when you're not shitting your pants every time you hear a helicopter. Let's update the Liberty Gardens of yesteryear with Tahoe trees and Sun Gold tomatoes. Corporal Mary Jane, America, reporting for service. Sad though it may be, pot growing is one of the last things we do better than most (you go ahead and argue, British Columbia, but you just keep it down, Netherlands). Hey, Missouri, don't you have a dreadful per capita income, a double-digit unemployment rate, and lots of arable land? I'd be more than happy to find you a team of suitable consultants. Get in touch, West Virginia. And it's a worthy export. Jesus, don't you think it's time the Chinese took a load off? I believe we can help. You know that popular collegiate pastime where you cut the bottom off a gallon milk jug, place it in a sink full of water, fill it with smoke, have someone place their mouth on the drinkhole, push it down really fast and then collapse in paroxysms of hilarity while they cough their balls off? I think that could be done with a conical hat. How many Chinese citizens are there again? Isn't it time we give back? Give them a way to really understand those garden gnomes and hula hoops and TVs and Rabbit Habits and wigs and picnic baskets they've provided us? Let's redress that pesky trade deficit!

Go mom-and-pops, keep growing so we can maybe help reduce corruption and assassination in Mexico. Seriously, when you think about it that way, which is not an illegitimate way to think about it, it just seems like the right thing to do. Why let the bank take your house when you can give it to the DEA later? At least you'll spend a few more months with some ready cash and a roof over your head.

Oh, and Monsanto? Fuck off. People have already been sharing and developing great ganja genetics for decades. Keep your fucked-up mutants out of the pot supply. We don't want to smoke them, eat them, or shit out the corny niblets our bodies won't digest. Mom-and-pop plant genetics have gotten us this far, though I'm sure you'd breed something spider mite–proof . . .

The Girls are, at the very least, surefire laugh bringers. And I mean, really, for all us puny humans, is not laughter the best medicine? Or at least an effective pain reliever? Jesus, doc, I lost my house, I lost my job, I have no fucking health insurance—is there something I can take for that? Yes, sir, here's an eighth of Chocolope, a *Family Guy* DVD, some saltines, and a tub of caramel. Call me when you need a refill.

Whoa. Didn't mean to get all polemical on your ass. I think that was a twinge of regret. Did I really just get out of the cannabiz? Remind me why again? I think I need to get myself some hot tub while the gettin's good.

THE BLUE-EYED BREATHER

WHILE PACKING UP THE LAST OF THE BATHROOM THINGS, I'M MESMERIZED by the amount of gray hair at my roots right now. When I moved here there were five strands, maybe ten. Now they can't be counted. Call me ma'am. Please. I've earned it. Have I?

What have I learned about how to grow?

1. Listen. If stems go purple, you're feeding too loud.
2. Bending is better than breaking.
3. Keep the main colas to four. Allow for focus. Colas are like priorities, which are like any limbs. If you've got more than four, you've got a problem—but cut too much and you just have less.
4. Remove anything that's more than fifty percent dead.
5. Let light hit as much surface area as possible.
6. Shit happens daily. If not, I'd have a serious problem. If only my mind had a sphincter.
7. The best a growgirl has to give is her attention.

The Girls were definitely medicine for me. They cured my hide.

The last things I pack are the note cards my mom left on the fridge. "Tread lightly. Trust in you." I think that means listen for the soften and the clench, accept that flux is not there just to fuck with me, any more than I was here just to fuck with The Girls—I was their tender, I wanted them to be their best, and so sometimes I pushed. That's how I brought the sugar up. Flux is there, regardless, and if I can meet it with ease it'll press me into new shapes around the blue-eyed breather at the core.

What do I still have to learn? Lots of things, but mostly the power of no.

I check for Buga one last time because you never know. He's still gone.

I get into the hot tub. Vito lays down on the ledge.

I haven't accumulated enough to burn again. No spectacular fire, just floating in water. I'm plenty buoyant with no hands under me.

The sun is headed down behind the pines. It's a white dot. I'm remembering Dorothy. Her lassoing breaths. It's not like there's some end point to letting go, some place of constant security awaiting me. I thought so when I did The Great Purge, but it's not like that at all. Dorothy was still learning to let go. She let go of her breast, her husband, her voice, and then her breath, becoming something else and something else until she became a memory; a speck—no—a spark.

Solidity is a trick of touch. Skin can't keep light out; there are no closed systems. The Girls can't help but choose awesome because they can't help but feed on light. That's as close as I have to a plan—keep aiming for the light, even if it comes from thousand-watt high-pressure sodium bulbs.

Acknowledgments

To my patient and intrepid early readers, Pat Miller, Shirley DicKard, Emily Bergl, Carson Becker, and Bronwen Williams. Without you I would still be in the woods.

To my late readers, Laura Goode, Sabrina Crawford, Lisa Richter, and once again, Miss Emily Bergl. Thanks for chucking in the eleventh-hour life raft, tugging me in along the tenuous line between honest and embarrassing.

To Matthew Zapruder, for letting me steal a line from your practically perfect poem, "The Prelude." A prize for the first reader who finds it. Seriously. Email me. And for making magic from the mundane in your own work and all those wonderful Wave Press books.

To Mary Roach, Joy Johannessen, Leslie Daniels, Jim Krusoe, and Po Bronson. Your generosity, guidance, and insight has meant the world to me. You are my best evidence that the universe will conspire to assist you at the moment of commitment.

To my final editor, Megan Newman. You waved the checkered flag with enthusiasm, experience, and aplomb.

To Gotham peeps Travers Johnson, Jessica Chun, Beth Parker, Lisa Johnson, and William Shinker. Thank you for your patience, faith, and support.

To Kathleen Schmidt and Jeremy Walker, a maven and a mensch, respectively. Thanks for spreading the word.

To my deeply awesome acquiring editor, Rachel Holtzman. You insightfully and subtly nudged at all the right cracks to break this book open. Ouch and thanks. You Growgirl!

To my kick-ass agent, Mollie Glick. What can I say? To you, well, you know. But to the other writers out there who think they have to choose between an agent who makes deals like an unceasing sea animal, and a career shepherd you can drink a margarita with? You do not. Choose Mollie. Hugs to Moose.

To the Grotto, for being. It's your fault I'm still paying San Francisco rents. Community can work. No matter how weird and neurotic and multivaried its members. Oysters may not make pearls in groups, but oysters are not people. So glad I didn't burn the place down in the microwave incident that time.

To the Schneidscums, Chris and Cindy. To Cindy for listening on long walks with dogs in the ditches. To Chris for being a patient physics consultant. All excruciatingly extended and inaccurate physics metaphors are due to my stubbornness.

To Kit, for the art and heart you bring to everything you do.

To Lucas, for the new light.

To Stefan, for the help and the cuddles. Of course we wanted more. Who wouldn't? But there's grace in noticing enough.

To Miranda, for never ever saying I told you so.

To Ryan and Caitlin, I dedicated this book to Mom and Dad, but it's for all the Donahues (you too, Hannah!). Who knew that not all families laugh and love like us? I love you guys and miss you more than words can make matter.

To The Community. For giving me this story. I hope you see the love in it.